# ON LOCATION

*In loving memory*

**CANDACE SPIGELMAN**
**1947–2004**

# ON LOCATION

*Theory and Practice in Classroom-Based Writing Tutoring*

*Edited by*

## CANDACE SPIGELMAN
## LAURIE GROBMAN

UTAH STATE UNIVERSITY PRESS
Logan, Utah

Utah State University Press
Logan, Utah 84322-7800

Manufactured in the United States of America
Cover design by Barbara Yale-Read

Earlier versions of these essays appeared as indicated:
Jennifer Corroy, "Institutional Change and the University of Wisconsin–Madison Writing Fellows
    Program," *Young Scholars in Writing: Undergraduate Research in Writing and Rhetoric* 1 (2003).
    Reprinted by permission.
Casey Gonzalez, "Building Trust While Building Skills in a Peer Writing Group," *Journal of Teaching
    Writing* 18:1–2 (2002). Reprinted by permission. (In this volume as Casey You.)
Laurie Grobman, "Building Bridges to Academic Discourse: The Peer Group Leader in Basic Writing
    Peer Response Groups," *Journal of Basic Writing*, 18.2 (1999). Reprinted with changes by permis-
    sion.
Candace Spigelman, "Reconstructing Authority: Negotiating Power in Democratic Learning Sites,"
    *Composition Studies* 27.2 (Fall 1999): 23–37.


Library of Congress Cataloging-in-Publication Data

On location : theory and practice in classroom-based writing tutoring / edited by Candace Spigelman,
Laurie Grobman.
    p. cm.
  Includes bibliographical references and index.
  ISBN 0-87421-599-4 (pbk. : alk. paper)
  1. Peer-group tutoring of students. 2. Writing centers. I. Spigelman, Candace, 1947- II. Grobman,
Laurie, 1962-
  LB1031.5.O5 2005
  808'.042'0711–dc22

                    2004021215

*For the writing fellows at Penn State Berks*

# CONTENTS

# PREFACE

My dear friend and colleague, Candace Spigelman, died unexpectedly shortly before *On Location* went to print. I want to take this opportunity to honor her life and her work.

Candace was a brilliant scholar, superb teacher, and committed colleague and campus citizen. My strongest image of Candace is seeing her at her desk, working side by side with students, challenging them to re-see and revise their writing in an effort to advance their intellectual capacities and writing skills.

Candace was particularly dedicated to our college's Writing Fellows program, which she designed, developed, and facilitated. Her devotion to the program and the tutors was based on her deep belief in students' capabilities. She always understood that if we encourage students to do their best, they will. She loved her Writing Fellows because of the work they accomplished and the good people that they are. Working with students and teaching them to work with one another, especially on location, were truly her passions.

Candace was an extraordinary colleague who brought her enthusiasm for students, her scholarship, the discipline, and the college to everything she did, and who inspired everyone around her.

Candace was a loving wife, mother, and grandmother. She was also a devoted and loyal friend. I miss her deeply.

Laurie Grobman

# ACKNOWLEDGMENTS

Experienced teachers know that they do not enter their classrooms alone: teaching, like writing, is largely the effect of manifold collaborations with fellow teachers and theorists, with significant texts, and with those who support their instructional activities. Likewise, we want to recognize the many wonderful collaborations that brought this book to publication.

We are enormously grateful to Michael Spooner for trusting in our project. His guidance and generosity encouraged us to take chances as we found our way. We appreciate the help of the publishing staff at Utah State University Press, Robin DuBlanc, Kyle Sessions, and Jessica Carver in preparing our manuscript for publication. We would also like to acknowledge the helpful comments of the anonymous reviewers. Our many contributors energetically discussed their drafts with us over electronic airways, met deadlines, and revised their essays with great goodwill. Finally, our thanks to classroom-based writing tutors everywhere—those who occupy the pages of our book and those we do not know.

**Introduction**

# ON LOCATION IN CLASSROOM-BASED WRITING TUTORING

Candace Spigelman and Laurie Grobman

In filmmaking parlance, actors work "on location" when they move from the sound stages, where the bulk of movies are filmed, to sites where geography and social life more closely represent the director's intentions. The clear connection between the notions of "on location" and "on the scene" suggests the film crew's submergence in the local environment, community, or culture. When one is working "on location," exigencies are less readily choreographed; variables, such as climate, local inhabitants, or political conditions, cannot always be controlled. Our title, *On Location*, marks the movement, or relocation, of tutoring to the classroom, a setting beyond or outside of traditional language and literacy support. On-location tutoring occurs in the thick of writing instruction and writing activity, and on-location tutors operate within complex, hierarchical, contested classroom spaces. Tutoring "on location" means carrying on one's back strategies and principles for sharing and building knowledge among peers in sites that—in myriad ways—threaten, contradict, demand, and support such projects.

In contrast to the more familiar *curriculum-based peer tutoring* model, *classroom-based writing tutoring* describes tutoring arrangements clearly integral to writing instruction—writing support offered directly to students *during* class. Classroom-based writing tutors facilitate peer writing groups, present programs, conference during classroom workshops, help teachers to design and carry out assignments, and much more. Their instructional sites range from developmental writing classes to first-year composition to writing across the curriculum classes to "content" classes where writing is assigned. Because on-location tutoring extends to a vast array of classroom contexts, its theories and practices have relevance for the many educators across the university who, in their varied and significant roles, advance writing instruction and strive to make writing central to students' academic work. We therefore offer this volume to faculty in composition and across the disciplines, writing center administrators and personnel, writing across the curriculum (WAC) administrators, graduate teaching assistants, and undergraduate tutors who seek continued discussion and assessment of classroom-based tutoring efforts.

In *On Location,* we argue that if classroom-based writing tutoring is to be staged and executed effectively, it must be understood by all stakeholders as a distinct form of writing support. Classroom-based writing tutoring is no less than an amalgamated instructional method, operating in its own specific space and time rather than as an extension of a single strand of tutoring principles. In the introductory discussion that follows, we borrow from genre theory and, in particular, from the concept of genre hybridity to conceptualize the distinctiveness of this tutorial form. While we acknowledge genre theory as, first and foremost, about texts and textual conditions, current research into the nature and application of genre for writing theory and for composition pedagogy succeeds in stretching (and sometimes breaking) existing textual boundaries.

We expand the concept of genre, taking quite literally what has been understood metaphorically in the notion of genre as *location.* Thus, Charles Bazerman describes genres as "environments for learning. They are locations within which meaning is constructed" (1997, 19). Anis Bawarshi contends that "genres do not just help us define and organize kinds of texts; they also help us define and organize kinds of situations and social actions, situations and actions that the genres, through their use, rhetorically make possible" (2003, 17–18) and further: "Genres function in the social practices that they help generate and organize, in the unfolding of material, everyday exchanges of language practices, activities, and relations by and between individuals in specific settings" (23). Locating and materializing genre in this way offers useful applications for discussions of teaching and tutoring in general and for classroom-based writing tutoring in particular.

It is our hope that *On Location* will signal a new phase in scholarly research on classroom-based writing tutoring. While earlier scholarship has focused on logistical and administrative issues and processes, emphasizing, among other points, the worthiness of such programs and how to set them up, this volume asks harder questions, which challenge, interrogate, and even critique classroom-based writing tutoring practices and principles. It poses new theories and offers alternative vantage points through which to reconsider long-standing theoretical controversies. At the same time, we are cognizant of newcomers' questions regarding logistical and administrative issues, especially as configurations of classroom-based writing tutoring multiply. In our concluding chapter, we suggest strategies for successfully implementing this important instructional practice, and we propose future sites of theoretical and practical inquiry.

This introductory chapter begins by tracing the intersecting instructional models that produced the hybrid genre we call *classroom-based writing tutoring*. To encourage our colleagues in their various roles to consider on-location tutoring, we discuss its value and importance for varied constituencies: from students to tutors to faculty to administrators. To acknowledge practical and theoretical difficulties arising from generic blending and blurring, we describe central conflicts for educators currently using or seeking to implement this form of writing support. Finally, we map the literal and conceptual territory that occupies our contributors.

## CLASSROOM-BASED WRITING TUTORING AS GENERIC HYBRID

Anis Bawarshi's definition of genre allows us to conceive of classroom-based writing tutoring and other forms of writing support as genres of instructional practice, each with its own conventions, paradigms, and heuristics (2003). In his recent book, *Genre and the Invention of the Writer*, Bawarshi characterizes genres as "*sites* within which individuals acquire, negotiate, and enact everyday language practices and relations" (31; emphasis added). According to Bawarshi, generic force is dynamic and constitutive: he identifies genres "not only as *analogical* to social institutions but as *actual* social institutions, constituting not just literary activity but social activity, not just literary textual relations but all textual relations, so that genres . . . also constitute the social conditions in which the activities of all social participants are enacted" (31–32; emphasis in original). Understanding genres as social practices helps us to notice their regularized (seemingly inherent) agendas and limits. As Bawarshi points out, "A genre conceptually frames what its users generally imagine as possible within a given situation, predisposing them to act in certain ways by rhetorically framing how they come to know and respond to certain situations" (22). In other words, each genre produces its own conceptualizing frameworks, "horizons," or particular ways of understanding the world.[1]

"The very nature . . . of contemporary genre theory," Wendy Bishop and Hans Ostrom explain in their introduction to *Genre and Writing*, "is to blur, dissolve, or at least cross boundaries; it is to violate decorum and trouble hierarchies" (1997b, xii). Crossing the boundaries of discourse and practice, we build on Bawarshi's explanation of the material and ideological aspects of genres to characterize classroom-based writing tutoring as a specific instructional genre. Blurring and dissolving boundaries lead us to recent examinations of genre hybridity to appreciate that classroom-based writing tutoring emerges as a combination of particular attributes, perspectives, ideologies, and conventions of several initiatives—writing centers, WAC programs, supplemental instruction, and writing group pedagogy—that gained authority in the 1980s as student-centered learning, writing in the disciplines, and academic support services became regularized features of higher education.[2] Fundamental to all of these programs is a revaluing of collaborative learning, with its dual emphases on peership and the social construction of knowledge. At the same time, each tutorial or collaborative initiative maintains its own perspective and conceptual orientation.

The potential of genre hybridity has been recognized at the discursive level (with blends of academic and personal discourse), at the textual level (with blends of fiction and nonfiction, autobiography and history, prose and poetry), at the rhetorical level (with blends of literary and critical analysis). According to Patricia Bizzell, a hybrid does not privilege or subsume competing forms; rather, it "borrows from [contributing discourses] . . . and is greater than the sum of its parts, accomplishing intellectual work that could not be done in either of the parent discourses alone" (1999, 13). In Bizzell's view, exploiting varied generic conventions—including informal language, subjectivity, emotional expression, consensus building, cultural and personal references—enables new ways of thinking and richer modes of scholarship (11–17). Encouraging hybrid or experimental forms of discourse in first-year writing, Bizzell argues, may better prepare students for writing in multiple contexts (8). In literary studies, Laura L. Behling's (2003) term *generic hybridism* is especially useful for our thinking, not about texts, but rather about textual processes. Describing multicultural works as blurred genres, Behling emphasizes generic interplay among a text's multiple origins.[3]

As we understand these and other hybridity theorists, the hybrid entity manifests two significant features: it emerges as something new that results from combining various features of its parent entities, but it also enacts the play of differences among those parent features.[4] From this perspective, writing centers, WAC programs, supplemental instruction, and writing group pedagogy each contribute important theoretical perspectives and practical strategies that together form the animated amalgam that is classroom-based writing tutoring.

*Writing center tutoring* is perhaps the most obvious "parent" of class-room-based writing tutoring, as many of the contributors' chapters attest. Undergirded by principles of democracy, student-centeredness, and peer interaction, writing center theory, research, and practice contribute these instructional and institutional values to classroom locations in which writing tutoring takes place. [5] What's more, writing centers can readily train tutors to work effectively with teachers and can intervene to ensure that students, tutors, and teachers achieve their instructional goals. Introducing writing center values to classrooms, and thus into the larger institution, helps to promote communication and build positive relationships among writing center practitioners, administrators, and scholars. Although on-location writing tutoring is a natural "next step" to one-to-one peer tutoring arrangements, it also modifies or altogether reverses some writing center principles, such as the tutor's autonomy from a classroom instructor. Relationships with faculty and tutors' immersion in classroom practices and assignments are among classroom-based writing tutoring's most powerful features. [7]

The theory and practice of *writing across the curriculum* also contribute to the generic hybrid we refer to as on-location tutoring. [8] In particular, WAC tutors, often referred to as writing fellows or writing associates, play an increasingly important role in WAC pedagogy. [9] WAC tutors usually respond in writing to drafts of assigned papers and often meet one-to-one with students in writing conferences. On-location writing tutoring adopts from WAC the practice of faculty-tutor interaction, as faculty in the disciplines gain the all-too-rare opportunity to respect and value the ideas and skills of undergraduates. Moreover, classroom-based writing tutoring continues WAC movement efforts to impress upon students, faculty, and administrators the important role writing can play in thinking and learning by way of student-centered, active learning pedagogies. Finally, WAC, like on-location writing tutoring, does not specifically or intentionally target "weaker" students in a particular class but considers writing instruction crucial to all students.

Classroom-based writing tutoring also benefits from *supplemental instruction* (SI), particularly its commitment to all students, providing resources for students as their needs determine. [10] Like on-location writing tutoring, SI acknowledges the importance of peers helping peers. However, on-location tutoring extends the role of the SI leader, whose sphere of instruction is confined to course material,[11] to help students master both the particularities of the course and the more general strategies of writing and critical analysis.

Finally, *peer writing group* theories and benefits extend to classroom-based writing tutoring as well. [12] Like peer writing group members, on-location tutors encourage peer discussion and provide immediate peer feedback. They participate in peer conversations, encourage the collaborative construction of knowledge, and promote revision as crucial to thinking and writing. Like peer writing groups, classroom-based writing tutoring can promote across the disciplines decentered classrooms and more democratic pedagogies.

We have described these multiple "parent" initiatives to on-location tutoring in order to emphasize their specific strengths and achievements as well as to argue that, at their intersection, classroom-based writing tutoring occurs as a hybrid instructional genre, yielding a different conceptual framework. Significantly, although classroom-based writing tutoring incorporates elements of writing center, WAC, SI, and writing group theories, its contributions as a distinct instructional genre derive from its engagement *on the scene* (and, therefore, *as* the scene) of writing. Tutoring on location performs our contemporary understanding of writing itself, reaffirming that textual production is intrinsically collaborative, chaotic, and recursive.

As a hybrid genre that varies, modifies, extends, or rejects characteristics of its "parents," on-location tutoring involves multiple, and sometimes competing, voices and complex choreographies. Engaging multiple voices and texts, this scene anticipates both consensus and conflict, collaboration and autonomy, agreement and resistance. Like writing itself, this scene of writing rehearses the often uncertain, recursive operations of discourse production, from inventing to composing to reviewing to revising. Like other writing acts, classroom-based tutoring is apt to be chaotic, even messy. Yet within this turbulent, hybrid classroom tutoring space, students, teachers, and tutors can locate themselves as writers.

## THE VALUE OF CLASSROOM-BASED WRITING TUTORING

Certainly, most contemporary writing teachers reject the notion that writing is a solitary and autonomous act of discovery, and those involved in writing support attest to the social nature of writing in all their practices. Nevertheless, composition textbooks and teachers who assign writing too often regard both invention and composing as practices "within the writer" that occur "before and outside the textured midst of things" (Bawarshi 2003, 4). Occurring as it does within the "textured midst of things," classroom-based writing tutoring *enacts* collaboration: on-location tutors suggest language, ideas, and strategies that student writers may incorporate directly into their drafts; on-location tutors encourage collaborative conversation among writers and responders; and on-location tutors point out useful text sources from which writers may expand their arguments.

Because tutoring on location brings together diverse cultures and perspectives, it creates new opportunities for productive dialogue and relationships among sponsoring units within the university, classroom teachers, undergraduates working to improve their writing, and classroom-based writing tutors. Below we highlight the benefits of classroom-based writing tutoring as suggested throughout this collection.

First, student writers benefit from the wide range of learning and teaching practices encompassed by classroom-based writing tutoring. These varied instructional approaches expose students to a number of collaborative models and hence meet the needs of many different kinds of learners. Peer group leaders, for example, encourage active response among students in basic writing—students who, because of their inexperience and their labels as basic writers, might be less likely to engage in productive peer feedback. Students in classes ranging from math to psychology benefit from peer tutors' writing expertise in the classroom and establish tutoring relationships that extend outside the classroom to the writing center environment.

Because on-location tutors bring assistance to the site where the writing is done, students benefit by having immediate answers to their composing dilemmas (even when they don't know to ask for it). In classroom workshops and in the peer writing groups, writing activity and talk about writing occur on the spot so that students have the immediate experience of the writing context. Successful peers also prompt and support students' use of writing as a form of inquiry; students across disciplines come to see that writing begins at the earliest—rather than at the latest—stages of research.

Equally significant, classroom-based peer tutoring performs for students the social nature of writing and of knowledge making; it enacts writing as collaboration. Prompted by "knowledgeable peers," student writers are more likely to invent together and to engage in higher levels of discussion and analysis than they might on their own. Support and stimulation from classroom tutors usually lead to more productive, group-generated revi-

sions of students' essays. Moreover, because of their experience as successful college students, classroom-based writing tutors can help developing
writers to appreciate the demands of the genres we call academic discourse.
As members of genuine scholarly communities, students gain intellectual
independence by engaging meaningful intellectual issues, opportunities
to think and write like scholars without the heavy-handed "right" answers
of teachers. With knowledgeable peers serving as models and facilitators,
student writers gain greater confidence in their own insights.

For the most part, classroom-based writing tutoring also helps to
decenter classroom power relations. The presence of tutors helps to
dismantle hierarchy: teachers see that students (both peer tutors and
enrolled classmates) can also be authorities. Likewise, it emphasizes the
importance of active learning, as students talk and write together on
site, in contrast to the kinds of passive reception learning styles, Freire's
(1970) "banking method" of education, that most students have been
conditioned to accept. More democratic teaching models give students at
least some voice and therefore some investment in their learning, while
new links, forged among disparate populations of students, tutors, and
teachers, create supportive, heterogeneous college communities.

While tutors are busily working in classrooms, they too are gaining
from their experiences. Like their fellow writing center tutors, classroom-
based writing tutors can develop skills that will improve their own writing, including enhanced detecting, diagnosing, and revising strategies,
greater audience awareness, and a more profound understanding of
grammar and mechanics (M. Harris 1988). Across-the-disciplines tutors
are building a repertoire of varied generic conventions while gaining flexibility and creativity in meeting multiple rhetorical situations.

In evaluating his on-location experiences, a tutor from the Penn
State Berks Writing Fellows Program wrote: "I found that my writing has
improved since the beginning of this program. I had always thought that
I was a fairly good writer, but now I consider myself even better. After
reading some of my group's papers, I noticed how important developing
my arguments was. This helped me for my history class. My first essay was
decent, but my argument was developed better in my second essay. I also
brushed up on a lot of basics, such as comma placement. My group [the
writing group he was facilitating] had comma trouble, so I made sure I
knew what I was doing."

Another writing fellow wrote that her activities as a classroom-based
peer tutor "contributed to my intellectual development" and helped her

"to critique my own work." She explained: "I have learned the valuable tool of depending on another writer or peer to help oneself get through obstacles and generate new ideas in writing."

Classroom-based writing tutors also develop skills beyond writing itself, including knowledge of how people learn and different kinds of strategies that are needed to explain or teach or communicate (M. Harris 1988, 29), which will be useful if they become teachers or if their professional fields require that they oversee the learning of others. With increased insight into how writers react to comments, positively or negatively, tutors learn to develop effective ways to respond to others' writing. In their relationships with students and teachers, they also discover how communication breaks down or is interpretive. At the same time, they are developing a sense of their own autonomy in addition to leadership skills for guiding individuals and groups to recognize a problem, to diagnose its causes, and to offer good recommendations.

Teachers also benefit because on-location tutoring programs provide important kinds of instructional support and instructional development. Classroom-based tutors may introduce teachers to composing theory, writing center theory, and peer group theory; they may guide instructors to clarify their expectations, offer more consistent instruction, or develop more coherent writing assignments. In "content courses," when writing tasks are grounded in composition theory, tutors and teachers benefit from current composition knowledge and practices not yet common to many disciplines. (For example, although for decades writing teachers have used peer groups, collaborative writing, and writing to learn exercises, such strategies have only recently found their way into the journals of higher education and journals of teaching in specific disciplines like science.) Moreover, tutors' advanced understanding of literacy practices has the potential, at least, to foster in faculty and students notions of social change. Thus, classroom-based tutor-teacher collaborations often result in better-informed and innovative teachers and more active kinds of learning. At the same time, many instructors quickly discover that on-location tutors make their job easier: there are extra "hands" or voices in the room, assistants who reduce the teacher-to-student ratio when guidance and feedback are needed. In the end, the advantages of on-location tutoring are realized by students and teachers simultaneously in the form of more consistent writing instruction, increased feedback mechanisms for writers at all levels, and the production of more carefully conceived written documents.

Among institutional supporting units, writing centers can gain as well as give by sponsoring classroom-based tutoring programs. In the past, faculty have typically misunderstood writing center operations, often distrusting tutorial instruction and even discouraging their students from seeking such instructional support (Clark 1999, 155). However, writing centers that provide classroom teachers with trained, knowledgeable personnel establish their credibility and achieve prominence within the institution. Instructors in various disciplines begin to understand what writing centers actually do, feel more linked to the center, and hence recommend its services to students who need assistance. And in the reciprocity of teacher-tutor engagement, writing centers learn more about what teachers are doing and what they want. Classroom-based writing tutors have "insider knowledge" of classroom activities and teacher expectations, and this knowledge enables adaptations during writing center tutoring sessions. Ultimately, faculty support and appreciation of writing center tutoring may be realized in permanent funding dollars that allow centers to continue their good work and outreach.

Finally, as classroom-based writing tutors traverse and bring together institutional structures and programs, including WAC, writing centers, and supplemental instruction, they introduce fertile opportunities for multiple collaborations, innovative learning and teaching, and resulting writing improvement.

## DISRUPTIONS AND AMBIGUITIES OF ON-LOCATION TUTORING

The essays in *On Location* illustrate that tutoring in classrooms can augment writing instruction and benefit students, tutors, faculty, and institutions in countless ways. Nonetheless, we realize that principles and theories underlying one-to-one tutoring, WAC theory and practices, SI, and writing group pedagogies may conflict with classroom-based writing tutoring efforts, producing confusion, ambiguity, and less effective instruction. Such uncertainties, we argue, are to be expected. If, as Behling and other genre theorists suggest, generic forms are themselves "unstable" (2003, 420), then the mixing of genres and the resulting hybrid forms may inevitably cause further turmoil.

Referring to literary texts, Behling argues that as genres shift, "our readings of these texts become unfixed, destabilized" (2003, 422). Likewise, our contributors show that, as a generic hybrid, classroom-based writing tutoring will be complicated, complex, and erratic. They reveal that associated theories and practices undergo constant adaptations and alterations, like the cultural hybrids Stross describes, which "are revised and refashioned as . . . needs dictate" (1999, 263). While Stross refers to "the cultural perceptions of the developers, whether these perceptions be economic or ideological" (263), we have in mind modifications that are educational, pragmatic, and theoretically sound. In the discussion that follows, we bring to light some of the disruptions, conflicts, and complications that we have noted in the ongoing discussions of this hybrid form. In the succeeding chapters, our contributors continue the work of refashioning and revising, modifying and adapting, as pedagogical considerations, theoretical advances, and institutional contexts demand.

First, in clear and definite ways, the physical and ideological isolation of the writing center conflicts with the notion of on-location tutoring, which brings writing tutoring into the classroom and thus into mainstream institutional culture. Most writing center theorists hold that a designated space or place, a "room of one's own," is crucial to successful tutoring operations. Peter Carino, for example, celebrates the "communal aspect of the [writing] center as a microculture in which camaraderie replaces the competitive atmosphere of the classroom" (1995, 43).[14] Likewise, according to Muriel Harris, the writing center's physically distinct location, its bustle and informality, create a relatively safe space for talking about writing (1992b, 157–58). Moreover, in their relations with the university at large, writing centers have traditionally been marginalized sites, peripheral to mainstream academic practices. Indeed, the radical, outsider status of writing centers has been a great attraction for compositionists who view peer tutoring as an opportunity for subverting institutional hierarchies (Kail and Trimbur 1987; Healy 1995; Grimm 1999).

For many compositionists, maintaining this separation gives writing center work its critical edge (Warnock and Warnock, qtd. in Carino 1992, 44; see also Grimm 1999). Common writing center wisdom supports Stephen North's "idea" that a writing center should be defined by the students who seek assistance; it should not "serve, supplement, back up, complement, reinforce, or otherwise be defined by any external curriculum" (1984, 440). Many writing center theorists hold with Harvey Kail and John Trimbur that in a setting relatively safe from institutional ideology, students can work together to understand themselves and to resist subordinating instructional forces (1987, 5). Inarguably, the autonomy that writing center supporters have battled so hard to attain may be lost amid the realities of tutoring in classrooms.

From an instructional perspective, established tutoring principles and classroom instructors' understanding of writing processes may also conflict. Instructors in the disciplines often hold traditional views of literacy; they may view tutors as editors rather than peer readers or consultants, or they may believe that the tutor's generalist training will not transfer to the specialist knowledge and disciplinary discourse conventions required for their specific writing assignments. Even in composition classrooms, nonintrusive methods advocated for one-to-one tutorials may not be the most effective strategies for in-class tutoring, where students and instructors expect immediate and direct answers to particular questions on specific writing assignments.

From a different angle, although the manifold classroom roles writing tutors can take (including classroom presenters, discussion leaders, workshop troubleshooters, conference consultants, and peer group facilitators) serve to promote an assortment of potentially powerful associations among tutors, students, teachers, and sponsoring constituencies, amid these crossings and connections the classroom-based writing tutor also occupies a space of ambiguity, a *relocation* fraught with potential conflicts among different institutional cultures. Like the writing center tutor, he or she straddles the role of both student and peer, but the classroom-based tutor must also contend with the competing claims of writing center theory and practices, WAC theory and practices, and classroom instructors, who are often untrained or differently trained in writing theory or WAC theory.

Classroom-based writing tutors may also find themselves working within competing systems of power. In some cases, the power and status of the sponsoring unit coordinator or the classroom teacher may restrict the tutor's instructional role and undermine her authority. Program coordinators may inadvertently undermine tutor authority in order to fulfill responsibilities—real or perceived—to other constituencies, such as faculty in the disciplines or college administrators, to ensure program continuation. Also, faculty who are institutionally or departmentally required to use classroom-based tutors may resent (and resist) sharing their classroom space. Moreover, even when instructors attempt to share authority, tutors' role confusion may lead them to reject it.

Across our chapters, then, these issues resonate, framing in their turn a set of oppositions—tutoring autonomy versus institutional immersion, nonintrusive versus directive tutoring approaches, traditional process-oriented strategies versus writing group pragmatics, tutors as peers versus tutors as specialists, and tutors as students versus tutors as "teachers." Such theoretical and practical oppositions are neither surprising nor disheartening, for we regard them as the logical products of genre hybridity. Thus, even as we recognize the forms of resistance, contradictions, and conflicts created by crossing locations and entering new territories, we also see evidence of the kind of dialogue bell hooks suggests is the real work of border crossing (although she believes it occurs too infrequently): individuals occupying different locations "sharing ideas with one another, mapping out terrains of commonality, connection, and shared concern with teaching practices" (1994, 130). We see faculty from various disciplines sharing authority with, and thus empowering, undergraduate writing tutors; and we find in tutors in our own projects and those of our contributors a certain strength that has allowed them to overcome the uncertainties of being on location in order to be effective, to varying degrees, in their new classroom roles.

The essays in *On Location* address the issues (both positive and negative) that we have touched on in this introduction. Overall, we have arranged our chapters into three broad sections intended to (1) highlight the alliances and connections on-location tutoring offers, both practically and theoretically, to supporting constituencies of teachers and students; (2) interrogate local strategies and resolve conflicts relating to the classroom scene of tutoring; and (3) address issues relating to institutional power configurations and role definition.[15] We acknowledge that these categories are not hard and fast, nor are they mutually exclusive. As a hybrid genre, classroom-based writing tutoring provokes discussions that invariably overlap and intersect. In their professional lives, our contributors assume many instructional roles–classroom instructor, writing center director, tutor trainer, graduate student. Each of our three main sections conclude with a "Tutor's Voices" chapter, in which we present an essay written by an undergraduate classroom-based writing tutor.

# PART ONE

## Creating New Alliances and Connections Through Classroom-Based Writing Tutoring

Fostering diplomatic relationships, building bridges, creating intensive-care communities, establishing trust and common ground: these are the concepts that resonate through part one of *On Location*. They point to the many connections that are fostered by and through the hybridity of classroom-based writing tutoring programs, and they emphasize new relationships formed between writing centers and students, tutors and faculty across the disciplines, tutors and students. These associations, in turn, yield additional benefits: writing group facilitation assists students to create knowledge together and improve their writing abilities; tutors develop their writing, critical thinking, and social skills; writing centers witness increased respect for and use of their services; and faculty across the disciplines find needed support to bring productive writing assignments to their students.

Thus, Teagan Decker describes the productive "diplomatic partnership" between the writing center and classroom instructors fashioned through on-location tutoring. Classroom tutors act as "emissaries," promoting conversations among teachers, the writing center director, and various groups of students. From a different angle, Mary Soliday addresses connections between disciplinary discourses, revealing that tutors with generalist literacy training can successfully bridge specialized writing situations in WAC courses. Taking a "writing in the course" approach that considers the teacher's specific expectations, she argues that peer tutors, regardless of major or course, can enhance undergraduate teaching by assisting with general writing strategies.

A very different kind of discursive bridging occurs when peer group leaders are effectively integrated into the classroom culture. According to Laurie Grobman, tutors can create a theoretical bridge between the discourses most familiar to students and those of academic communities. She argues that undergraduate classroom-based writing tutors are best suited to this task because they can simultaneously model academic response, guide writing group conversation, and maintain their status as college-level peers. Also focusing on basic writing, Jim Ottery, Jean Petrolle, Derek Boczkowski, and Steve Mogge discuss peer tutors' central role in a successful summer Bridge Program learning community. They describe how classroom-based writing center consultants were able to provide academic support and, even more important, to foster a welcoming and caring environment for their students. In so doing, peer tutors helped Bridge students establish a college identity while giving faculty a unique opportunity to consider their roles as teachers. Likewise, Casey You reveals that peer group leaders can foster a sense of connection and community among writers of varied proficiency by encouraging students to take on leadership roles within their groups and by validating each student's accomplishments.

As we reflect on and celebrate the varied connections and new relationships that these chapters suggest, we note that these collaborations are never without tension and never completely settled. From our perspective, this is exactly what makes hybrid practices so exciting.

# 1

## DIPLOMATIC RELATIONS
### Peer Tutors in the Writing Classroom

Teagan Decker

Of the many things that define a writing center, one of the most crucial is the relationship it has with those who assign the writing in the first place. Some centers, especially those connected with basic writing programs, are thoroughly intertwined with the classroom and may serve as labs that students attend as an extension of their composition classes. Others are more autonomous and may have spun away from their home departments altogether, housed in a central location such as a library or undergraduate center. Many are connected with a department, usually English, but are autonomous within that relationship, free to practice forms of pedagogy that diverge from the writing program they are associated with. This type of center attempts to provide students a place separate from the classroom, a place where they can find a different perspective, an interested audience, a place to be free from the authority of the instructor.

In 1984, Stephen North articulated the frustrations and desires of many writing centers by declaring independence from the writing classroom and the writing instructor: "In short, we are not here to serve, supplement, back up, complement, reinforce, or otherwise be defined by any external curriculum" (440). As directors of writing centers, those of us who share his views try to maintain a separateness from the classroom, which serves to strengthen our authority and allows us to offer an alternative learning experience to students. Writing centers don't want independence because of animosity toward instructors. Most writing center directors have been or are instructors, and many tutors plan on making a career in teaching. The real reason for our quest for autonomy has to do with our fundamental belief that students can become better writers and learn from writing better if they have a place to practice writing and share writing that is separate from a writing classroom.

### DECLARATIONS OF INDEPENDENCE

For many centers, this desire for separateness has resulted in a place that is, in fact, separate. Far from being combative about autonomy, many writing center directors no longer have to think about these issues: others in the department, although they may not all fully understand or appreciate what goes on in the writing center, leave it alone. The writing center may even operate under a different pedagogical theory than the writing program. Writing centers have achieved an institutional independence that is no longer in need of defense—we are constantly fighting small battles, but the larger one has for the most part been won.

However much we value this independence, we must allow that a strict approach to autonomy can create a climate of poor communication between center and instructors. We lament on listservs, at conferences, and in print that some instructors don't understand what we do, send us their students for the wrong reasons, or don't recommend us to their students at all for equally wrong reasons. We must admit that this is partly due to our declarations of independence. We exist apart from the classroom, so we are misunderstood by instructors. We try to bridge this gulf with flyers, brochures, and presentations, but until they see for themselves what goes on in the writing center, instructors will never really understand what we are doing.

The writing center I work in is independent, autonomous, and has the freedom to experiment. The manner in which we are experimenting, however, seems at odds with the autonomy we have worked so hard to maintain. We have begun sending tutors into the writing classroom. The tutors are not simply visiting the classroom to give an informational speech about the writing center—they are becoming part of the instruction. This bringing together of the writing center and the classroom, on the instructor's turf, may cause writing center advocates to cringe. How can a writing center maintain its integrity when its tutors are being sent to the classroom to do the bidding of an instructor? Doesn't this compromise the autonomy, the separateness, of the writing center and do exactly the opposite of what North advocates: reinforce an external curriculum?

I believe that there is a way to send tutors into the classroom without compromising integrity. Further, I have found that far from compromising the writing center, peer tutoring in the classroom can forge a diplomatic partnership between the center and the instructors that is healthy and supportive. Inviting instructors to work with us allows for a dialogue between instructor and writing center director that is much richer than the usual exchange of information. Tutors visiting the classroom can act as emissaries, sharing their perspective on writing collaboration with instructors and students. If the relationship between the writing center and classroom is built upon a diplomatic model, with careful negotiation and a mindfulness of the role of the tutors, not only is the integrity of the writing center spared, the classroom becomes a fertile ground, with writing center theory infusing the curriculum and instructors witnessing collaboration in action.

## THE UNIVERSITY OF WASHINGTON'S ENGLISH DEPARTMENT WRITING CENTER

The climate at the University of Washington is the epitome of autonomy: the UW has no central writing center; instead, various departments have created their own centers to serve their students exclusively. The English Department Writing Center, where I am the assistant director, is the only center open to anyone on campus. One main group of the students who visit us are taking lower-division English classes, another significant component consists of those seeking help as second-language students, and a heavy sprinkling come from departments that don't have writing centers of their own.

In short, we are a small center in a very large university. Ten to twelve tutors make up the staff, each working an average of fifteen hours per week. They are almost all undergraduate English majors in their third, fourth, or fifth year. We require all new tutors to enroll in a full-credit training course that provides plentiful theory and practice, preparing students for the complexity of their roles as tutors in the writing center and, more recently, as writing center tutors who occasionally visit classrooms. I try to engage tutors in some of the theoretical problems writing centers face, including the debate over definition. I feel it is especially important for tutors to have a sense of the complexity of their place in the university when they leave the writing center and visit the classroom. If they are able to define themselves as tutors, as opposed to helpers or preteachers, they are better able to maintain their roles as writing center representatives when they enter the classroom.

My motives for initiating a classroom-based tutoring service were twofold. Our relationship with the English department's expository writing program (which offers composition courses that fulfill general education requirements for undergraduates) is positive and complementary, but we operate independently of one another. Most of the composition instructors are graduate students, many of whom are teaching their first or second year. They are introduced to the writing center at their orientation and again through e-mails detailing our specific services. Part of my job description is to act as a liaison between the writing center and the teaching assistants (TAs), but one short presentation and a few e-mails never seem like enough to me. My social skills are simply not advanced enough to develop relationships and engage in fruitful professional dialogue with ninety busy graduate students, most of whom are studying literature and don't have a natural interest in writing center theory. Since there are few formal links between the classroom and the writing center, I began searching for a new way to connect with instructors.

Another goal of mine was to incorporate group tutoring into what we do at the writing center. As an undergraduate tutor, I worked in a curriculum-based lab connected to a basic writing program. One of the instructors occasionally used lab time for peer response groups with tutors as group facilitators. I always enjoyed these groups because I was able to encourage students to tutor each other, which gave them confidence in their own abilities as writers and critics. Although committed to this idea, I couldn't devise a way to bring groups of students into the writing center regularly enough for this new group tutoring program to work. So I decided instead to try sending tutors into the classroom. A group of two or three tutors would attend class during peer response group day and sit in on the groups, helping them respond to each other's work. Not only would students benefit from an experienced peer group facilitator, the TAs (especially the TAs new to teaching) could get help with conducting successful peer response groups, and we would be able to do all this during slow weeks (the first weeks of the quarter), when often tutors are underworked. As a purely practical matter, this idea seemed like it would benefit everyone, but I felt that we were wading into dangerous waters theoretically. How could I send tutors into the classroom without compromising our center's independence? What stakes are involved in such a venture?

## THE DEBATE OVER CENTER/CLASSROOM RELATIONS

Since Stephen North's initial declaration of independence, many writing center theorists have engaged in the struggle to define a writing center's relationship with the classroom. As Thomas Hemmeter points out in his review of the literature, "These repeated calls for self-definition form a distinct segment of writing center discourse" (1990, 36). What he finds is that we routinely define ourselves in terms of difference: we are different from the classroom, different from the institution at large, different from expository writing programs. This habit of perception, he maintains, is to our detriment: "The metaphorical contrast of writing center with class-room has been expressed so literally as an environment that the discourse becomes constricted, inhibiting effective communication" (38). The communication he is addressing is that between composition instructors and writing center staff. When writing centers pursue the path of isola-tionism, setting up a polarity between center and classroom, communica-tion and collegiality are put at risk. The real losers in this communication block are students: instructors may distrust a place they have no ties with, wondering just what goes on in there, and not recommend us to students. Alternatively, they may misunderstand us and misconstrue our agenda to students, who will either not visit or visit under false expectations.

In "Revisiting 'The Idea of a Writing Center,'" North agrees that his original polemic, while useful to writing centers as they have worked to define themselves over the years, is heavy-handed and "presents its own kind of jeopardy," limiting the role of writing centers with its polarized conception of the relationship between writing center and classroom (1994, 9). He now advocates a writing center that is more integrated with the instructional end of things: "I want a situation in which we are not required to sustain some delicate but carefully distanced relationship between classroom teachers and the writing center, not least because the classroom teachers are directly involved with, and therefore invested in, the functioning of that center" (16).

The notion of separation that North's 1984 article advocates has been revised and questioned by North himself and others, but its opposite, inte-gration, has its own pitfalls. In an integrated, or curriculum-based, writing center, tutors are part of the classroom instruction for a full term. They are usually attached to a specific class and perform various duties, includ-ing one-to-one tutoring, group tutoring, responding to papers in writing, and even giving presentations to the class. The curriculum-based model has met with enthusiasm and success by writing center practitioners like Mary Soliday, who, although frank about problems she encountered and that may be looming in the future, considers her program beneficial to all involved and argues that it "popularize[s] the writing center's services . . . so that classroom tutors also function as 'gateways' to the writing center" (1995, 70).

Although these curriculum-based programs may be effective in meet-ing certain pedagogical and practical goals, they undercut important aspects of writing center identity. As Harvey Kail and John Trimbur warn, "the curriculum-based model makes the peer tutors an extension of the faculty" (1987, 6). This violates one of the main tenants of writing center ideology: the absence of professorial authority. Although it is difficult for tutors to truly be peers, most of us can agree that a tutor should not serve as a teacher. When tutors do become teachers, they "suppress the crisis of authority precipitated when students work together, domesticate it, and channel the social forces released by collaboration into the established structures of teaching and learning" (11). In other words, the writing center is often conceived as (and this is true for my writing center) a site of liberation from the traditional regimes of the academy. It is a place to question and investigate the seemingly untouchable expectations, goals, and motivations of the power structures within which undergraduates (and those at all levels in the university) operate. Combining writing centers with classrooms retains the more obvious benefits of peer tutoring and provides much-needed help to overworked instructors, but leaves the political and social energy of the autonomous writing center behind.

Writing center theorists often position autonomy and integration at opposite ends of the pedagogical spectrum, each extreme having its costs and benefits. Writing centers like mine, which try to be what Kail and Trimbur advocate—a site of political awakening, a place where students can "remove themselves from the official structures" and "reengage the forms of authority in their lives by demystifying the authority of knowledge and its institutions" (1987, 11)—suffer from a loss of communication between center and classroom. Curriculum-based centers, however, lose the very "crises of authority" Kail and Trimbur describe by merging the writing center with the classroom, compromising the separateness that allows students to become aware of institutional assumptions about writing and learning in the academy.

Dave Healy, who, like Kail and Trimbur, argues for the political benefits of a separate classroom and center, nevertheless urges us to "recognize the fluidity of both classroom and center" (1993, 26). He suggests a solution much like the program my writing center has been experimenting with: "On writing workshop days, tutors could join the instructor in circulating around the room and doing short conferences." Even an advocate of dualism like Healy is comfortable with tutors in the classroom if the visits are isolated, not every day. With the instructor in the classroom, and the structures of the classroom in place, it is probably too much to expect that students will experience a "crisis of authority" when tutors visit the classroom, but if tutors are able to retain their identity, certainly students will experience something of what the writing center is able to offer them.

Also, if tutors visit only once per term, the writing center itself remains the primary locus of the tutor. Handled properly, then, my program can bring instructors closer to the writing center and reach more students, while still retaining writing center integrity.

## A DIPLOMATIC PARTNERSHIP

If the goal is to promote stronger relationships between classroom and center while closely guarding the benefits that only an autonomous writing center can offer students, then a model of diplomacy can work well to structure this relationship and offer a theoretical framework to operate in. This type of structure also allows us to transcend the duality that pushes us to one extreme or the other. Instead of fostering a strained, cool relationship, or, conversely, uniting the two into one homogenized entity, we can make connections and negotiate agreements across institutional borders that we all feel comfortable with. In this model of diplomacy, classroom and center are analogous to nations sending representatives across borders to forge a mutually beneficial relationship. Both states keep their identity but are able to share ideas, services, and responsibility to citizens (in this case, students).

Tutoring in the classroom allows for two diplomatic events. First, the negotiations between instructor and center: before sending tutors to the classroom, a conversation takes place between the instructor and the writing center staff, planning when and how the visit will happen. If handled properly, this conversation can communicate the pedagogy of the writing center without alienating the instructor. At the same time, the instructor can communicate his or her goals, and together the instructor and center can work out a lesson plan that reflects the pedagogy of both. Second, when the actual visit occurs, tutors function as emissaries. If what the tutors do in the classroom is reasonably consistent with what they do in the writing center, then instructors and students are educated about the writing center in a far more immediate and experiential manner than an informational class visit could ever hope to achieve.

## NEGOTIATION IN ACTION

The word *negotiation* can carry the implication that two parties are at odds and need to solve a problem. "The Middle East peace negotiations" is an example. In the case of classroom and writing center, however, we can begin with the assumption that we are peaceable neighbors hoping to work together on a mutually beneficial project. Initiating a negotiation gives us a chance to have a meaningful conversation with instructors as we work toward an agreement. In their book *Getting to Yes: Negotiating Agreement without Giving In* (1981), Roger Fisher and William Ury describe negotiation as a process of mutual gain, even when the two sides are adversaries. In their program, negotiation begins with each side learning about the other and then using this information to find solutions to problems. This stance seems especially helpful to classroom/writing center relationships since one of our goals in promoting tutoring in the classroom is increased communication. The very act of negotiating the visit can begin to accomplish that goal.

We have been in negotiated diplomacy with instructors at the University of Washington for four quarter-long terms and have visited quite a few classrooms. Some visits have been successful, some have not (at least from the point of view of tutors). The actual goal of our visits, of course, is to help students respond to each other's writing. I can't say for certain how effective we have been in the long term, but since instructors who have participated often ask for us to visit again the next quarter, there is at least a perceived benefit. What I have noticed from my desk in the writing center, though, is a marked increase in the frequency and quality of my interactions with instructors.

I begin the negotiation process with an offer of help. I know from my own experience as a graduate student TA that the first term especially can be overwhelming. TAs are taught about peer response groups in their training course but may be wary of the potential for unsupervised, unfocused groups. An offer of help in this area can be very attractive.

I sent this e-mail to all first-year English instructors: "Writing Center tutors are now available to help you make peer response groups more effective. A group of two to three tutors can come to your class on peer response day and join the groups. The tutor's function in this case is not to be a tutor, but to be a facilitator—sparking group conversation about a student's writing, encouraging constructive feedback by asking questions, and modeling appropriate comments and questions. This works especially well for students new to response group work."

This e-mail offers our assistance with peer response groups but at the same time defines the role of tutor, which is the one point we are not prepared to negotiate. Beginning the conversation with a definition of tutors' roles helps ensure that TAs understand from the beginning what we are offering.

When an instructor replies to the e-mail, either requesting the service or wanting more information, I send them this second e-mail, which introduces negotiable items:

Thanks for your interest in peer response group facilitation. Based on our prior experience with these sessions, we have come up with a few suggestions for ways to structure your class time in order to make the session successful. During the class period before the peer response day:
- ask students to bring in multiple copies of their paper
- introduce class to the idea of peer response groups;
- have students form groups of three or four and pass around copies of their papers;
- ask them to read the papers at home (or during class time);
- also for homework ask them to write down comments;
- discuss appropriate types of comments.

On peer response day:
- set aside an entire fifty-minute class period for response;
- introduce tutors, explain their role;
- ask students to form their groups and get started.

We suggest having the students read the papers beforehand because we have found that otherwise much of the fifty minutes is spent reading. Also, the students have the chance to think about what responses they might make ahead of time.

These are some basic guidelines, but feel free to experiment. Just let us know what you are thinking, and we will discuss the possibilities.

This set of guidelines informs TAs that we intend to be involved in the planning and that this will be a joint venture. It also is designed to allow for negotiation: the word *suggest* is repeated, and the last sentence makes it clear that we aren't laying down the law on how this visit will be conducted. We are opening up the conversation and setting the stage for a negotiation.

The next step in this process is to invite the instructor to the writing center to meet with me and the tutors who will be visiting the classroom. They bring copies of the assignment the students are working on and the readings they are working with. This is where we hash out the details, where the true negotiation takes place. This negotiation has both obvious and underlying purposes. On the overt side, we must figure out some logistics: How many tutors should go? How big should the groups be? Will the session follow the above plan or diverge from this in some way? The underlying, less obvious, purposes of the negotiation are to bring the instructor physically into the writing center in order to develop a good working relationship and promote understanding of our purposes and methods. (I have also conducted this conversation via e-mail with good results.)

It is interesting to try new things, so we are willing to brainstorm with the instructor and work with the ideas that come up. Fisher and Ury tell us that "joint brainstorming sessions have the great advantages of producing ideas which take into account the interests of all those involved, of creating a climate of joint problem-solving, and of educating each side about the concerns of the other" (1981, 65). Being receptive to ideas generated by the brainstorming and demonstrating a willingness to develop new approaches to the logistics of the peer response group sessions show the instructor that the writing center is a partner. As Fisher and Ury write, "communicating loudly and convincingly things you are willing to say that they would like to hear can be one of the best investments you as a negotiator can make" (26).

One of our more interesting meetings with an instructor resulted in a substantial departure from the recommended guidelines. He asked the tutors to identify the biggest problem that they had when facilitating peer response groups. One tutor told him that students are often so worried about offending each other that they won't say anything critical about other students' work. After discussing this situation for a few minutes, one of the tutors had an idea: using an anonymous paper for a practice response group session and then, later in the week, having the tutors work with the current writing assignment. This would allow students to experience a response group without the anxiety of sharing their work. When they did actually share their essays, they would be more skilled and comfortable with the format. We tried this approach, and the tutors thought it was highly successful. The instructor was pleased and from then on had a close relationship with the writing center. This negotiation allowed the instructor to get what he wanted out of the visit and to feel involved in the planning. Furthermore, even though the writing center deviated from the standard plan, the tutors' role was consistent with our original definition. They remained writing center tutors acting as facilitators, not classroom assistants, and the writing center remained autonomous while creating a positive relationship with a classroom instructor and his students.

## TUTORS AS EMISSARIES, TUTORS AS FACILITATORS

The core of a writing center is its tutors, and so any deviation from their standard role must be investigated carefully. I have referred to the importance of a well-defined role for tutors as they cross the borders of writing center and classroom, and here I will explain more fully what the tutors in my writing center have been doing when they visit classrooms.

The best term I have come up with so far to describe what tutors do in the classroom is *peer response group facilitation.* This is cumbersome but, I hope, descriptive enough to help tutors and TAs navigate this new territory. In this facilitative role, tutors help students in peer response groups use writing center skills, such as open-ended questions, comments such as "I don't quite understand how this connects to your main claim," and specific rather than general praise and criticism. In other words, they show students how to tutor each other.

The pedagogy of peer response groups is similar to that of writing centers: focused on collaboration, student-centered learning, and students keeping authority over their work. In many ways, what instructors expect of students in response groups amounts to what we expect of tutors in one-to-one sessions. Often, though, students are unable to manifest the skills of an effective group collaborator, even with examples and practice offered by the instructor. Tutors have the benefit of being practiced responders, with an understanding of the types of questions to ask and the types of dialogues to encourage. This helps students to take themselves seriously as writers and to see their written work's potential for revision. Tutors can share this experience and training with students by sitting in on response groups and prompting students to ask questions of each other. They facilitate the conversation, encouraging the group to focus on the larger concerns of thesis and organization rather than punctuation, modeling appropriate questions and comments, asking the responders to offer revision suggestions to the writer. They become meta-tutors, encouraging students to tutor each other. In this capacity, tutors are not doing what they would be doing in a one-to-one conference in the writing center—they are showing students how to do it. Their role, then, does change, but at the same time remains consistent. A tutor, Todd, writes about his role in a class visit: "I definitely felt like a tutor showing students how to respond to each other's work."

This is, of course, an ideal that is not always easy for tutors to live up to amid the individual demands of students and instructors and the general chaos that peer response groups create. Todd continues his comments: "There were a few students who had specific questions for me, and I did my best to answer them without usurping classroom authority from [the instructor]." Here Todd is carefully monitoring his role, trying not to be a teacher, as students often expect from anyone placed above them in the academic hierarchy. What the tutors are encouraged to do in this case is to quickly either answer the question or pass the question on to the teacher, then turn the group's attention back to peer response. Tutors must be aware that they are entering a climate in which anyone who is not a student is traditionally a teacher, and they must be confident enough in their roles to resist that climate. Mary Soliday uses the metaphor of cultural assimilation to describe the choices tutors have when they enter the classroom: "A stranger can assimilate to a new place by shedding old values, identifying with the 'other,' but this is only one possibility. Another might be to resist identification with the new culture, thus experiencing continuous conflict, or, more daringly, revolutionizing the dynamics of the culture. A third way could be to assimilate critically, holding differences in tension so that a dialogue between individuals from different cultures can occur" (1995, 68).

Soliday encourages her tutors to pursue the third way, but I believe it is better for writing center integrity if tutors take the second path. Since they visit any particular classroom only once or at most twice per term, they are more able to avoid assimilation than tutors in Soliday's curriculum-based program, which expects tutors to attend a class every day. Even though students, instructors, and tutors (who are often aspiring teachers themselves) will automatically rank each other in terms of teacher/student, if tutors are aware of this climate, they can actively resist their own urge and the students' expectations to assume a teacherly role and instead share their skills as responders. Tutors in our program try to maintain their identity as writing center tutors, resisting assimilation into the classroom culture; instead, they introduce writing center culture into the classroom for a day.

This is how tutors become emissaries in a diplomatic mission: bringing the writing center closer to the classroom without compromising the center's integrity. And here also lies the potential for tutors to "revolutioniz[e] the dynamics of the culture," as Soliday put it (1995), and create the type of event Kail and Trimbur describe. If tutors are resisting student's expectations of authority, then students may indeed experience a "crisis of authority" in perhaps even a more profound way than they do in the writing center, because it takes place right in the heart of the instructor-as-authority's domain: the classroom.

## CONFUSION WITH AUTHORITY

Many instructors I have worked with value the revolutionary aspect of writing center/classroom collaboration. As advocates of student-centered instruction, they resist the authority that comes in a classroom but can never truly escape the structures of hierarchy inherent in the classroom. In fact, in one class visit, the tutors and the instructor were so eager to give up authority that the entire visit backfired. One tutor laments: "He [the instructor] obviously didn't know what he wanted out of the session. . . . some students had 2.1 essays, others had 2.2, a few had no essays at all. . . . the students were all at different points in the writing process, so were really not into doing peer reviews. To make matters worse, we as tutors were reluctant to take control over the session, and over each other. . . . things were happening in sessions that were more instructive than facilitative, and because there was no real authority involved, I feel that the session was a flop."

Even with the benefits of short visits as opposed to extended stays, then, we have experienced some confusion in tutors' roles. Instructors and tutors are often not sure who should have authority. Some instructors prefer the tutors to run the class, introducing the lesson plan and organizing students into groups, whereas some tutors feel uncomfortable taking over a classroom while the instructor is present. In order to bring tutors and instructors into the same location, there must be an understanding between them first. If not, tutors and instructors lack confidence in their roles, which leads to awkward moments in the classroom; students notice, lessening their confidence in the whole plan. Like Mary Soliday's experience, our first few tries at sending tutors to the classroom met with some confusion. Soliday found that "several tutors said that teachers didn't know what to do with them or 'didn't know what my role is.' While a few noted that the teacher seemed to expect them to take the lead in defining their role in the classroom, others thought that their teachers exerted too much control over the role of tutoring" (1995, 63). This has been the case in our program as well, and tutors have reported similar feelings of dissatisfaction or anxiety, especially during the first few minutes of class when someone should be addressing the students.

New problems and challenges are bound to continue to crop up given the dynamic nature of this experiment. In the above case, we were forced to examine more closely the need for some authority, at least initially. The classroom is different from the writing center, and we must take that into account. Bringing tutors into a foreign context throws our own pedagogy into high relief even as we are sharing it with instructors and students.

## CONCLUSION

In political terms, my writing center is making a transition from an isolationist to a globalist model. The danger of this is the possibility that the writing center will become homogenized into the academy. By use of careful diplomacy and insistence upon autonomy, though, we can avoid being swallowed up by the classroom as we become more engaged. By use of negotiation that is focused on positive outcomes and building relationships, we can strengthen ties, thereby strengthening our positions in the academy. By sending tutors to the classroom under our pedagogical conditions, we can promote the writing center and foster communication while keeping our integrity intact.

Far from compromising the writing center, I suspect that tutors facilitating peer response groups may ultimately bring the more revolutionary aspects of the writing center into the classroom, showing students that even the most entrenched site of the academic hierarchy can be subverted—within its own borders—and all with the approval of the instructor. On a more basic level, students benefit from tutors' skills in peer response. The visit can give students the confidence to conduct response groups on their own for the rest of the term without a tutor facilitating. Also, a positive experience with a tutor/facilitator in the classroom often encourages students to make an appointment with that tutor for a one-to-one conference, initiating a relationship with the writing center that can last far beyond the term.

The relationship between the classroom and the writing center has been a major theoretical struggle for decades; there is no quick and easy answer. The peer response group facilitation program that I have described may not work for all centers, but I think that imagining the writing center as something like a nation-state making its way in a complicated world shows us that, through good use of diplomacy and negotiation, we can retain our autonomy while fostering ties with those whom we share interests. And the place to send our delegations is most logically the classroom. We have established our independence; now it is time to initiate a diplomatic relationship with instructors, sending tutors into the classroom as emissaries, creating stronger relationships with instructors through positive negotiation experiences, lending our expertise in peer collaboration to students and instructors alike.

## 2

# GENERAL READERS AND CLASSROOM TUTORS ACROSS THE CURRICULUM

Mary Soliday

With the rapid expansion of writing across the curriculum (WAC) programs, many of us wrestle with understanding the differences between teaching writing in composition courses and teaching writing across the disciplines. While a lively debate has long existed over whether we can teach writing effectively in composition courses, it has gained fresh life from WAC scholars like Aviva Freedman, who "question the value of GWSI," or general writing skills instruction (1995, 122). A similar debate has also spilled over to tutoring programs, where scholars and program directors wonder whether tutors trained in GWSI can cope with the more distinct forms of writing that readers trained in special fields may assign and evaluate.

Peer tutors in WAC classrooms or in writing centers that support WAC face complex challenges when they read a range of different assignments (see Mullin 2001; Soven 2001). How will these tutors best support WAC, which stresses faculty development and writing in specialist settings, as opposed to their more traditional support for composition programs, which stress student empowerment and writing for broad audiences? Can tutors translate their generalist training to new learning environments? Can an English major cope with a lab report for a biology class or a research paper for an upper-level chemistry elective? Can a psychology major cope with an essay exploring the causes of the American Civil War? A dilemma results when we wonder whether readers trained in a generalist tradition can be reasonably expected to read and react to so many distinct assignments.

In this chapter, I will examine how content knowledge affects the success of classroom tutors in WAC programs. Adopting a perspective called writing in the course (Thaiss 2001), I will focus on the fit between general rhetorical knowledge and what naturalistic research shows that professors in content courses expect from student writing as well as how students respond to those expectations. Generally speaking, writing in the course suggests that even within the same discipline, professors can diverge widely in their purposes for assigning writing. The goals professors may have for their students' writing evolve partly throughout the life of a course (Prior 1998) in response to the rhetorical situation of a class. Several factors could influence the situation—the quality of students' responses to an assignment, the professor's alignment with a discipline, the different resources that students draw upon during the semester, or the relative importance of the writing to the overall course design.

For these reasons, writing in the course suggests that a tutor's knowledge of content is an important but not exclusive factor determining his or her success. The quality of a tutor's relationship to the course professor or understanding of the assignment would also influence how a tutorial unfolds. From this perspective, classroom tutors—peers who participate in the ongoing life of the course—are admirably situated to bring their general strategies to bear upon a dynamic rhetorical situation where, at a given moment, content may be more or less significant. Linking tutors to courses in their majors surely enhances their work (and their confidence), and therefore is advisable whenever possible. But content knowledge is not the major precondition for success, especially in liberal arts and general education courses.

Despite the fluid differences between the rhetorical situations in WAC classes, WAC faculty do share a common ground. Within disciplines, for instance, many assign official genres that tutors can learn to recognize. Another similarity concerns how WAC faculty organize writing in their courses: many use peer group learning in their classrooms, and professors often assign research projects that involve writing as a mode of inquiry. Peer tutors from any major can act as peer group leaders in content courses, and they can also, again regardless of their majors, promote writing as a form of inquiry across the curriculum. Though classroom tutors will have to adjust to their new circumstances, they can play influential roles in promoting those aspects of writing that are common to all the disciplines and in this way contribute to WAC's overall mission: to improve undergraduate teaching.

## THE GENERAL AND THE SPECIALIST TUTOR

The best illustrations of what I call the general approach to tutoring can be found in Muriel Harris's *Teaching One-to-One: The Writing Conference* (1986) or Emily Meyer and Louise Z. Smith's *The Practical Tutor* (1987). While the latter offers sample dialogues from courses outside English, both texts lean heavily on conversations where tutors and students discuss essays written for English courses. Sample dialogues exemplify the peer's general strategies: careful, nonjudgmental listening; nondirective questions that apply to the global qualities of texts; and personal skills that help to establish a trusting relationship between reader and writer. In the generalist tradition, which the Rose Writing Fellows Program at Brown University has helped to popularize, a reader's specific knowledge of content is less important than the ability to engage with the writer's text and to ask questions that prompt global revision (e.g., see Soven 2001). Encouraging a richer writing process in a safe environment remains the overarching purpose of, and motivating ideal behind, generalist peer tutoring at the writing center and in curriculum-based programs.

But with the growing demands of WAC, program directors debate whether the generalist strategy is enough when peer tutors work with students on case studies for business, research papers for upper-level sociology, or critical essays for art history. In her review of curriculum-based programs, Margot Soven (2001) shows that two perspectives have framed the debate. On the one hand, students benefit from readers who don't know the content because they tend to ask questions and use strategies that push writers to consider how an educated but nontechnical audience will read their work. From her long experience with both writing centers and WAC programs, Susan Hubbuch (1988) notes that generalist tutors are less directive if they aren't familiar with the content, but sometimes assume a teacher's role if they are tutoring in their majors. Successful curriculum-based programs at liberal arts schools, as Soven notes, traditionally privilege the role of the general reader, perhaps because this stance reflects the mission of these institutions—to prepare students to communicate to well-educated, as opposed to technical, audiences. Again as Hubbuch points out, peers should become familiar with different forms across the curriculum. But she suggests that an acquaintance with rhetoric—writing for different audiences at different times and places—does not necessarily entail a specific knowledge of the content.

On the other side of the debate, program directors often consider a peer tutor's major when pairing him or her with classes because experience and some research suggest that knowledge of content plays a role in successful tutorials (see Soven's 2001 survey). For example, Jean Kiedaisch and Sue Dinitz (1993) videotaped twelve tutorials in which students brought drafts from literature courses to their writing center. The researchers asked the professors who taught these courses to rate the

tutorials' success and found that the teachers thought there was a relationship between the tutor's content knowledge and the quality of the session.
Kiedaisch and Dinitz then examined the videotapes of the sessions and
found "that the 'ignorant' or generalist tutor sometimes has limitations"
(65). Only the English majors tutored at the global level—they started
with the quality of the thesis and its relationship to the assignment (69).
At the same time, as Hubbuch might predict, one of the English majors
simply edited a paper (71).

Despite the small sample of tutorials, this study persuasively indicates
that the tutors' content knowledge enhanced their confidence as readers who skillfully pinpointed a global problem in a draft. As a result, the
English majors suggested fruitful revision strategies for the critical essays.
However, as the teachers only inferred from the transcripts that the
tutors' majors affected their superior diagnosis of drafts, this study also
asks us to determine further how other factors—the tutors' knowledge of
the critical essay, which cuts across disciplines, or their past experience
with professors they knew—might also influence successful outcomes.

## COMPLICATING THE DEBATE: WRITING IN THE COURSE

From a theoretical perspective, the debate over the status of a general
reader reflects our beliefs about whether some qualities of writing cut
across all disciplines or whether disciplines use language in highly par-
ticularized ways. Some research indicates that the dualism might not
clearly exist in all courses. For example, Ann Johns (1995) notes from her
experience with ESL students in content courses that many faculty across
the disciplines don't introduce their students to specialized discourse but
assign the essay form. Christopher Thaiss and Terry Zawacki (1997) lent
credence to this experience when they examined portfolios containing
papers for many courses at George Mason University. They found that
faculty across the disciplines appeared to accept and even privilege qualities of writing we associate with composition courses—the use of personal
experience to support arguments, the grammatical first person, and the
essay form with a thesis up front.

This lack of fit among professional discourses, content, and what faculty expect students to write further complicates a dualism between general and specialized kinds of writing. If both specific content and general
rhetorical knowledge come into play, then the classroom tutor trained
as a general reader is well situated to interpret assignments in a variety
of courses. If several factors, such as the professor's relationship with a

student, also affect a professor's expectations, then the classroom tutor's knowledge of this rhetorical scene may be especially influential.

Writing in the course assumes that an array of rhetorical factors might further explain a tutor's success. For example, Judith Levine (1990) evaluated the role of a peer tutor, an English major, in her introductory psychology course and found that, compared to a similar course she taught that didn't employ a tutor, the papers were more likely to be handed in on time. Also, the students said they spent more time working on their papers and expressed greater satisfaction with the writing assignments. However, since the grades for the papers were similar in both courses, Levine speculates that having a tutor with a psychology major may have enhanced the papers' overall quality. On the other hand, Levine's description of her teaching reveals that her course is not fixed but evolves each semester as she continues to evaluate her success. Thus, she suggests several other factors might have influenced the tutor's work: the quality of her assignment, its relative importance to the course grade, and a revised curriculum (58).

As she describes it, Levine's assignment is not tightly aligned with a professional conception of the discipline of psychology. She required students to write a series of short anecdotes based on personal experience and to analyze them using psychological concepts. While knowledge of these concepts would be a plus for a tutor, understanding how narrative works—how the writer must analyze or interpret, not just retell, a personal experience—would be helpful to a reader in this situation. The analysis of anecdotes, of course, is a skill often taught in composition classes. I have frequently seen versions of this assignment in anthropology and psychology classes at my institution, perhaps because it contains features typical of the case study. Nevertheless, this assignment has not achieved the status of an official form such as the lab report. What may really help a tutor in Levine's course is to know what she expects with an assignment whose local origins define it as a classroom, not a disciplinary, genre.

Our experience at the City College of New York with classroom tutors in content courses further underscores how more than one factor affects their success. For instance, in 1999, we attached peer tutors, from both English and psychology, to introductory and upper-level psychology courses taught by the same professor. In these courses, the professor was also collaborating with a writing fellow, one of six Ph.D students from the City University of New York (CUNY) Graduate Center who work on my campus to implement a WAC program. This fellow (from English) worked with the professor to integrate writing into both courses and to develop discipline-specific assignments. For example, they created sequenced assignments that reflect writing as a process, explicit descriptions of the lab report, and rubrics for students to use in peer review groups and to assess their own progress (see *Innovative Teaching at City College* or www.ccny.cuny.edu/wac). In addition to conferences with peer tutors in class, students were required to make an appointment at the writing center. At the end of both courses, the professor surveyed students about what they had learned about writing, and she also asked explicit questions about the peer tutors.

When we read the students' evaluations of the writing assignments, we saw that the writing fellow involvement had been highly successful from the students' point of view. Their responses echoed those found in other institutional assessments of WAC: students spoke specifically about the purpose that writing plays in their discipline and described particular generic features they had learned; they thought that writing helped them to learn the content; and they felt that their writing had improved.

On the role of the tutors, students gave mixed reviews in both classes, focusing their criticism on two factors. One strand of criticism concerned the tutors' specialized knowledge of disciplinary style and content. Students indicated that tutors who didn't know about writing in the social sciences tended to focus on language issues. While for many of the ESL students this was helpful, others dismissed that role and asked for tutors in their majors. Several wrote comments like "My tutor could not answer my questions on APA style. The tutors should represent the student population in majors." Or: "I liked the fact that they helped me correct my grammatical errors but in terms of helping me with my research paper for psychology, it was only beneficial if you had a tutor who was actually a psychology major." Another student remarked, "The writing tutor who came to help was actually no help. He said he was used to working with students taking ESL courses." Not all the students reacted negatively, of course; many thought that tutors had helped them to understand assignments and to revise their work, particularly the literature review section.

Another equally significant strand of criticism in the surveys involved students' complaints about scheduling problems at the writing center. This emphasis on institutional problems alerted us to the possibility of alternative interpretations of the factors most responsible for the tutors' success in these classrooms. In our earlier study of peer tutoring in English classes (Soliday 1995), we found that when students and tutors complained about scheduling, this institutional factor correlated with the tutor's lack of an authoritative role in the classroom. In this case, the writing fellows wondered whether the required appointments at the center and the mandatory time limits for in-class tutorials might have affected outcomes, especially the comfort level of the English major who was used to a different role at the writing center. Again, the 1995 study suggested that the tutors' success is deeply influenced by the authoritative role they are able to assume—their relationship to the professor helps to shape their relationship with students. For instance, a professor could grant the tutor who is a major in the field a more legitimate status. In any case, a naturalistic study focusing on the professor's relationship with the tutors and their level of comfort in a new environment could explain how institutional tensions affect success.

In light of these factors, it's no wonder that the definitive role content plays in determining a tutor's success remains unsettled. For while we know that specialized knowledge does play a role in successful tutoring, we also can see how content is entangled in other factors typical of writing in the course: an assignment's local or disciplinary features; the professor's alignment with a discipline; the quality of assignments and their weight in a particular course; the professor's relationship with the tutor and the tutor's consequent status in the classroom. While Margot Soven concludes that content knowledge is a crucial component of tutoring, especially in advanced courses, she too wonders whether "we have exaggerated the influence of knowledge in the major as the factor most responsible for shaping the role of the peer tutor and determining his success" (2001, 215).

Writing in the course is a useful concept that also helps us to see why a generalist tutoring strategy remains a flexible option in WAC programs. Writing in the course highlights how professors in the same discipline (even those teaching the same course) do not necessarily share the same expectations for writing. In part, this is because professors align themselves more or less tightly with disciplinary norms—some promote generalist goals and purposes for writing, while others stress specialized forms and audiences. For instance, the professor of psychology whose classes I described above had a distinct disciplinary purpose in assigning writing for both the advanced and introductory courses. Like some of the teachers described in Barbara Walvoord and Lucille McCarthy's case studies (1990), the professor at City College saw her students as professionals in training. A well-known scholar, she hoped to prepare students to write like future researchers, especially in the advanced course, and a tutor in her class had to be familiar with the lab report to be successful. In Judith Levine's psychology course as she describes it, the assignment calls for a classroom genre with which many composition students might be familiar. For the professor at City College, the writing weighed heavily in the final course grade, while Levine indicates that she did not weight the writing assignments as seriously. A classroom tutor in both these courses would need to assess the teacher's expectations because not all of them are universally typical of psychology classes.

## PEER LEARNING IN WAC PROGRAMS

Writing in the course suggests that when readers assess a piece of writing, they rely on both their special knowledge of course content and a more general rhetorical sensitivity. In our writing fellows program, we have examined peer reading groups in different content courses to ascertain the success of a pedagogy that WAC programs widely recommend to faculty overburdened with paper grading. What kinds of knowledge do students bring to their reading, and how might tutors intervene in reading groups?

So far, we have found that during peer reading sessions, students use different types of knowledge typical of writing in the course to evaluate drafts or finished papers. For instance, the writing fellows audiotaped peer reading groups in a large introductory lecture course in the art department. The groups participated in a demonstration workshop organized and then led by a team of writing fellows and peer undergraduate tutors from the writing center. In demonstration workshops, writing fellows and peer undergraduate tutors visit classes to structure and then help to lead writing workshops. In class, fellows and tutors usually demonstrate some aspect of writing, such as developing a works cited page, and then invite students to come to the writing center for individual or group conferences on their drafts.

In the art class, writing fellows and peer tutors gave a demonstration workshop on an assignment that required students to go to the Metropolitan Museum of Art, take notes on two paintings, and then compare and contrast their visual descriptions in a short analytical essay. The writing fellows met with the professor and obtained models of introductions that they presented to the students in the class to read and discuss. With the help of peer tutors, they broke students in this large class into groups to read and analyze four model introductions of varying length and overall quality.

Here is a sample of a group's discussion of two model introductions that is typical of all the conversations the fellows audiotaped and then excerpted for our faculty handbook, *Innovative Teaching at City College.*

*Student 4:*    I like this [model] better than the other one. Because it was like he said—it was like an introduction to what the entire paper is about. He set it up so that he can do one painting, talk about that, go onto the next one, compare them and contrast them, and then his conclusion would sum this up.

*Student 1:*    What do you think of the size of this one compared to the size of what we read here? [referencing the two introductions]

*Student 4:*    I don't always think more is better. But I don't know. This one wasn't so descriptive, detailed of the work. . . .

*Student 3:*    Because an introduction has to be broad. It doesn't have to be detailed like in the first.

*Student 4:*    The body has to be detailed.

*Student 1:*    What did you write?

*Student 2:*    He set it up in a way that you want to continue reading it. He has a problem in the beginning. Here he says when comparing two pieces of work on the same subject, both of them are like different subjects. One of them was a Gerard David painting— it's like religious leaders, like a religious painting, you know.

*Student 1:*    But they both had the mother and the child.

*Student 3:*    The same subject is the mother and child.

*Student 2:*    Oh, he meant the mother and the child.

The writing fellows concluded that the students in this peer review session did not rely exclusively on content knowledge to read the models. This conversation and others reveal that students also depended upon their familiarity with the class assignment and general approaches to writing when they assessed the text. The students in this art class leaned on both types of knowledge: the rhetorical situation of the particular course and that of writing papers for humanities classes more generally. The students knew about David's paintings and they knew what the professor meant by "the same subject" as a basis for comparison. Their talk also focuses on the qualities of introductions that any well-trained tutor can join and expand: the scope of a thesis and its relationship to the body of a paper, how to focus an opening, or what constitutes the basis of a good comparison.

Because the professor of this course is a practicing artist—his alignment with an academic discipline is loose—students were required to show that they had learned to "think visually," rather than to produce a particular academic form. Again, then, the unique rhetorical situation of this class forms a powerful context for writing that a classroom tutor is well situated to interpret and understand. It is the context of the course rather than that of an academic discipline that shaped the assignment and guided the professor's responses to student writing.

The transcripts from this workshop also highlight the powerful role tutors can play as organizers or leaders of peer reading sessions, regardless of their backgrounds. As the number of writing assignments increases in content courses, students call for more feedback from their professors (Hilgers et al 1995). While they prefer their teachers' responses, students also rank peer comments very highly (Beason and Darrow 1997). But often when content faculty import peer learning into their classrooms, they experience some of the problems that Laurie Grobman describes in her review of the scholarship in chapter 3 of this volume. For example, students stray from the task, focus on local as opposed to global issues, or hesitate to provide constructive criticism. Similarly, we've found through survey and naturalistic research in two biology classes that peer review was not successful for all these reasons. In a third biology class, however, we compared students' comments to the professor's on a set of drafts for a lab report and found a close match in the focus and quality of peer and faculty response to the writing. In all three biology classes and the art class, students were given clear, specific instructions to perform group work, and they had rubrics to use for peer review. But the successful biology class and the art class had something the other two classes lacked: peer tutors who were present to help structure the workshop (art) or to lead the review sessions in small groups (biology).

Peer tutors, as Grobman shows, can focus discussions in reading groups and help students elaborate their comments on drafts. For instance, in the art class, most students were used to working in groups because they were enrolled that semester in a block program, or learning community, that featured English courses that had a peer tutor attached to them. Our 1995 study suggests that the tutors' satisfaction with the 1999 project meant they played active roles in the English classes. Possibly, the peer group sessions in English helped to prepare students to work seriously on their drafts in another class like art. Particularly when peer tutors have an explicit rubric to follow, as they did in the successful biology class, they can help to focus group readings, and they gain confidence that they might otherwise lack if they are working with an unfamiliar content.

Guided peer reading during class remains a common tool for learning that faculty across the disciplines can share.

## WRITING AS A MODE OF INQUIRY IN WAC PROGRAMS

Along with peer learning, WAC programs promote using writing as a mode of inquiry across the disciplines. From any major, classroom tutors can be especially effective in helping students to use writing as a form of discovery and to understand how writing fits into the flow of a course. In writing for the course, the writing process takes distinct shapes. For instance, in some WAC courses, students are required to produce low-stakes assignments that do not require revision. In other WAC courses, professors often expect that students will use writing to conduct research—even when faculty don't call the task research. Tutors can help students (and faculty) distinguish between low- and high-stakes writing assignments and learn to use writing as a mode of inquiry when that's appropriate.

WAC professors sometimes assign formal research papers, but at other times, they require students to perform research without calling the task by that name. WAC faculty may assume students will use writing at the earliest stages of a research task—or, just as often, they may not have clarified for themselves their tacit assumption that writing is integral to inquiry in their fields. Yet a successful final paper may depend upon the healthy use of writing at the earliest stages of invention. Barbara Walvoord and Lucille McCarthy (1990) asked students in four disciplines to keep logs and protocols to document their actual writing processes. They found that the less successful students did not have a rich invention process—they didn't use writing as a mode of inquiry at the earliest stage of a research project, for instance. Some of these students tended to rely upon the concept of "the thesis statement" they had learned from English. Their problem was that they tended to adopt a thesis prematurely before clarifying their purpose or gathering solid data.

Promoting writing as a tool for discovery is a special talent of the peer tutor, who more than any other person can help students to think about what they want to say before establishing a thesis statement. Developing a writing process—especially good invention strategies—remains central to students' struggles with writing across the curriculum, as Walvoord and McCarthy show in business, psychology, history, and biology courses. In a business class they describe, students had to go to fast-food restaurants and observe their management; if they hadn't collected good data from the start, no amount of content knowledge would help them. Similarly, in the art class I described, if students had not taken good notes at the museum, no amount of content knowledge or revision strategies would have improved their papers. In both cases, the professors are asking students to gather primary data, and students are most successful when they use writing at the scene to record their observations. And in both cases, professors expect students to use writing to perform research even when they don't give the task this name and even when they don't explicitly organize their assignments around writing at the invention stage.

As our writing fellows have discovered in chemistry, anthropology, sociology, literature, and architecture classes, research projects involve using writing as a tool for inquiry in the earliest stages of the process. Since scientists, social scientists, humanists, and faculty in professional schools alike use writing in this way, we can infer that peer tutors with any major can play a central role in showing both students and faculty where the actual writing begins—at the moment of reading or gathering data, not afterward. Using writing as a mode of inquiry remains a common ground many of us share regardless of our discipline.

## FUTURE ORIENTATIONS

While I want to end by reaffirming the role of the general tutor in WAC programs, tutors must orient themselves to classrooms that may constitute foreign territory for them. Tutor training must address the demands of writing-intensive courses: the rhetorical situation will now have to include those curricular and institutional aspects of WAC that differ from the traditional writing course. We will have to expose tutors to a robust notion of genre: as an official set of expectations that exists before a course begins (like the lab report) and as a set of expectations more distinct to particular classrooms (like Judith Levine's anecdote assignment). Similarly, tutors will have to learn to distinguish writing to learn or low-stakes assignments from more formal high-stakes assignments that often involve writing as a mode of inquiry. As Susan Hubbuch (1988) recommends, we will have to introduce tutors to conventional forms that differ subtly from one another: a thesis and a hypothesis, a conclusion in an essay and a discussion section in a lab report. Above all, we need to stress that these forms take on life within the rhetorical context established by a course. Classroom tutors who are present at the rhetorical scene are very well suited to read and help decipher assignments and their fit into the flow of the semester.

To understand how general readers can work effectively in content courses, we need also to continue to research the interplay between different kinds of knowledge when readers encounter various assignments. Margot Soven (2001) recommends audiotaping tutorials, following the Kiedaisch and Dinitz study (1993) I described earlier; Laurie Grobman in chapter 3 offers a model for studying the dynamics of peer group learning. This semester at CCNY, we are planning exit interviews with students enrolled in a writing-intensive biology course focusing on understanding how the students interpret the professor's assignments and how they draw upon their general knowledge of writing to complete their tasks in a science course. If we use naturalistic research methods to contextualize peer tutorials, surveys, or interviews, and if we adopt writing in the course as a theoretical lens, we can deepen our understanding of the extent to which different factors shape the overall success of classroom tutors.

Many professors join WAC programs not only because they want to improve students' writing, but also because they share a common desire to improve undergraduate teaching. These programs attempt to improve writing, but WAC began originally with the mission of reforming undergraduate teaching. Over the years, some of my most pleasurable teaching experiences involved classes in which I worked alongside a peer undergraduate tutor. Peer tutors enhance WAC because they can energize teachers and help to put into practice techniques, such as peer group learning, that faculty hear about in workshops and seminars. The widespread success at CUNY of the writing fellows program owes in part to our faculty's willingness to form classroom partnerships with outsiders—the basic tenet of curriculum-based tutoring. Similarly, when they are given the proper room to do what they do best, peer tutors can enhance the life of any classroom, regardless of the discipline.

## 3

# BUILDING BRIDGES TO ACADEMIC DISCOURSE

*The Peer Group Leader in Basic Writing Peer Response Groups*

Laurie Grobman

David Bartholomae's landmark essays "Inventing the University" (1986) and "Writing on the Margins: The Concept of Literacy in Higher Education" (1987) locate the basic writer outside academic discourse, lacking the authority academic writers possess. This exclusion is manifested, among other ways, in peer response groups, where basic writers often shy away from critiquing substantive issues of content or organization in each other's work. Their hesitancy is understandable, given that the university has told them (by virtue of their placement in a "remedial" writing course) that they do not know how to write.

The theoretical support for peer response groups in composition is by now well known: social theories of language and learning suggest that students should construct meaning not in isolation but within the context of social interaction. Although the use of peer response groups is common practice in writing classrooms, research on peer response groups offers mixed reviews, largely because students typically lack the skills and knowledge for peer response (see Zhu 1995). Indeed, much of the research on writing groups focuses on ways to promote more effective, substantive response in students (see Zhu 1995) and on the causes and characteristics of successful and unsuccessful peer response groups (see Bishop 1988). Furthermore, a great deal of this research focuses on composition rather than basic writing students.

Nevertheless, Bartholomae's work with basic writers has led many researchers and instructors, including myself, to use peer response groups as a way to empower basic writers (Weaver 1995, 31). Basic writing pedagogy emerging from social constructivist views of writing encourages students to see their written texts as part of academic discourse, a larger conversation taking place in writing. This approach presupposes, as do I, that developmental writers can produce intelligent writing if instructors challenge them with serious content and enable them to enter academic conversations. Peer response groups are one means through which students can potentially enter these conversations.

However, Wei Zhu notes that the opportunities for peer interaction offered by peer response groups often go unfulfilled (1995, 517). Though many factors influence peer response group efficacy and inefficacy, group members' lack of confidence in peers' expertise and members' fear of offering criticism are among the most salient characteristics of peer response group failure (Bishop 1988, 121). Clearly, these problems are more pronounced for basic writers, whose reluctance and/or inability to offer substantive critique hinders meaningful learning from knowledgeable peers. Basic writers' precarious position as outsiders in the academic community and subsequent lack of confidence in their own writing abilities lead these students to shy away from assuming any measure of authority in offering meaningful response. Basic writers tend to resist honest and authoritative critique, even in electronic classrooms that otherwise contribute to community building (see Gay 1991; Varone 1996). Indeed, Sandra Lawrence and Elizabeth Sommers (1996) conclude that many instructors doubt the value of peer response groups for inexperienced writers.

In the study under discussion, implemented in the fall of 1998, I sought to increase the efficacy of basic writing peer groups by using a *peer group leader*—a sophomore student who guides basic writers during peer response sessions—in an electronic classroom with online peer response sessions.[1] Moreover, I attempted to promote meaningful and valuable writing groups in which basic writers, like their composition counterparts, reconceptualize substantive issues in their writing, countering Joan Wauters' claim that for basic writers, "there is an excellent rationale for offering only positive reinforcement, if the goal is to encourage confidence on the part of reluctant writers" (1988, 157). Basic writers should be treated as intellectuals learning a new discourse, and peer response sessions should reflect such academic work.

In this chapter, I suggest that the peer group leader builds bridges between basic writers and academic writers. Acting as a link between basic writers' and academic communities, the peer group leader encourages basic writers to model academic discourse as they authorize themselves as participants. David Bartholomae and Anthony Petrosky suggest we "engage students in a process whereby they discover academic discourse from the inside" (1986, 36). Peer group leaders make academic discourse's inside visible, so basic writing students do not have to invent it blindly. At once insiders and outsiders, peer group leaders provide a vital link between writer and audience, writer and academic discourse (64). As James Gee argues, discourses are mastered by "enculturation into social practices through scaffolded and supported interaction with people who have already mastered the Discourse" (qtd. in Zhu 1995, 518). Straddling the fence somewhere between academic and basic writers' communities, the peer group leader provides the scaffolding and supported interaction upon and through which basic writers enter academic discourse. In so doing, peer group leaders provide what Kenneth Bruffee (1984) would call a "conversation" to model or what subscribers to the competing model of academic authority would see as a means to challenge it. Making academic discourse *visible* to students, the peer group leader assists students in their understanding and appropriation of academic literacies.[2]

## BUILDING BRIDGES IN PEER COLLABORATION RESEARCH: PEER GROUP LEADERS IN BASIC WRITING

Using limited funds from an internal grant,[3] I selected Tyisha, a student I had known from my basic writing class a year earlier, as the peer group leader.[4] She was among the strongest writers in my class (and I knew she had been successful in English Composition), but more important, I felt she had characteristics that would suit the peer group leader role: leadership, integrity, maturity, and sensitivity. Tyisha, the peer group leader, attended my class during peer response sessions, joining one or two groups and guiding them through and participating in response. I instructed her to be descriptive and to pay attention to global issues of meaning, content, and organization rather than mechanical issues in students' writing. I expected Tyisha to model these responses for students as well as guide them to similar modes of critique. I also informed students that they could seek Tyisha's help outside of class through e-mail, phone calls, or face-to-face meetings.

The peer group leader thus straddled the roles of the two primary types of peer collaboration in basic writing: peer response in basic writing classrooms and peer tutorials in writing centers. In my experiences, the peer group leader acts as an intermediary between peers in a peer response group and tutors in writing center tutorials, and bringing the peer tutor *into* the peer response group draws at once from the advantages of both peer response groups and peer tutorials. Of course, there is a flip side as well, for peer group leaders have the potential to degrade the collaboration of peers in peer response groups.

Muriel Harris's widely known and respected work on the similarities and differences between peer tutorials and peer response, though now over a decade old, remains a significant contribution to the study and practice of these important collaborative methods in basic writing classrooms. Harris asserts that both writing center tutorials and peer response groups are "collaborative learning about writing" (1992a, 369) in which "one writer claims ownership and makes all final decisions" (370); moreover, the goal of the tutor and peer group members is the same: "all are working toward more effective writing abilities and heightened awareness of general writing concerns" (373).[5] Bringing peer group leaders into peer response sessions leaves these important general similarities unchanged.

It is the distinctions Harris makes, however, that interest me more in the context of peer group leaders, particularly in terms of how the peer group leader can take advantage of these distinctions and become a force in basic writers' peer response sessions and meaningful learning in collaboration with knowledgeable peers. Among the most significant of these differences is the widely accepted view that peer tutors in writing tutorials become "neither a teacher nor a peer" as they assist writers with writing issues beyond "fixing" a particular paper under consideration, while peer response readers focus on and critique a specific draft (1992a, 371). Peer tutors explain issues and problems and give instructional assistance. As Stephen North notes, the tutor's job "is to produce better writers, not just better writing" (qtd. in Harris 1992a, 372). In tutorials, tutors individualize and personalize the concerns, while in peer response groups, readers offer mutual assistance in a back-and-forth interaction that deals with general skills (373).

Peer group leaders take on both roles, neither entirely teachers nor completely peers, straddling multiple communities as they join the peer response group. In their unique role, peer group leaders can bring individualization to peer response groups since they do not have writing to be critiqued and do not seek assistance themselves. This difference from other members of the peer response group allows for an additional layer of instruction in peer response groups, beyond a focus on the writing under scrutiny to more general writing concerns, including instructional assistance on *how to respond to peers' writing*, which the tutorial lacks. Learning the nuances of critique can in and of itself lead to improved writing abilities. Thus, Harris's assertion that peer tutors' methods and concerns for uncovering writers' problems are not appropriate for peer response groups no longer holds when we introduce peer group leaders into peer response groups. Peer group leaders can individualize response, and, more important, can lead students away from purely directive response.

Harris's distinction in terms of collaboration is important in this context. She argues that peer response groups are closer to collaborative writing (i.e., joint authorship) than writing tutorials, for peer response group work emphasizes informing, while writing tutorials emphasize the student's own discovery (1992a, 377). At first glance, it may seem that using a peer group leader might move the peer response group away from collaborative writing, since peer group leaders do emphasize students' own discovery. However, peer group leaders can simultaneously increase the level and quality of informative modes. Peer group leaders raise peer response beyond simple informing on specific issues, a goal of many instructors who use peer response groups, despite Harris's claim that these groups tend to be prescriptive (see Benesch 1985; Zhu 1995; Bishop 1988). Peer group leaders guide group members into larger, substantive issues and thus students' own discovery of the writing process. Moreover, unlike tutorials, peer response groups with peer group leaders also facilitate students' discovery of group processes; that is, peer group leaders guide and model peer group response and critique, so students discover not only their own writing issues but how to benefit from and contribute to peer response. In peer response work with peer group leaders, basic writing students not only attempt to critique their peers' drafts but themselves learn about the possibilities for revision in the process. Therefore, despite the potential to undermine collaboration among peers, the peer group leaders can enhance it by raising the efficacy of peer group members' informing *and* multiple layers of discovery.

In their multiple roles, peer group leaders thus provide a bridge between what Thomas Newkirk calls peers' and instructors' distinct "evaluative communities" (1984, 309). His study suggests that peer response groups may reinforce students' abilities to write for their peers but not for the academic community, and, subsequently, that "students need practice applying the criteria that they are now learning" and should thus be viewed as "apprentices, attempting to learn and apply criteria appropriate to an academic audience" (310). Newkirk argues for teachers' active role in peer response; however, I believe peer group leaders can more effectively "mak[e] the norms of that community clear and plausible—even appealing." Ideally, peer response enables students to enter academic discourse through working with knowledgeable peers, breaking free from one evaluative community to enter another, and it empowers students who do not see themselves as academic writers. However, in practice, students' crossover is more problematic. Peer group leaders can expose students to the conventions—appealing and not so appealing—of academic discourse. Peer group leaders do not impose on students what Benesch calls the "teacher's code" but instead allow them to respond to writing issues "in their own language" (1985, 90), since peer group leaders have, in Harris's words, "a foot in each discourse community" (1992a, 380). With the use of peer group leaders, therefore, basic writers develop this language more independently of the teacher and in collaboration with peers.

Using peer group leaders in peer response groups also bridges what Tim Hacker describes as the two main approaches to peer response: the broad categories of "teacher-directed" and "modeling" (1996, 112–13). The former category includes teacher intervention in the form of worksheets (a set of heuristics for approaching an essay) and/or instructions on how to proceed, while "modeling" consists of teacher intervention prior to actual student-directed peer response sessions through teaching students how to evaluate and critique their peers' essays before peer response sessions. Using peer group leaders, however, reduces the need for teacher intervention in either instance.[6] That is, with peer group leaders, students can "model" effective response, but they do so in process, and they do not need a set of heuristics provided by the instructor. Moreover, with peer group leaders, more authentic collaboration occurs because peer response groups remain decentered. Students cannot blindly invent the language of academic discourse, but peer group leaders make its inside visible. With peer group leaders as facilitators, basic writers take on a more active role in the invention of academic discourse. Like peer tutors, peer group leaders can empower student writers who "want to have power over their environment, to be in control of what happens to them, . . . and manipulate language the way their teachers do before they will be able to play the academic game the way the insiders do" (Hawkins 1980, 64).

Harris makes the further point that students in peer tutorials typically trust peer tutors and have confidence in their skills and knowledge (1992a). Students' perception of the peer group leader is also an important component of the peer group leader's usefulness in peer response groups. For peer response to work, peer group members must have confidence in their peers' knowledge. However, for basic writers especially,

trust in peers' knowledge is suspect, mainly because they have been designated as underprepared for college writing. Peer group leaders can play a
significant role in leading basic writers to see themselves and their peers
as knowledgeable, skilled writers. Moreover, because peer group leaders can pass their knowledge to basic writing students, they more evenly
distribute knowledge in the classroom. As a result, the classroom becomes
a more authentic decentered, collaborative learning environment, in
practice as well as in theory.

While peer group leaders can bring the advantages of both peer
response groups and peer tutorials to their roles in peer response sessions,
they may also degrade peer response. Harris points out that because peer
tutors are more acquainted with academic discourse than the tutees, "the
further they are from being peers in a collaborative relationship" (1992a,
379). Students come to them seeking prescriptions, thereby making it
difficult for tutors to remain collaborators rather than coauthors and
frustrating both student and tutor. Certainly the potential exists as well
when we bring peer group leaders to peer response groups. Peer group
leaders, straddling both the basic writers' and academic communities, are
not completely "equal" to other peer group members. Without writing of
their own "out there" and under scrutiny, peer group leaders have less at
stake than the other peer group members. Harris makes the point that
the peer tutor's unique position as interpreter of academic jargon is in
peril if the tutor, "enamored of the jargon of the field, moves too far into
the teacher's world" (380). Clearly, this risk of coauthoring and co-opting
student writing exists with peer group leaders in peer response groups,
but can be minimized with effective training and guidance.

Relatedly, peer group leaders may interfere with what Harris identifies
as peer response groups' give-and-take process of negotiation that leads
to consensus about how the group will undertake peer response (1992a,
374). With the peer group leader's participation in peer response, the
negotiation among students will likely be less democratic, for part of the
peer group leader's role is to help guide students to specific kinds of
response. Moreover, as in tutorials, the tutor's and students' goals may
often conflict, since students want particular papers fixed while the tutor
attempts to address larger issues (374–75). Clearly, if students have the
goal of fixing a particular piece of writing in their peer response group,
they may find themselves in conflict with the peer group leader, who will
be guiding them to more global issues as well. On the other hand, since
peer response groups with peer group leaders can effectively address both

specific and general writing concerns, the conflicts between students and peer group leader are likely to be reduced.

Harris's identification of the tutor's "unique advantage of being both a nonjudgmental, non-evaluative helper—a collaborator in whom the writer can confide" (1992a, 376)—cannot be ignored when we bring the peer group leader into peer response. Arguably, the peer group leader may face difficult hurdles in getting group members to perceive him or her as nonevaluative and nonjudgmental, given the peer group leader's connection to the instructor. Instructors can make it clear to students that the peer group leader is there to offer assistance, not to evaluate or judge them. Instructors can also inform students that even though they will consult with the peer group leader throughout the semester (much like peer tutors in writing centers confer with instructors), the peer group leader will not be involved in grading the students in any way. In my class, students' participation in peer response did influence their grades to some degree, but it was my assessment of the logged transcripts of the sessions, not anything the peer group leader told me, that affected our evaluation of students' participation in this process. Thus, while I do not think I was able to completely overcome my students' association of the peer group leader with myself, I believe they did come to see her as nonevaluative, enabling her to evoke honest and authoritative response.

## BUILDING BRIDGES TO ACADEMIC DISCOURSE:
## THE PEER GROUP LEADER IN BASIC WRITING

How well did using a peer group leader work in this particular class? What advantages and/or disadvantages did this young woman bring to basic writers' peer response groups? Since most of our response sessions occurred online, I was able to use these transcripts to monitor and assess the peer group leader's effectiveness in leading students to substantive response.[7]

In the basic writing class under study, I challenged students with difficult work, connecting content with methodology as we studied varied aspects and definitions of literacy, each assignment building off the others so that the writing assignments, as Ann Berthoff suggests, "encourage conscientization, the discovery of the mind in action" so students "learn . . . how meanings make future meanings possible, how form finds further form" (1984, 755). Moreover, class content, focused on academic literacy itself, wedded content with methodology and put discourse itself at the center of analysis. Thus, course content and methodology began the process through which basic writers could enter academic discourse. The peer group leader helped these students make this difficult leap, as the following examples demonstrate. At the same time, however, her work illuminates some of the potential perils of peer group leaders' interventions in basic writing peer response groups.

One strength of the peer group leader was her ability to both inform and model. In the following example, Tyisha guides students away from mechanical issues, without specifically instructing them not to consider such surface features.

| | |
|---|---|
| *Stan:* | yo Paul i guess you read my review |
| *Paul:* | yup |
| *Paul:* | it was good |
| *Stan:* | good content |
| *Paul:* | yes |
| *Stan:* | i found it very interesting |
| *Paul:* | but I found a lot of little mistakes |
| *Paul:* | did you catch any? |
| *Tyisha:* | I liked your paper also Stan, it was really good, Paul is there anything in his paper that you thought he could work on, besides a few spelling mistakes. |

Tyisha's language effectively downplays "a few spelling mistakes" and refocuses students' attention to more substantive issues, without specifying what these should be. This exchange demonstrates Tyisha's ability to simultaneously focus on the essay under consideration while leading students to discovery.

In the next example, Tyisha successfully keeps the group focused and elicits effective critique.

| | |
|---|---|
| *Tyisha:* | what can he do about that 5th paragraph |
| *Stan:* | break it up |
| *Tyisha:* | It is too big—break it up how? |
| *Stan:* | hold on i have to read it again to get that answer |
| *Paul:* | I think I could break it up at the word people |
| *Larry:* | LEHIGH IS BETTER THAN BERK |
| *Paul:* | yea yea |
| *Tyisha:* | Larry we're having a discussion |
| *Paul:* | Larry is the man |
| *Stan:* | ok i just want to get to main soooooooooooo i don't really care |
| *Stan:* | but berks has more than one building and we have a guy |
| *Paul:* | that really doesn't bother me |

| *Tyisha:* | Anyways, what can we do with this para. lets get back on track |
|---|---|
| *Tyisha:* | just 5 more minutes |
| *Paul:* | I could break it up at the word "people" |
| *Tyisha:* | Good and from there what could he do Stan |
| *Stan:* | that is what i was just about to say |
| *Stan:* | back up the ideas in greater detail |
| *Tyisha:* | should he change the intro. sentence to that paragraph or keep it the same. |
| *Stan:* | just make sure you have good transition between the two paragraphs |
| *Paul:* | ok |
| *Stan:* | yep—change the intro. |

When Larry interrupts Paul and Stan's academic conversation, Tyisha takes on a leadership role, trying to get them back on track. Although Stan momentarily gives in to Larry's disruptions, he does refocus his attention on the task. This is an important example of the peer group leader's potential role, for all too often, basic writers get off track—and stay there. Tim Hacker (1996) claims that students in writing groups tend to take on the role of teacher, but I rarely see this occur with basic writers. It is difficult for these students to get back on track on their own, perhaps because they are afraid to take on such a leadership role, questioning their own authority as writers.

Furthermore, the above exchange also illuminates the ways in which the peer group leader can simultaneously focus on a particular piece of writing and more global writing instruction. Even though Tyisha and the peer group members are discussing Paul's essay, Tyisha's comments are directed at Stan, the responder. Paul's comment, "I could break it up at the word 'people'" and Stan's comment, "That is what I was just about to say" indicate their understanding of both how to "fix" this particular paragraph and its applicability to issues of paragraphing generally.

Similarly, the following exchange also illuminates the peer group leader's ability to straddle the roles of tutor and peer, focusing on specific and general concerns.

| *Sara:* | In some of the papers I write, I start out with a question |
|---|---|
| *Tyisha:* | so how does this help Joes paper |
| *Tyisha:* | what idea do you have for Joe that he could use with a question in his paper |
| *Sara:* | He could have started out with "What is Technical Literacy?" |
| *Tyisha:* | and then what could he have done in his intro to support this? |

| | |
|---|---|
| *Joe:* | why would I want to start with a question that I don't know the answer to? |
| | . . . |
| *Sara:* | Explain how many definitions it had and use each definition to start a new paragraph |
| *Tyisha:* | good point how would you answer that, you went right to the point in your starting paragraph. |
| | . . . |
| *Sara:* | Joe what do you say? |
| *Joe:* | The point that I am attempting to say is that I do not know the exact definitions. |
| *Sara:* | Did you try looking them up? |
| *Joe:* | no, because we are suppose to find our own. |

Sara begins this exchange over Joe's introductory paragraph by pointing to her own strategy for introductions. Tyisha then pushes her to apply it to Joe's essay. Despite Joe's disagreement, Tyisha effectively guides these students to consider not only Joe's essay but a particular rhetorical strategy more generally. Sara and Joe debate the issue in academic terms, Joe responding that "looking it up" is not what academic discourse is about. Instead, Joe realizes the role he must play as a knowledge maker.

The following example demonstrates an impressive interchange of substantive ideas among Tyisha, Jennifer, and Stan that occurred fairly late in the semester. Jennifer begins by asking both her peer and the peer tutor for response:

| | |
|---|---|
| *Jennifer:* | Tyisha, do you think I stay on track or do I drift off my topic? Also, do you think my thesis is okay, or more like what do you think my thesis is? Stan, give me some input. What do I need to change? Remember I did this late last night. |
| *Stan:* | well you talk about culture and beliefs and than you jump to standard english. It just needs something to blend the idea that even though a person likes to keep their beliefs that they still need standard english. |
| *Tyisha:* | Your paper is very good however, Stan can you identify Jennifers thesis, and does it go along with her paper. |

Tyisha directs Jennifer and Stan to consider a particular problem in Jennifer's essay, the lack of a clear thesis/focus, specifically responding to Jennifer's request for help but in the process guiding Stan to respond. The discussion continues:

| | |
|---|---|
| *Stan:* | well i think it can be improved upon. I really did not understand what the article was going to be about when I read it. |
| *Jennifer:* | I think I am still talking about Standard English. I throw in culture and beliefs because that is why people stray from Standard English, it is so they can keep close to their culture. |
| *Tyisha:* | Okay, so then how does all this information tie in to Rachel Jones facing disadvantages—what do you think Stan. |
| *Jennifer:* | I don't understand. Didn't I introduce my thesis in the opening? I thought I made it clear what I was talking about, but I could be wrong. |
| *Tyisha:* | Your thesis should be in the introductory paragraph last sentence before you get into you supporting paragraphs. |
| *Jennifer:* | I used Rachel Jones because I like how she expresses that people are faced with disadvantages without speaking Standard English. |

Tyisha presses Stan to help Jennifer with this problem of purpose and simultaneously propels Jennifer into thoughtful consideration of her rhetorical choices. Even though Jennifer notes, as a writer questioning her own authority, that "I could be wrong," she continues to explain the reasoning behind her own understanding of her thesis and its placement in the essay. Tyisha's presence has helped this basic writer gain confidence in her own and her peer's knowledge and writing. The conversation concludes this way:

| | |
|---|---|
| *Stan:* | try adding something like this; Standard english pulls from cultural independence. Some people feel that without there cultural distinction they will be lost. For a person to truly accelerate in our society they must have a little of both. Cultural diversity is not acceptable in todays world and for a person to not understand or use standard english they will be lost. |
| *Jennifer:* | so, she was my spark for this paper. I am responding and giving my idea of her views. |
| | . . . |
| *Tyisha:* | It's good you used Jones however, what is your thesis, is it that last sentence, because if so then you could talk about the things SHE FACED, I think it could be the second and third sentences combined, how do you feel Stan? |
| *Stan:* | well I write what I think it should be |
| *Jennifer:* | Thanks Stan, I like that response you gave me previously. I wrote it down because I like it a lot. |

Tyisha's membership in the academic community is evidenced by her more nuanced reading of Rachel Jones' essay, "What's Wrong With Black English?" (1992) and her clearer sense of incorporating textual references effectively in her own writing. She prods Jennifer into a deeper reading in a way that both models and guides Jennifer and Stan in the conventions of academic discourse. Benesch argues that peer response is often disconnected—that is, utterances are left suspended, other comments are raised, and an emerging conversation rarely materializes (1985, 93). With the aid of Tyisha, we see a substantive conversation emerge (temporarily interrupted by the lag time inherent in online synchronous conversations), because Tyisha enables them to "enter *imperfectly* into peer group conversations" (93; emphasis added), as Stan's misstatement that "Cultural diversity is not acceptable," indicates. Indeed, Stan's rewriting of Jennifer's introductory paragraph (which shows his own sense of authority as a knowledgeable peer) illuminates the perils of peer response generally. Other experiences with peer group leaders have demonstrated to me that peer group leaders can lessen the impact of such difficulties, although Tyisha did not "catch" it this time.

The above examples and analysis point to the strengths of peer group leaders in basic writers' peer response, but there were some pitfalls as well. Mainly, these occurred when Tyisha became overly prescriptive, as the following two examples demonstrate:

| | |
|---|---|
| *Stan:* | overall the paper was good. Some things that need to be worked on is unity. Also what is that delta 9 stuff about? Is that the code for the tetrahydrocannabinal? |
| *Stan:* | is that the code for the tetrahydrocannabinal |
| *Paul:* | yea |
| *Tyisha:* | define cannabis in your paper so your reader knows what it is. |
| *Paul:* | ok |

. . . . . . . . . . . . . . . . . . . . . . . . . . . . . . . . . . . . . . . . . . . . . . .

| | |
|---|---|
| *Tyisha:* | what can Joe do to make his first sentence sound interesting? |
| *Tom:* | Joe could tell the reader what his point of view is |
| *Tyisha:* | yes or he could also do what |
| *Tyisha:* | where are you Joe |
| *Tom:* | he could state what the controversy is |
| *Joe:* | I don't want to include my opinion in the beginning because I was writing from a non-bias point of viewpoint |
| *Tyisha:* | Tom, do you think you would pick up an article like Joe's why or why not? |

. . .

*Tom:*  I would because in reading the first sentence I want to know what the controversy is

. . .

*Tyisha:*  Joe your paper is good, just work on making the introductory sentence sound appealing to the reader, by having a sentence like, As I looked into the subject of cultural diversity, I noticed how it was such a controversial topic.

There are probably a number of reasons why instances such as these occurred, beginning with Harris's identification of the peer tutor's tendency to become "enamored of" their more authoritative role (1992a, 380). There were times when I observed Tyisha reveling in her role as more knowledgeable, and why not? She was a former basic writer, and her work as a peer group leader by its very nature indicated how far she had come. At the same time, like peer tutors, Tyisha was still very much a part of her peers' community, only one year ahead of them in school, as her comments from various peer response sessions reveal: "What can Paul do to make his paper more personal to his audience?"; "Maybe in your intro you could mention that there are bad effects of weed"; "Let's flip to Paul's [essay]"; and "You're a nut Paul." In the first comment, Tyisha uses academic terminology ("audience"), though somewhat awkwardly. In the second sentence, her use of the word "weed," rather than the more formal "marijuana" (as I would call it), discloses her ties to the basic writers' community. The final two comments also reveal her connection as peer with the basic writers in my class.

I also believe that Tyisha was genuinely concerned about the writers in my class, and she wanted to help them improve their essays and get good grades, perhaps losing sight of her alternate roles. Her impulse to jump in with ways to "fix" their essays may have been a result of this concern. Moreover, there were times when she probably became frustrated with students in her group, as she prodded and pushed them to areas they did not want to go.

Relatedly, Harris's identification of the conflict over objectives of tutor and tutee may also explain some of the difficulties I experienced with the peer group leader. In the impressive exchange between Tyisha, Stan, and Jennifer previously discussed (I reproduce it below), there are also some signs of discontent.

*Stan:*  Try adding something like this; Standard english pulls from cultural independence. Some people feel that without there cultural distinction they will be lost. For a person to truly accelerate in our society they must have a little of both. Cultural diversity is not acceptable in todays world and for a person to not understand or use standard english they will be lost.

*Jennifer:*    Also, she was my spark for this paper. I am responding and giving my idea of her views.

. . .

*Tyisha:*    It's good you used Jones however, what is your thesis, is it that last sentence, because if so then you could talk about the things SHE FACED, I think it could be the second and third sentences combined, how do you feel Stan?

*Stan:*    Well I write what I think it should be.

*Jennifer:*    Thanks Stan, I like that response you gave me previously. I wrote it down because I like it a lot.

The transcript itself shows less of the conflict than did Tyisha's comments to me after class. In Tyisha's view, Jennifer was defensive, rejecting Tyisha's input and guidance. The dialogue above highlights two of Harris's points. First, it is possible that Jennifer saw Tyisha as judgmental, since Jennifer clearly felt strongly about her essay. The fact that the peer group leader does not have writing to be mutually critiqued alters the dynamic of peer collaboration and may have led Jennifer to feel defensive about her writing. Second, I think it is conceivable that Jennifer wanted what Stan gave her: a more direct answer to her questions about the thesis. Indeed, Stan rewrites the paragraph for her. Tyisha, on the other hand, prods Jennifer into making the discovery for herself, which may have been frustrating for Jennifer. Moreover, Tyisha's use of capital letters when she wrote "you could talk about the things SHE FACED" may have been offensive to Jennifer, although I think Tyisha meant only to emphasize the point she was trying to get across. Jennifer's "thank you" to Stan at the end of the discussion, absent one to Tyisha, may be further evidence of the conflict Tyisha sensed.

## PEER GROUP LEADERS AND BEYOND

Five years after this initial study and subsequent projects with peer group leaders in my classes, I remain confident of the potential for peer group leaders to aid basic writers' appropriation of academic discourse. I am grateful to my colleague, Candace Spigelman, for spearheading a more formal writing fellows program at our college, thereby intensifying tutors' training and enabling instructors to take advantage of in-class tutoring in myriad ways as appropriate to each instructional situation. In my spring 2004 Basic Writing class, I used successfully writing fellows in one-to-one "troubleshooting" roles during drafting and revising workshops throughout the semester. As a committed basic writing teacher, I am especially excited by the many configurations of classroom-based writing tutoring discussed in this volume; the good work being done by administrators, faculty, tutors, and students in institutions across the country and at various levels of writing instruction bodes well for basic writing students everywhere.

# 4

# WRITING AND READING COMMUNITY LEARNING
## Collaborative Learning among Writing Center Consultants, Students, and Teachers

Jim Ottery
Jean Petrolle
Derek John Boczkowski
Steve Mogge

Columbia College is located in Chicago's South Loop, which is a rapidly gentrifying commercial and residential downtown area. Columbia has been an anchor in the South Loop for three decades, and with its student population of nine thousand it is recognized for the opportunities it provides to young men and women who aspire to careers in the arts and communications. While it graduates talented artists who go on to "author the culture of our times," as the school's mission declares, it also graduates, and too often fails to graduate, fledgling artists and future employees in communications fields—students who may not author their culture, but who nevertheless punctuate the culture with the understanding that the arts should flourish with widespread, unlimited access.

Columbia College, Chicago, recognizes its commitment to the arts as a democratic undertaking. To that end, Columbia has always had an open-admissions policy, enrolling any students who wanted to pursue their ambition, regardless of portfolio, and regardless of high school GPA and college entrance test scores. However, despite more than three decades of open admissions, it wasn't until the mid-1990s that Columbia College, in response to its low retention rate, began offering developmental courses or even assessing students' reading, writing, and math abilities. By 1997 it was becoming apparent that assessment and developmental courses were making a positive difference, but more needed to be done to help Columbia's underprepared college students succeed. A blue-ribbon panel was formed to study the school's open-admissions policy and its consequences for the school.

After two years, the special commission, still unable to reach a definitive "thumbs-up or thumbs-down" decision on the school's open-admissions policy, offered a surprising compromise: the creation of the summer Bridge Program for students who were deemed underprepared for college. During the fall semester of 1999, the developmental reading and writing faculty, along with the director of composition, created much of the curriculum for a summer 2000 Bridge Program.[1] In this program, students with high school GPAs of 2.0 or lower participated in a five-week intensive program with writing center consultants and writing and reading teachers.

The Bridge Program was comprised of students, teachers, and writing center consultants who met for three hours per day, three days per week, with up to fifteen students in each class. Six tutors were chosen for the three sections of Bridge—three males and three females, all undergraduate students or recent graduates. During the writing skills session, students worked most often in a computer lab, drafting and revising essays, doing online peer evaluation workshops, and so on. The class was divided into four groups, with a teacher or a writing center consultant working with each group. Thus, groups of three or four students each had the full attention of one writing "expert." Once a week, the writing center consultants led class discussions as teachers conferenced one-to-one with students regarding their class progress. In large-group discussion, if the students were "stuck" on a question of understanding or interpretation, consultants would volunteer their knowledge and then discuss how they arrived at what they had talked about. In smaller groups, the consultants became teacher/facilitators in their own right.

In this distinctive learning community, writing center consultants, working as tutors, facilitators, mentors, and teaching assistants in the classroom, played a pivotal and significant new role. The consultants aided the Columbia College faculty in fashioning an "intensive-care" learning community experience for Bridge students, a way of helping students to establish a successful college identity. Equally important, working with consultants provided unique opportunities for faculty members to reflect on and revise their pedagogical approaches. This chapter reflects the central role played by the writing consultants in the Bridge Program and reveals how invested collaboration among consultants, students, and teachers constructed a model community of learners.

## THE CONSULTANTS' ACADEMIC FUNCTIONS

As a result of their experiences as tutors in the writing center, the consultants were well prepared for the Bridge Program students. However, the learning community model, which allowed for "continuous help," meant that there were new factors for them to manage. Most significant, they were now "on location" in the writing and reading classrooms themselves. All of the consultants found the chance to work in the classroom a welcome, exciting, and rewarding break in routine. While both Joe and Ben asserted that at times trying to ply their skills in the classroom was more difficult, as the classroom did not afford the privacy of the cubicles in the center—and, indeed, both retreated to the center after class with students who desired more one-to-one tutoring and a more focused ear—the consultants often found the group setting advantageous. Dana, for example, noted that whereas tutoring in cubicles in the center was "immediate," that immediacy could sometimes seem "stifling" because students felt as though their role in the give-and-take of tutoring required rapid response. Dana said she enjoyed the environment in the classroom, where the students needn't feel "on the spot," as they could defer to the group when trying to work out a problem.

However, this change in territory also prompted a change of their role. Being a writing consultant in the writing center meant striving for peer status (which was moderately achievable in the neutral ground of the writing center); in the Bridge classroom, where the students knew the consultants were meeting with the teachers each day, no one could reasonably assume a peer relationship. Thus, the consultants described their roles in many terms: "model student," "class mentor," "sympathetic listener," and, out of a defiance to labeling, just plain "Julie." Julie saw her active listening in the class as a kind of active teaching. She contrasts her classroom practice with her work in the writing center, which she describes as exhuming knowledge the student already has: "Observing students learning put me in a different seat, viewing the learning process in a totally different angle. I wasn't merely sucking out the knowledge most students who visit the center already have." Julie felt that being involved in the classroom meant she was helping to shape the students' creative minds. Sharon also felt more like a teacher than a writing consultant: "We helped plan the day in the morning, we led discussion groups, and we circled the room, helping people individually." As a matter of fact, Sharon, Dana, and Ben saw this experience in the Bridge Program as a step toward a teaching career.

At the same time, the consultants were asked to follow along with the work the students were doing in class. They had to complete the reading, be prepared to discuss it in class, and write in their journals. "I learned along with them," Julie offered, explaining that the tasks became more manageable when the students saw how someone else did them. The modeling also helped the consultants become better resources. Whereas in the writing center, the consultant finds it impossible to be familiar with the subject matter of every student assignment, as Dana noted, in the Bridge Program, doing assignments along with the students empowered the consultants to guide students through activities.

One foot firmly planted in the teacher and student camps (Sharon saw it as traveling between two different worlds), the consultants provided an important link in the functionality of the Bridge classroom, a link with the purpose, as Dana described it, of "community building." Not quite instructor, not quite student, the writing consultant stood between the "two worlds," becoming perhaps the human evocation of this bridge of learning.

Notably, the consultants had opportunities to confer with the class instructors directly, in contrast to their more lengthy process of writing session reports. Working and meeting with instructors and the program coordinators offered tutors a chance to affect procedure and pedagogy, as they were able to provide the instructors with information about how the students were reacting to the class. They were also able to discuss personal issues pertaining to the students, issues consultants might feel reluctant to put into the writing session reports. The consultants were heartened by the fact that the faculty for the most part sought their regular feedback.

However, consultants had mixed views toward their weekly meetings with faculty and administrators. Some felt intimidated by the "professionals" and held back their observations. Joe even wished he had not been privy to such meetings, as he felt he was betraying his camaraderie with students in the class because he was asked to weigh in on their standing as potential college students; he said, "I don't like deciding the students' fates."

Overall, however, the Bridge Program experience left a lasting positive impression on the consultants. While the slightly higher pay the program provided them and the feeling of "slight privilege" offered "material" rewards, the consultants felt that just as important was the program's contribution to their professional development: it taught them to be better consultants.

## THE CONSULTANTS' LISTENER FUNCTION

The Bridge Program at Columbia was designed in part to raise our retention rate which is low, even for an urban, nonresidential, open-admissions college. Being an open-admissions institution serving a commuter population poses significant challenges to us in our mission to educate students and prepare them for careers in arts and communications fields: to those students whose high school experiences contain nothing to make success in college a likelihood, how can we offer the possibility of change, the possibility of a more satisfying educational outcome? The Bridge Program was designed as a strategy for doing this: helping students to reverse the tide, to chart a fresh course.

Thus, one of our central goals was to reexcite students about learning and strengthen the skills we assumed were lacking. Surprisingly, few of the Bridge students had any significant skills weaknesses, certainly no more so than many successful students have. Instead, what these students had were histories of conflict—inside school and out—that had left them quite distracted from the possibilities of learning, bereft of any really nourishing sense of their own talents, and discomfited, wrapped up in a feeling of *unbelonging* and not "fitting." A number of them wrote quite well; some placed out of Composition I and had the option of entering Composition II directly. Bridge writing instructors realized quickly that, whereas they had prepared to cultivate invention, arrangement, revision, and sentence-level skills, their more important task involved *enfranchising* students *as* students—as readers, writers, thinkers, time managers, capable doers.

This process of helping students with histories of failure see themselves as capable students is far more abstract and mysterious than talking about paragraphs or sentences, especially since the space of the classroom is not a therapy session or encounter group. Somehow, while remaining focused on the practice of writing and reading, the Bridge instructor needs to bring to the classroom and conferencing a kind of presence with an attention to students that *says* (without saying anything), "You're bright! You're capable! Your past experience with education may have been flawed, but you're actually *just* the kind of person who can read, write, think, graduate from college, and make your way well in the world!" All committed teachers do this—whether consciously or unconsciously—but in a Bridge Program, it seems impossible *not* to make this central to the educational mission.

The process of enfranchising students—of contributing to the alteration their self-concept—amounts to a kind of witnessing function that teachers, other students, and consultants fulfill. In fact, many of the consultants who served in the Bridge classroom considered their informal interactions with Bridge students—their listening, advising, and personal sharing—to be their most significant contribution. In the Bridge classroom, consultants play a crucial social role that teachers could not appropriately play. Consultant Julie Shannon, for instance, reported that she and many Bridge students "became instant friends" and that "some of the students . . . still come to me at the campus with their questions about their classes, or registration, [or] financial aid" (e-mail, 24 July 2002). In such informal ways, consultants often served as friend and mentor at once, giving the students a social foothold in a bewildering mass of new information and personalities that comprise their first-year experience. The friend/mentor role also gave Bridge students another forum to share the high school struggles that led to their spotty academic histories and inclusion in Bridge. Consultants served an important listening function as students told the stories that could help them raise their own awareness about where they had been and where they wanted to go.

Mary Rose O'Reilley, in her book *Radical Presence: Teaching as Contemplative Practice,* suggests that students can be "listened" into existence, into stronger senses of self (1998, 16–21). There's a simple, powerful dynamic at work in listening intently to a student that helps that student see him- or herself freshly. During our time together in Bridge, students told such stories in the process of responding to Ron Suskind's *Hope in the Unseen* (1998)—a chronicle of an African American boy's journey from a DC ghetto to graduation from Brown University—stories about their own epic quests for success in school; their own epic descents into underworlds of family trauma, peer group troubles, substance abuse; their dearly won heroic comebacks, of which attending Columbia College was the latest. They read about educational experiences, wrote about educational experiences, spoke about educational experiences, all the while piecing together a narrative explaining what had happened to them in school, and what could be different this time around. Listening intently—through attentiveness during class discussion, through careful responding on drafts, through student-directed conferencing, through e-mail and phone conversations, and through student contact with consultants—somehow enabled the teaching team to create a hospitable space for a student's unfolding.

Almost all the consultants, when asked to reflect on their experiences teaching in Bridge, ranked listening as a number-one priority. Sharon said, "My relationship [with students] was partly that of a sympathetic listener and then partly that of an advisor. . . . There were a lot of people [struggling with their identity] who just needed someone to listen to them, and then *what* they revealed through their writing and art once they felt [listened to] was amazing" (e-mail, 24 July 2002). Another consultant, Joe, also reported being useful to students in his capacity to listen, especially since his own background includes a victorious struggle with challenging learning differences. Joe wrote: "With the hardships of having a learning disability myself, I understood their feeling of embarrassment when it comes to being involved in a `special program' like Bridge. While I didn't announce my learning disability in front of the class . . . I was able to encourage selected students on moving forward in education even if they suffer from a problem learning. Their eyes would light up when they heard that someone with a learning disability was able to succeed in college" (e-mail, 24 July 2002).

Sharon reports in an e-mail that another writing center consultant, Julie, similarly struck by the centrality of listening in the consultant/student relationship as a result of her experiences in Bridge, wrote an essay for one of her classes about "how listening, collaborating, and observing [are] the three main components to tutoring" (e-mail, 24 July 2002).

The kind of listening that occurred throughout the Bridge Program takes time. By sharing responsibilities with other teachers and especially with the consultants (who read about educational experiences, wrote and spoke about their educational experiences, all the while piecing together a narrative explaining what happened to them in school, and what made it different for them when *they* found success), intensive listening became our most important teaching tool.

## THE CONSULTANTS' TEAM-TEACHING FUNCTION

Teachers are usually alone in their classrooms—alone in their successes and alone in their failures with students. This professional isolation, unless mitigated by outside opportunities for exchange, makes it difficult to perceive one's own pedagogical idiosyncrasies, appreciate one's own strengths and weaknesses, evaluate objectively one's own effects on one's students. In addition, the teacher-student ratio in the single-instructor classroom makes it difficult for even the most skillful writing teachers to expand their relationships with their students beyond the students' writing within the context of the class. With students at risk of failure or attrition, this lack of time and energy for developing holistic relationships with students can seriously jeopardize an instructor's opportunity to help a struggling student bring forth the resources necessary for academic success. In structuring Columbia's Bridge Program as a team-teaching, consultant-supported learning environment, we turned teaching into a more public activity, making the Bridge Program an unusual learning opportunity for *teachers* and consultants as well as for students, and securing much-needed time for intensive contact with our students.

The team-teaching environment, in addition to enlarging the time and space of contact between instructor and student, enlarges contact between instructor and consultants, who intern help "Bridge" the time and space between teachers and students. This environment creates an extraordinary and rare professional development opportunity. When developing a syllabus, planning class sessions, responding to writing, and assessing student growth in collaboration with others, one's pedagogical assumptions, logic of sequencing, and teacherly priorities become more openly articulated and subject to revision. The colleague-to-colleague feedback is indispensable. The feedback from our classroom mediators, the consultants who have become our teachers' aides, is a bonus.

Most of the consultants commented on their role as mediators when they gave feedback about their Bridge experiences. Sharon wrote, "The tutors sort of went between both worlds, and explained the teacher's assignments to the students and the purpose of working on them, and explained some of the students' feelings to the teacher." Suggesting a Foucauldian-panoptical dimension to the mediator role that instructors acknowledge but didn't intend, Julie wrote about her experience: "We were sort of like secret agent spies who interviewed the students and kept their thoughts and concerns in mind to tell the instructors" (e-mail, 24 July 2002).

As Petrolle explains, the mediator role played by consultants enabled her coinstructor and her to make changes in their plans and mode of presentation quickly enough to respond to the constantly evolving and sometimes unpredictable needs of struggling students. When Petrolle is alone in the classroom, she may realize communication breakdowns and logjams too late to change an approach to facilitate better learning outcomes. Accordinaly the consultant, Joe, is right when he compares instructor perceptions with consultant perceptions, and notes that, "Due to our different observations [of] students, we noticed different things.

We were able to collaborate together on how to help the students succeed" (e-mail, 24 July 2002). Consultants often noticed signs of student
struggle that an instructor missed, or identified a shortcoming in his or
her approach: a failure to explain something that was mistakenly considered obvious, a slowness to realize that certain students were not completing assignments, or an overestimation of what was possible to achieve in
the short span of five weeks.

In addition to acquiring an additional ear to the ground, one develops
as a result of consultant support in the classroom the healthy self-con-
sciousness of the observed. No matter how self-reflective an instructor
tries to be, the privacy of the public space of the classroom can breed
a degree of complacency. To teach in the light of another colleague's
observation, and in light of observation by the consultants—who are half
student/half teacher—to teach in the light of observation is to observe
oneself teach.

In sum, the benefits of the community approach to teaching and learning extend to both students and instructors. In the team-taught, consultant-supported environment, struggling students benefit from expanded
opportunities to be seen and heard by supportive and experienced
companions on the journey toward academic and professional success.
But instructors benefit from heightened visibility and contact as well: the
enlarged and reconfigured community of the team-facilitated classroom
offers greater insight into one's public teaching persona. Greater insight,
of course, offers possibilities for greater effectiveness. O'Reilley also
suggests that a key ingredient for effective teaching and learning is an
atmosphere of intellectual "hospitality"—that is, an atmosphere in which
students are invited in, welcomed, and made comfortable in a realm of
ideas and communicative strategies (1998, 8–11). The spaciousness and
variety fostered by team-teaching methods helps the Bridge community
cultivate this atmosphere. It is our hope that this atmosphere will have
the same effect on retention that hospitality usually has on any warmly
received guests: they visit again and again and again, until they no longer
feel like a guest, but like they are at home.

## CREATING AN "INTENSIVE-CARE" COMMUNITY WITH STUDENTS, CONSULTANTS, AND TEACHERS

In Ottery's classes, students write a weekly journal that they e-mail to him
(thus, an "e-journal") in which they reflect upon their college experience. The purpose of the exercise is to get them to articulate what goes

well for them in and out of school (or not so well, as the case may be) during the week, so that they may be able to internalize their strengths and shortcomings and adopt behavior that identifies successful college students. The information the students provide also helps him as a teacher make adjustments in the classroom to enhance the chance of success for the group or to intervene with a student on a one-to-one level if necessary.

E-journals from the summer Bridge session of 2000 and 2001, as well as spring 2002, confirmed that the problems that most of these students had in high school often had little to do with their literacy skills and more to do with social situations that placed them at risk. So it was not surprising that in this program designed to provide the space, time, and *personnel* to begin to create socialized identities of successful college students, students chose most often to write about how important that "abstract and mysterious" yet "enfranchising" intensive care was to their sense of well-being in the program and in their futures at Columbia College. The consultants' presence and development of academic and social relationships with students indicates that such a presence is essential on location in a classroom that turns underprepared students in transition into college students who have a real chance to be successful.

Almost all of the students echo comments like those from Nia and Tony, who wrote about "meeting people" and "getting to know more about them" as being what was working best for them in the program (e-mails, 27 August 2000). For many of these students, "meeting people" did not come naturally or easy. One student wrote about shyness connected to feelings of insecurity that led to near deep depression: "A lot of the time I feel as if I'm the lowest thing on earth. . . . I do my best to ignore this feeling, but it's very hard, it makes me afraid, and it makes me angry. . . . Nobody knows how it feels to be me" (e-mail, 2 September 2000). Ten days later, after making a new friend, he writes: "So I think I finally got the hang of talking to people. . . . All through High School [*sic*] I was so shy and I couldn't figure out why, I wouldn [*sic*] never start a conversation with someone unless they talked to me first. . . . See this [Bridge] experience helped me to build confidence in myself and maybe I'll start talking to more people and get out of my shell (e-mail, 12 September 2000).

The intensive practice of two consultants and two teachers working with rotating small groups in class allowed students to provide their own "intensive care" to and about themselves and other students—these students had "histories of conflict" that prevented them from feeling as though they fit in anywhere, in school or out, and thus became academic underachievers at best.

Anthony, another student in the summer 2000 program writes, "I've made some new friends and I just keep making more. I don't have to hide my true self or sensore [*sic*] what I say" (e-mail, 27 August 2000). "[S]chool is becomeing [*sic*] my social life" (e-mail, 3 September 2000), he writes, indicating that a new identity based upon being a successful college student is forming.

In one of her e-journal entries, Nia affirms the value of classroom experience being about "personal relationships" as much as it is about teaching and learning content and also as "interaction between persons." She writes that she is happy to feel like learning in school "instead of outside of school" and attributes this new attitude to her feeling that "meeting people was great, but now getting to know more about them is even better" (e-mail, 12 September 2000). Another student writes of the importance of being accepted for who he is, a relief because he came from a "narrow minded" town that condemned people for differing life-styles (e-mail, 22 August 2000). He continues later in the same e-mail: "The reading and writing program is another one of the key factors of this program. Through our discussion, we get to see each individuals [*sic*] outlook on the reading, just because we all read the same portions of the book, doesn't mean we all think the same about it (e-mail, 22 August 2000).

Students in the summer of 2001 continued to make similar observations about themselves and the program. Leilani writes, "This week I feel a little better about the people I am around. I guess I'm learning to be myself more, and I'm starting to adjust to the amount of time it will take to get all my work done" (e-mail, 2 September 2001). "I've learned to give people more credit for their abilities," notes R. E. (e-mail, 4 September 2001). James builds on that theme by writing: "I think the one main thing I learned about myself is that I can become a social success, and still work hard for school. I think I learned that others can do this as well" (e-mail, 4 September 2001).

The intensive-care Bridge learning community created the time and space and opportunity—the hospitality of home—to help students learn, as Justin did, "that I have a lot inside of me that I didn't even know I had" (e-mail, 17 January 2002). As Jean notes, the constant classroom presence of writing center consultants allowed us what some might consider to be "the luxury" of fulfilling our *real* roles as teachers in facilitating the discovery of hidden potential and the desire to learn, even as we taught some of the skills that students require in order to take advantage of that potential and desire.

It will take many years for us to realize the statistical success (or failure) of the intensive-care learning communities comprising the Bridge Program in the first years of its existence.[2] But the numbers are encouraging. Ninety percent of the students who volunteered to join and successfully completed Bridge were retained through the spring of 2001 compared to 76 percent of the entire first-year class. The figures for the summer of 2001 might be considered somewhat less encouraging: 75.5 percent of those Bridge students mandated into the program were retained through the spring of 2002 compared to 79.6 percent of the entire first-year class. Still, the program's accomplishment is substantial if one keeps in mind that Bridge students are selected according to criteria that indicate that they are the least likely students to succeed in college. Statistics aside, however, what the consultants, teachers, and students themselves have said and about the program provides a clear picture in words of intensive-care, on-location, learning community success.[3]

# 5

# BUILDING TRUST AND COMMUNITY IN PEER WRITING GROUP CLASSROOMS

Casey You

Every semester, thousands of college students encounter their first experience with college writing. Most of them have no idea what is expected from them at this academic level, how to write using appropriate college discourse, or how to become better writers. If they are basic writers, their difficulties and anxieties are that much greater. This is why many writing teachers arrange their developmental writing students into peer writing groups, where they are given the opportunity to read their papers aloud and to develop their ideas with the help of others. Much research has shown that peer groups can be an important contribution to writing improvement (Bruffee 1978; Gere 1987; Brooke, Mirtz, and Evans 1994). However, many basic writers have not had experience in group work, or they are insecure about their writing or uncomfortable criticizing their peers' essays, and because of this, writing groups are not always as productive as they might be (Spear 1988; Bishop 1988; Zhu 1995).

As part of a project intended to encourage more active collaboration in one basic writing class, I was one of five specially selected education majors who were invited to serve as peer group leaders at a branch campus of a large university. As a peer group leader, I had responsibility for meeting with three first-year writers in their developmental writing class. My job was to model positive group behavior and to help my group of basic writing students learn how to respond to their peers' essays. In this role, I wanted to encourage my group members to develop confidence in their individual and collaborative decisions as writers and readers, since these group discussions were intended to guide group members as they revised their essays. However, I soon discovered that while writing groups can help students develop their writing skills, the question of trust among members must be addressed if students are to be confident in their ability to establish effective written communication. This is particularly important when students in the group reveal different levels of writing competency.

This small case study of three developmental writers attempts to discover how peer group collaboration contributes to writing improvement. Specifically, it concentrates on the question of trust and on the role of the peer group leader in building trust among group members when students have a wide range of skills and abilities. What follows is a description of the writing difficulties faced by three basic writers involved in the classroom writing group and an investigation into how the development of trust within the peer group helped the writers to overcome the difficulties.

## BACKGROUND TO THE STUDY

As a peer group leader, I met with my assigned peer group once a week during their fifty minutes of class time. I also attended a weekly peer tutoring seminar with four other peer group leaders, in which we assessed our classroom experiences, discussed assigned readings in composing theory and writing group theory, and planned for subsequent peer group sessions. In order to stay in touch with my students' progress as group members and as individual writers, I often took notes about what happened in our workshop sessions and described these exchanges in my weekly journal entries. This helped me to see whether the suggestions made during peer group meetings were really used in their revised papers and whether revising, based on the suggestions, helped the students to write stronger papers. My notes also allowed me to review the sessions to determine recurring individual writing problems, so that I could plan ways to help the group intervene for further progress. In addition, following a strategy described by Byron L. Stay in "Talking about Writing: An Approach to Teaching Unskilled Writers" (1985), I asked my group early in the semester what each of them considered the most difficult part of writing. Their answers gave me a good stepping-stone to understanding how they perceived themselves as writers in relation to how I perceived them based on writing samples. These insights were particularly helpful as the semester progressed, for students' perceptions of their own and their peers' writing abilities had enormous influence on the work of the peer response group.

To determine who is placed in this basic writing class, all incoming students take a placement exam (a sixty-question objective test) that is supposed to test overall facility with language. At the time of this study, students who scored below twenty were placed in basic writing. On the first day of class, students complete a writing sample; based on the instructor's assessment of their writing skills, they may be recommended to move to first-year composition. Based on those factors, my students, Mark, Paul, and Bob, stayed in basic writing.[1]

For their basic writing course, the students whom I taught were required to write seven essays. (The professor of our seminar group was also the basic writing instructor.) After writing their first drafts, they participated in a peer response session, which I facilitated, where they received oral feedback from the peer group. Then they revised their papers based on each other's suggestions and comments. The essays were then submitted to the professor, who gave each student additional feedback. This allowed the students to further revise their essays and learn as they progressed. This "loop" of events reinforced the idea that the writing process is recursive, not linear. It was helpful for the students to receive lots and lots of feedback.

In order to complete this study on trust among group members, I collected a variety of data. I read the students' first writing sample as "college writers." I also collected most of the essays written by my group, including first, second, and final drafts. I reviewed the drafts and looked for improvements and inconsistencies. I considered the relationship between these observations and my journal entries, which were kept over the entire course. As I reviewed their drafts, I noted which feedback came from the group members, from the writer, from me, or from the instructor. Journal entries that related to a specific writing piece and the English instructor's changing comments on their continually revised copies helped me to form fairly accurate judgments on their development. I also used an initial questionnaire that gave me some feedback about how they viewed themselves as writers as well as a final questionnaire to see how they felt about their development as writers and whether they thought the writing group had been helpful. I measured all activities against each writer's individual progress. I used this material to reflect on how they had developed and what problems were still common occurrences in the group.

## WRITING ABILITIES AND THE PROBLEM OF TRUST

According to Rick Evans (1994), trust is an essential element in the peer writing group relationship. If students are to trust each other, Evans says, their workshop meetings must allow members opportunities to get to know one another, provide an environment that feels safe and secure, promote feelings of "mutual dependence" and "shared involvement," and encourage a sense of community. Initially, the students seemed friendly to me and to each other. Since all of the group members felt that they had problems with organization in their written work, they seemed to have a common bond. However, tension occurred when members started to notice the level of difference in their writing abilities. They soon became self-conscious about their peers' response to their papers and about what they should say to each other. This led to discomfort, silence, and, at times, some evidence of hostility in the group.

I became aware of these differences in writing abilities early on in the semester, mainly from their writing samples, the questionnaires, my conversations with them, and from seeing their writing early on in the course. Mark was the strongest writer in the group. It is likely that Mark should have moved to the first-year class, but his ability didn't show itself in his writing sample. He was a very conscientious and serious student, but his early essays lacked organization. He initially wrote long papers with more than one focus topic and a lot of rambling in between central points. When I asked about his writing style, he recognized his problems. This was an important first step. He explained, "The biggest problem I have with my writing involves thought and organization." Basically, he didn't know where he was headed with most of his papers, so he would start in one direction and end in another, often going off on tangents along the way. This was perfectly fine for a rough draft, but for the final product he needed to learn techniques of organizational development. For example, early in the semester he wrote an opening paragraph that talked about his future in the Marine Corps. Then he went on about boot camp and later returned to his senior year of high school. This made his paper difficult to follow.

Bob initially limited his writing ability to a "frame" style, using a five-paragraph writing formula for every essay. At the beginning of the semester, Bob told me that he didn't know much about writing "good essays." He felt this way because he had a preconceived notion of how the essays were to sound and couldn't quite get his there. Bob found it difficult to write because he did not want to leave the comfort zone of the five-paragraph formula he had learned in high school. The instructor commented on one of his early essays that it was "too easy—your essay shows no tension, no human side, no exploration." This was common in most of his early writing pieces. Although he was initially self-conscious about his writing and nervous about peer feedback, he was the most willing to accept his peers' suggestions and to use them when revising his essays.

Paul was extremely unfocused, and he often underanalyzed crucial issues in his essays; therefore, he found it very difficult and frustrating to write. Initially, neither the instructor nor I knew that he had learning disabilities. On a questionnaire given at the beginning of the semester, he wrote that he had "a slight spelling disorder" and that "I don't really write very well at all." He said that he had earned a B in English his senior year at a Mennonite high school.

Paul had many difficulties and was the weakest writer of the group. When I asked him what he thought was his biggest problem with writing, he said, "I don't really write very well at all." He recognized that he had to search for ideas to write about, and he often forgot the purpose of his paper. Because he seldom read or wrote outside of school, he tended to run out of ideas and his writing sounded fake. Much more than Mark's, Paul's essays lacked focus and organization, and late in the semester he disclosed that he had ADHD. At the start of the semester, both Bob and Paul were clearly working below college level in their writing.

My students' varied writing abilities as well as their perceptions of themselves and each other negatively impacted our early peer group sessions. It seemed as though Paul knew that the others were better writers than he was, and this made it difficult for him to feel confident enough to offer suggestions about their writing. Mark wanted input from the group, but they appeared reluctant to comment because they viewed him as a "good writer." Often in the early sessions, Mark asked for comments but the others remained silent, looking at each other and me to give feedback. Usually, if I began the discussion, Paul and Bob would join in, but only to agree with my comments or add specific details to what I had already said. It was a rare occasion, especially early in the semester, when Paul or Bob submitted helpful feedback. Even when Mark asked specific questions in regard to a passage from his paper, they would give only very limited responses or tell him not to change it. I saw this as a common response, probably because Paul and Bob saw making changes as hard work, so they did not want to impose that writing process on a peer whose writing they admired. In addition, Mark had received an A on his first paper, while Paul and Bob had each received instructions to "rewrite." The group often felt that his essays didn't need further revision or help exploring new ideas. The group sometimes helped him with organization or development, but they did this with reluctance and only as a result of my constant encouragement.

On the other hand, when Mark offered suggestions to Paul and Bob, they felt he was probably right and that his insight was valuable. Both young men would immediately jot notes and make changes to their papers. As I look over some of my past journal entries, I notice that never did either disagree with a suggestion of Mark's.

In their essay "Our Students' Experiences with Groups," Brooke, Mirtz, and Evans discuss the need to build trust in writing groups. Presenting "some of the ways our students experience their small response groups and some of the major challenges they face as they interact," they note "the challenges are often located in differences" (1994a, 50). For my students, the differences had to do with their varied writing abilities, or at least their perceptions of differences. As a result, instead of trusting the group members to help them solve their writing problems, each student felt he had to bring a "perfect" paper to the workshop session. As the peer group leader, I knew that perfection could not be their goal, that if they were to develop as writers, they needed feedback, and that building trust would be an important way to get them to open up and get their ideas out there. It became clear to me that if the group was going to help each other write more clearly organized and more fully developed essays, I would need to promote trust within the group or the process would not be successful.

## BUILDING TRUST

To develop the kinds of conversations that would promote trust in my peer group, I borrowed from writing group theorists. Evans (1994) stresses the importance of on- and off-task conversation to develop this crucial trust among members, and together with his coauthors, Robert Brooke and Ruth Mirtz (1994a), he offers suggestions about warm-up and friendship-forming activities and strategies that can be used to help the students successfully negotiate the differences among them. At our first meeting, we got to know each other by talking about ourselves rather than our writing. In addition to early "get acquainted" activities, I had the group comment on all positive aspects of each paper before talking about what needed to be changed. This relaxed the writer, and once the ball was rolling, harsher criticisms from the group were not taken as defensively but were assumed to be a way of making good writing better.

One strategy that helped to build trust in the group members' suggestions came from Sandra W. Lawrence and Elizabeth Sommers's "From the Park Bench to the (Writing) Workshop Table: Encouraging Collaboration among Inexperienced Writers" (1996). Each student read his paper aloud and then everyone responded to it by writing what was good about the piece, what they liked and disliked, what confused them or needed further expansion. Then we discussed everyone's ideas. In this way, a lot of feedback was given to every writer, and they started to revise more actively when they had each other's comments to look at. Further, individual feedback was valued because everyone had something to say, and each member's opinion seemed to be valued more because it was personal, not just an extension of someone else's idea. In my log entry, I described the result: "This method worked really well and it allowed them to run the session more independently and productively." However, the differences in students' writing ability remained a central problem throughout the semester, and I developed particular strategies that helped to address the individual concerns of each group member.

Learning to trust was a two-way street for my group members. They had to develop confidence in other group members and they had to believe that they could trust themselves to offer significant comments. In the case of Mark, it seemed to be more difficult for him to trust the others' suggestions, and they were certainly more hesitant to offer advice when it came to Mark's essays. It therefore became necessary that they understand the different roles they could play in the writing group. Emphasizing the importance of talk for student writers, Michael Kleine's "What Freshmen Say—and Might Say—to Each Other about Their Own Writing" (1985) describes four particular kinds of verbal response that should be promoted in peer workshops. Kleine suggests that group members respond (1) as evaluators to find surface-level or formal criticisms; (2) as immediate readers by giving extended suggestions about content and clarity; (3) as helpful listeners to help the writer brainstorm additional ideas; and (4) as a role-playing audience serving remote readers outside of the group and the teacher. In Kleine's view, all four kinds of talk are necessary and should take place at various appropriate moments during any workshop session.

I used the ideas from Kleine's article to explain that it wasn't always necessary to find things to change; they could also find things they liked and build on those ideas. The peer group could be used to further blossoming ideas. Within two sessions, they picked up on this point, and this set us in a new direction early in the semester. Everyone had something to say and everyone could trust each other's ideas of "development," not "corrections." In a later interview, when I asked Mark if he had been helped in any way by the peer group, he said, "Yeah. I get my ideas down on paper first and then I go back and organize them into a well-developed paper from the input of my group." Mark could see that the results of peer input were positive: the English instructor commented on his paper, which was revised by the group, saying, "You have done a remarkable job of taking a complex issue and systematically examining the arguments—this paper is as good as it can be." In respect to Mark, my students came to see that they could make good suggestions so that Mark could benefit from what they had to offer. In this way, they learned to trust themselves and, using Kenneth Bruffee's term, to view themselves as "knowledgeable peers."

Because Bob had a negative view of his writing ability, he was more open to suggestions, especially from Mark, so developing trust was not as difficult for him as it was for the other writers. In the first month of working with his peer group, he established a good working relationship with Mark, whom he viewed as a superior writer. Stay, whose article builds upon Robert Zoellner's work on the benefits of conversation for composition students, asserts that since basic writers are often better at talking than at writing, "talking helps unskilled writers to formulate and clarify their ideas while they gain confidence" (1985, 248). In our workshop sessions, we helped Bob reword his ideas and expand on his thoughts so that his essays were much less formulaic. This greatly improved his papers and his writing style. After one of the peer sessions, I interviewed him about the changes that he had made in his essay and asked if his new way of thinking about the ideas for his essay had emerged during the peer group meeting. He replied that he had a better handle on how to organize his information now that he had talked the ideas over with the other members of his group. Bob commented that he trusted the input of the group members because their feedback was always helpful in developing his papers, so that he didn't have to "rewrite" each one for a grade. He said, "The group really helps to get my ideas organized and put into writing. I have a very hard time trying to put my words onto paper so that all the readers know what I'm trying to say."

On the following paper, he showed us that he had earned an A. His papers became full of ideas. He had clear statements, supporting ideas, and nicely developed paragraphs, and his personality began to shine through in his writing. With notable changes in his development and

style of writing, his papers were more interesting for his specific audience, including his peers, his instructor, and me. The last paper that we
reviewed together also received an A. He had a few grammatical errors,
but his essay had good structure with meaningful support. At the bottom
of his paper, the instructor had written, "You've come a long way." I had to
agree. I believe that Bob's willingness to trust his peer group was key to his
progress. Rather than trying to bring a "perfect" draft to the workshop, he
took more time on his later papers because he wanted them to be good,
and he knew that he could count on the help of his group to shape his
essay so that he expressed what he wanted it to say.

Helping the group to deal effectively with Paul's writing and helping
Paul to trust and consider his peers' suggestions was probably the most
challenging aspect of my work as a peer group leader. At the beginning of
the semester, Paul's drafts were very difficult for the group to understand,
as this early introduction reveals:

> Well, this past summer a very defining event happened when I was chosen to
> be on staff at a summer camp. It was my first year on staff but I had been a
> camper for the past nine years. The summer brought many interesting chal-
> lenges and problems that I had to deal with. The one that sticks out in my
> mind the most was as follows: At the beginning of the week the campers fill out
> information forms so staff knows a little bit about them. All of mine checked
> out fine. Tuesday night I was covering someone's supper table and one of the
> campers was crying her head off. I asked her what happened but she didn't say
> a word. I then asked her friend what happened and she told me that this girl
> (Becky) had just gotten a letter in the mail from her mom.

The introduction continued on for several more lines, and its lack of
focus was evident to the group. It seemed as though Paul was wandering
around trying to find something to write, and, as a result, his peer group
members were unable to offer him meaningful feedback. When Paul
finally disclosed that he had a learning disability, he took a gradual step
toward developing peer trust. He showed that he felt comfortable sharing a personal characteristic with the group, and the group was in turn
sensitive to this. Also, learning about Paul's ADHD was useful to me as
the group leader as I tried to promote trust among these students who
had such different writing styles and such different peer group needs. I
now knew that Paul would need more specific feedback from the group
on fewer content areas. I was able to model this type of feedback late in
the semester by choosing only one or two things to work on for the next

paper, such as a topic sentence and good transitions as a focus point for the next few sessions, while for the other members, I usually gave two or three suggestions to focus on at each session. Soon Mark and Bob began to realize that when reading Paul's papers they should focus on the major problems, such as paragraph organization and thought completion, not the details that could be corrected with more careful revision.

For Paul, peer group collaboration was the main ingredient in developing trust. I would usually ask Paul to explain the point of his paper before he began to read it aloud to the group. If he could tell us what it was about in a sentence or two, he could usually develop a focus for his paper that the group could attempt to follow. If he could not specifically state his topic or point, then the group helped him to develop a thesis. From there, the group could also help him develop each paragraph and make it support the thesis.

Asking the group to comment on the positive aspects of his paper before moving on to the problems was especially important to Paul, and the group sessions became a big part of his revision process. In particular, the group suggested ways of forming solid introductory paragraphs, which seemed to contribute to improvements in his focus and organization at the same time. By the middle of the semester, with help from his group, Paul was writing introductions like the following:

As I walk through the front door of my Aunt Bert's house in Harrisburg PA, I see many things. I see a big grandfather clock that has been in the family for many years, an oak table in the dining room that is loaded with food, a big screen television set with Sony Playstation hooked up to it. I also see a many number of people. I see Adrienne, who came all the way from New York, Brian who came all the way from Italy and occasionally a stranger or two. With all of these people gathered for one big party, there are a countless number of presents. The thing I look forward to most during the whole year is our family tradition on Christmas Day.

The instructor commented positively on this introduction, saying, "Great opening, Paul. This tour of the family invited your reader to travel along." I agreed that his strong introduction led to a much more sophisticated and detailed essay.

Unfortunately, overcoming his own self-doubts and distrust of the group process came too late for Paul, and his writing did not develop to the extent that the other members' did. Although Paul's writing showed a fair amount of improvement over the semester, his writing never achieved the level I had hoped for him. If I had I known about his learning disabilities earlier in the semester, I might have used a different approach. I could have shown him ways to organize his papers in stages, a strategy we tried to develop toward the end of the semester, instead of going all out in one sitting. I could have guided the group in providing more help-ful suggestions for him, but Paul was wary about sharing this informa-tion with his peer group members or me, probably because he doubted acceptance.

I also found it interesting that Paul was the least likely to use the advice from the workshop when he revised his papers. This might have been because he could not remember exactly what he was told or because he didn't know how to integrate the suggestions. However, Stay stresses that students whose writing has been evaluated as "deficient" may feel "social and psychological pressures" that make them reluctant to resee and revise what they have written (1985, 249). In either case, it suggests that some issues of trust cannot be easily resolved, even when the peer group seems to be functioning productively. Also, it is crucial to take writing disabili-ties into account during workshop time, as would be done with any other subject.

Finally, my position as the peer group leader also played an instru-mental role in the relationship among group members. As Karen Spear explains, students in peer groups will often take up the teacher's role rather than offer advice to each other as peer readers (1988, 54–57), and when there is a peer group leader, this is even more likely to occur. My peer group members wanted to transfer all the authority to me. In order to stay away from this role and give responsibility back to the students, to encourage them to trust each other as well as me, I simply accepted every member's initial suggestions and then pushed them to clarify and develop their ideas and suggestions in the workshop. Because I did not want to be viewed as the "expert," I liked having everyone equally contributing. Offering my insight and suggestions along with the suggestions of the peer group members contributed to their self-confidence and to their trust in each other as writers and readers. They began to see that all the writing in their essays was not merely corrections from the teacher, but group and self input that ultimately improved their writing.

After all my peer group had learned about enhanced communica-tion and learning to critique and accept criticism, the biggest factor in developing trust within the group was maturation over the semester. In order to build a higher, more intense level of trust and therefore a greater degree of productivity, the three men had to mature into their new role, a college role, in which they learned to be proud of what they wrote and learned to make others feel confident and accepting in their own writing ability. When each student learned how to give and accept suggestions, this showed me that they trusted the input coming from the other members. This trust eventually led to peer-dominated sessions, rather than teacher-dominated or peer group leader–dominated sessions.

## PEER GROUP LEADERS AND THE QUESTION OF TRUST

Although my group consisted of only three students, all male and all from similar educational backgrounds in central Pennsylvania, this small study of one peer group shows that collaborative peer feedback can help basic writers. Each of my students benefited individually by gaining an understanding of their specific problems as writers and learning how to develop their skills individually. They also learned how to revise together as a group so that every member had a stronger paper. They found techniques they liked and didn't like, but they developed a style that worked for them and their audience. This is important for all writers.

This was a useful study for me as a future teacher because it gave me an insider's look at the development of basic writers as they learn from peers, leaders, and instructors. Working as a peer group leader has given me new knowledge of the writing processes of basic writers. I have also become more conscious of the difficulties basic writers face and why these difficulties occur. In my group, peer group leader intervention was important for building the kind of trust that sustained a positive and progressive learning environment. There was a lot of on-task talk and some off-task talk in my group, but, for the most part, everyone left feeling as though he had been heard. Once the trust was established and ideas were flowing, the three students could have easily worked in a collaborative group without a leader. When I talked to the other group leaders, however, they told me that trust was not a constant consideration in their groups, and that this might be why their groups were not as coherent or helpful for the students.

My experience with peer group writing sheds new light on the ways in which teachers should consider peer group organization. In conversations with my instructor when the semester ended, I learned that many instructors experiment with different peer group configurations. In our class that semester, our teacher chose to place a strong, middle, and weak writer together. My research on trust and writing abilities in peer groups leads me to believe that teachers must be more cognizant of the way they organize groups. With different levels of writing abilities, students are seemingly less trusting of the peer response situation. But I can also confidently say that peer group leaders can mediate in these kinds of situations to engender trust and create a positive peer response environment.

The positive effects of peer group collaboration have been well researched by many scholars. Hopefully, this project will contribute to ongoing research by giving teachers and students a greater understanding of how a peer group leader can build trust and thus enhance the productivity of writing group response. The peer group's small size and comfort level nurtured honest conversation. Whether students like group work or not, sharing and developing ideas with others is a significant way to develop their roles as communicators for life, learning to write by writing and collaborating.

# PART TWO

## *Reconciling Pedagogical Complications in Classroom-Based Writing Tutoring*

The essays in part one highlighted collegial, institutional, interdisciplinary, and discursive connections that classroom-based writing tutoring may foster. Yet, as a hybrid genre, those same intersecting forces that provide transformative possibilities simultaneously create new hurdles for students, tutors, faculty, and administrators. In this section, our contributors describe the day-to-day operational decisions participants must address when tutoring takes place in classrooms. (We deliberately bracket issues of power and authority, which serve as the focus of part three). These decisions are often at odds with deeply entrenched alliances and beliefs about the "right" kinds of tutoring practices, which are, in turn, tied to tutors' training and the ideology surrounding that training.

As Barbara Little Liu and Holly Mandes reveal, problems can emerge when the demands of a classroom environment clash with more familiar nonintrusive tutoring approaches. In their study, tutors found that their writing "center(ed)" training did not equip them to deal with students unwilling or ill-prepared to ask for assistance. Liu and Mandes suggest that tutors take a more interventionist approach, and they turn to recent writing center theory to legitimize these alternative strategies. Steven J. Corbett likewise argues that on-location tutoring often warrants more directive tutoring techniques, which may clash or meld with traditional minimalist approaches. By modeling the communicative practices students need and desire for academic success, Corbett contends, tutors can reconfigure their roles as authoritative but not authoritarian, and, in this way inspire writing group and whole-class conversations.

A different kind of conflict can occur when tutors trained in one-to-one tutoring are asked to facilitate classroom-based peer response groups. They may, as Melissa Nicolas discovered, be unprepared to handle the immediacy of writing groups or the duality of roles expected of them as group members and simultaneously as knowledgeable peers. Nicolas suggests that tutor-training methods and writing students' training must clearly distinguish between peer response groups, writing center tutorials, and writing group tutoring.

Even if the training is on target, even if the appropriate modifications are in place, the involuntary nature of classroom-based writing assistance introduces conflicts that go to the heart of the tutoring situation. As tutor Kelly Giger found, developing writers, in particular, may resist revising suggestions, going through the motions of the revising activities without making real changes to their essays. Giger's experience reminds us that instructional interventions usually require negotiation and diplomacy and a heavy dose of optimism.

In the classroom, conflicts between theory and practice, among theories, and even between tutors' and students' desires add additional layers of complexity to the work our tutors do. The essays in this section explore these conflicts while providing theoretical and practical strategies for overcoming them.

# 6

# THE IDEA OF A WRITING CENTER MEETS THE REALITY OF CLASSROOM-BASED TUTORING

Barbara Little Liu and Holly Mandes

Stephen North's essay "The Idea of a Writing Center" (1984) stands as the touchstone for much subsequent writing center theory and writing tutor practice. The essence of North's essay (and, hence, of most writing center philosophy) is summed up in this oft-quoted idea: "[I]n a writing center the object is to make sure that writers, and not necessarily their texts, are what get changed. . . . our job is to produce better writers, not better writing" (438).[1] The work of a writing center tutor, then, is not to help the student writer "fix" or "correct" the current draft of a particular assignment or even to improve a single draft in more complex, logical, organizational, and intellectual ways than are suggested by these mechanical-sounding verbs. The work of a writing center tutor is to engage the student writer in an intellectual process that will result in more fully developed and carefully crafted writing in general. A particular paper is not the focus—but rather the writer's processes and strategies for producing and crafting any piece of writing.

How does that philosophy work in practice? Usually it means keeping the writer in control—not writing on her paper or making specific prescriptive suggestions for wording or organization. Descriptions of such tutorial approaches emphasize that tutors ask questions rather than provide answers. For example, in *The Allyn and Bacon Guide to Peer Tutoring* (2000), Paula Gillespie and Neal Lerner suggest that a tutor begin "by asking writers a few basic questions [about the assignment, the writer's main argument, the writer's concerns about the draft] before they even consider the draft" (26). Then the tutorial proper begins, with the writer reading his entire draft aloud as the tutor listens and takes notes. "Listening to the whole thing from start to finish and taking notes puts you in the role of the learner, and the writer in the role of the expert. . . . You're taking notes, listening. . . . [H]e's the expert since it's his paper. . . . [I]n a good tutorial, the tutor asks questions, and the writer decides what to do with a draft" (26–27).

In their discussion of the ethics of writing center work, Irene L. Clark and Dave Healy (1996) provide an overview of similar scholarship in tutor training, illustrating the degree to which the nonintrusive tutorial model dominates. They quote a variety of authors who, by advocating "Socratic dialogue" and "minimalist tutoring" and by castigating the editing or improving of papers or mentoring of students, make "the concept of tutor restraint a moral imperative, dictating a set of absolute guidelines for writing center instruction." Clark and Healy's ultimate example of this dogma comes from Thomas Thompson's description of the Citadel's writing center: "[T]utors try to avoid taking pen in hand when discussing a student paper. They may discuss content, and they may use the Socratic method to lead students to discover their own conclusions, but tutors are instructed not to tell students what a passage means or give students a particular word to complete a particular thought" (35).

North's model of writing center work has been adopted enthusiastically in writing centers in universities and in primary schools, from the Northeast to California, but does it travel as well outside the realm of the writing center? What about when writing tutors move into the classroom? As coordinator of First-Year Writing (Barbara) and a well-trained and experienced peer tutor (Holly), we were involved in establishing a classroom-based tutoring component for a developmental writing course at Eastern Connecticut State University. We quickly discovered that the nonintrusive, writing center(ed) model in which Eastern's tutors had been trained did not always meet the needs of the students with whom they were working in the classrooms. In what follows, then, we will offer a description of our situation as one example of the difficulties writing center(ed) tutors can encounter in making the move into the classroom, the ways in which some of our tutors began to respond to their sense that a different kind or kinds of tutoring might be appropriate in the classroom, and the ways in which these responses are reinforced by a growing body of writing center theory that offers alternatives to the dominant nonintrusive model.

## CLASSROOM-BASED REALITY AT EASTERN

Eastern Connecticut State University lacks a full-fledged writing center. Therefore, our classroom-based tutoring program did not develop as an extension of such a center; however, it did grow out of a writing center(ed) program developed by the English department. For many years, Eastern has provided some tutoring in writing through the university's Learning Resource Center (LRC), which also provides tutoring in math and a variety of other academic subjects. Several years ago, the director of the University Writing Program began to realize that the tutoring in writing provided by the LRC was inadequate in regard to the number and availability of tutors and the quality of their training; therefore, the writing program director began the Writing Associates Program, in which promising English majors (who were first identified and recommended by English faculty) were recruited to act as tutors for the first-year writing course. Writing associates received internship credit for tutoring students in particular sections of the first-year writing course to which they were assigned; however, the tutoring took place outside the classroom, by appointment, in much the same way that it would in a writing center. Writing associates were trained by taking a junior-level course in composition theory and pedagogy that included an introduction to writing center theory and practice. Thus, although these tutors were not literally working in a writing center, their work as tutors was writing center(ed) in many ways.

Eventually, the Writing Associates Program added a classroom-based tutoring component for a new developmental writing course, English 100Plus. However, tutor training at Eastern remained the same, so that the key differences between writing center and the 100Plus classroom contexts were largely unaddressed. Therefore, tutors assigned to 100Plus entered the classrooms with a number of assumptions from their writing center(ed) training that didn't necessarily jibe with the classroom-based context in which they had their initial (and much of their ongoing) contact with student writers. The first several tutors to work in 100Plus were left to make their own adaptations and philosophical adjustments, in part because they brought with them key assumptions derived from their training in writing center theory. The following assumptions became especially problematic in the 100Plus classroom-based context:

- *Writers* come to writing tutorials of their own accord, in their own time, and through their own motivation.
- *The writing tutorial's purpose* is to help the writer improve as a writer, not to help the writer improve a particular piece of writing or to support the curriculum or coursework of a particular class.
- *The writing tutor's role* is of learner, listener, and questioning partner in dialectic, not that of writing expert, teacher, or teacher surrogate; therefore, the writer carries the authority in the interaction among writer, tutor, and text.

Hence, English 100Plus tutors had to develop new strategies for classroom-based tutoring that either adapted or put aside their writing center(ed) training.

After we share our tutors' intuitive strategies for adapting to their new tutoring environment, we will discuss how these accommodations are validated by a number of writing center theorists who are suggesting alternatives to the dominant nonintrusive tutoring model. Finally, we will share our plan for a revised approach to tutor training that draws on these theorists and our tutors' experiences.

## MOTIVATION IN ENGLISH 100PLUS TUTORING

One of the largest differences between the context for our classroom-based English 100Plus tutors and the context assumed in the writing center(ed) model is that writers do not initially come to the tutors; the tutors come to their classroom. In North's description of the writing center, the catalyst that brings the writer and tutor together is the writer's own commitment to his or her current writing project and motivation to make it as good as it can be. Writing centers, he argues, do their best work not when students have been required by an instructor to make an appointment, but when they are "deeply engaged with their material, anxious to wrestle it into the best form they can: they are motivated to write" (1984, 443). English 100Plus tutors, however, cannot wait for motivation to strike. They often need to prompt the motivation. If they are to do their job and earn their pay, they must become the catalyst that brings about productive writer/tutor interaction.

This catalyst role is one of the most fundamental differences between traditional writing center tutoring and tutoring in the English 100Plus classroom. In writing center settings, a writer's motivation to seek help with her writing will likely occur when she has a finished (or nearly finished) draft that she feels needs revision. North notes that these moments of motivation (while they may occur in other stages of the writing process) do not always coincide "with the fifteen or thirty weeks [students] spend in writing courses—especially when . . . those weeks are required" (1984, 442). In English 100Plus, most of a tutor's time is spent working with students whose presence in the classroom is required, who do not have finished drafts, and who may (as so-called developmental writers) be particularly apprehensive about sharing their writing.

For the student writers in English 100Plus, apprehensions about sharing often stem from their awareness that they are (or at least have been labeled by their placement as) inadequate writers. Most are also insecure about their abilities because of their lack of experience with writing. They do not know how to talk about their writing and, more important, are probably nervous about their skill level. When a student writer enters a writing center, while she may be quite apprehensive about the tutoring process, she has still reached a point where she feels that she can show another person her thoughts. When students are working during an English 100Plus class, however, the tutor often approaches them, whether they have reconciled themselves to the need to share their work or not. Therefore, in their efforts to reach out to writers, tutors may invade the writers' comfort zone when they are not necessarily ready to show their work to someone else. When a tutor approaches these students without their permission, she treads a thin line between help and invasion. While our tutors are sensitive to this problem, they also know that it is part of their job to make each class session productive, for both themselves and the student writers.

This is perhaps one of the most difficult conundrums for the tutor working in the classroom environment. How should one approach a student who is in the middle of writing? The student who isn't really writing yet? Or the student who is unsure if what he is doing even constitutes writing? Many tutors, like Holly, find that, through taking a gentle, peer-centered approach to instigating in-class writing conferences, they can make the classroom-based tutoring process comfortable for both themselves and the student writers with whom they work. Once initial contact is made, students and tutors can then learn that their conversations about writing can be helpful, not just when it seems most obviously necessary, but at many other points in the writing process. The key to this gentle approach is a gradual easing from social conversation into the talk of a writing conference.

Tutors who have adopted this approach feel that it is unwise for a tutor to simply sit down next to a writer and immediately ask to see his current progress. Rather, it is better for the tutor to first approach the writer in a way that builds on her status as peer, then expands to include the use of her expertise. Holly found that inquiring about the student's general mood (his relative confidence or apprehension) about his progress with a writing assignment was a good place to start. She might begin with a relatively nonthreatening icebreaker such as, "How are things going?" While some students would share their apprehension, leading to some commiseration on Holly's part and then some suggestions for how to get over that apprehension, most students responded as briefly as possible: "Fine." Holly noted that the easy thing to do at this point was to leave her interaction with the student at that, but she realized that if she didn't press further she might never get beyond this level of conversation with the student. Her next step, then, was often to express curiosity about the writer's general topic and what he had done with it so far. After a bit of discussion along this line, Holly would express interest in a particular aspect of the writer's description of his work and ask the writer to read that part of his paper. In most cases, however, she didn't need to ask to see the writing. By that point in their conversation, most writers had already read parts of their work to her because reading it was easier than explaining it. Thus, Holly was able to engage most students in their first writing tutorial relatively painlessly.

Another experienced English 100Plus tutor, Mandee, finds that she is uncomfortable trading too much on her status as student peer. She feels she has more to offer if she maintains a more professional (yet still empathetic and supportive) role in the class. She still tries to lay the groundwork for productive interaction gently and as early as possible, but her approach is different. On the first day of class, Mandee introduces herself to the class as a whole. Her introduction often goes something like this:

> I'm here to help you with your writing no matter where you may be with it. Even if you're stuck because you're not sure what to say or how to say it, I can help. If you are unsure about the assignment and have questions you don't want to ask Dr. Liu, I can help you with that. I took this class with Dr. Liu, I've tutored for her before, and I know her assignments inside out. I'm also really interested in your writing. I've learned some really interesting stuff from reading student papers and seen some perspectives I otherwise wouldn't have seen. To best help you with your writing, I'll need to get to know a little about you, your interests, your concerns about your writing, and your writing itself. So don't be surprised if in the next few days I come over to you to talk a bit. I'll want to get to know you and read some of your writing, so that I can work with you to figure out how I can best help you.

Mandee's introduction sets the professional tone she finds most productive, and it prepares students for her interruption—not only by letting them know that she will be interrupting them, but also by letting them know the role those interruptions will play in establishing an ongoing tutor/writer relationship. When Mandee sits down next to students, then, they are prepared for it. They may have already chosen a writing sample that they are comfortable showing her, and they are prepared to talk to her about writing. She reintroduces herself to each student and asks his or her name, often offering her hand to shake. Many students find this formality reassuring; they know what to expect from Mandee.

## DIFFERENT PRIORITIES IN ENGLISH 100PLUS TUTORING

Once students begin to feel comfortable with having the tutors around and working in the classroom, they will start to raise their hands and ask for help with specific concerns. Because the tutor is in the classroom and students are expected to be working on the writing assignments for that class, the questions students have and the kind of help they want is always related to their English 100Plus coursework, usually the specific assignment due next on the syllabus. In many instances, writers' questions will be even more specific: about a particular grammatical or syntactical puzzle they are dealing with in their writing at that moment, for example, or about the clarity, effectiveness, or relative improvement of a particular idea, sentence, or paragraph (i.e., "Does this sentence make more sense now?"). While such questions are asked in writing center tutorials, the mandates to (1) improve writers and not necessarily particular texts; and (2) serve the writer rather than a particular course curriculum, lead writing center tutors to redirect the students' immediate attention to so-called higher-order concerns. In *The Allyn and Bacon Guide to Peer Tutoring*, for example, a boldfaced heading in the chapter on "The Tutoring Process" announces "HIGHER ORDER CONCERNS COME FIRST." Here, Gillespie and Lerner remind tutors that "one of the most important things you can do as a tutor is to deal first with . . . higher order concerns. As a tutor, you'll save grammar and correctness for later." They go on to note that "if we help writers proofread first, a lot of writers—especially those who are inexperienced or hesitant—won't want to change anything in their papers, even to make things better, because they feel that once they have their sentences and punctuation right, all will be well with their writing" (2000, 29). Redirection to higher-order concerns makes sense in the context of the writing center, not only philosophically but practically. Writing center tutors are able to put higher-order concerns first because of the amount of time they have for each student writer. Out of the sixty minutes a tutor has with a student, he may be able to afford to devote fifty to higher-order concerns, and then help the student recognize and deal with syntax or punctuation in the remaining ten minutes (or in a subsequent session). Additionally, when a student comes to a writing center tutorial, she has completed her writing for the moment, left the place where she was working on it in order to travel to the writing center, and is not currently actively engaged in the act of composing.

The situation in the English 100Plus class is quite different, however, and hence, a different response is needed. Students spend much of their time in class writing. When a student chooses to interrupt his composing momentarily to ask a tutor a specific question, that student believes that his question is of the utmost importance to his writing at that moment. He plans to receive an answer or advice and continue writing immediately. He does not usually plan on getting his answer, applying it to his writing, and then working no further to complete or improve his writing. Therefore, most English 100Plus tutors and instructors feel that student writers are best served when the tutor acknowledges the question and immediately offers an answer or advice on the specific concern the student has raised.

As Gillespie and Lerner note, embracing North's idea of a writing center, "writing centers are not about editing. We are about teaching and maintaining a much larger view than correcting the immediate paper: our goals for sessions are to help the writer learn the skills needed to improve not just this paper but subsequent papers" (2000, 40). However, in the College Writing Plus class, if tutors ignore the initial questions they are asked by students, they invalidate the students' writerly instincts and thereby damage their ongoing working relationship with those students. By not answering their questions, tutors may make writers feel belittled and unheard, which will ultimately lead to less and less worthwhile interaction between tutor and writer. Many of our tutors find, therefore, that it is simple enough to answer the writer's initial question, and then—if time permits and several other students aren't vying for the tutor's attention—the tutor might respond, "Now that we've figured that out, if you're okay with it, can we look at the rest of the paper to see if you have any other concerns?" Sometimes this is all it takes to move the writer toward higher-order issues, but at other times, the writer may not be ready to discuss more of her paper with the tutor just yet. As working relationships are established throughout the semester, tutors no longer need to impose themselves; rather they can allow the students to initiate and set the limits for their class-time tutor/writer interactions. If tutors have done a good job establishing productive working relationships with student writers, the students know that tutors are always available for them and that the writer's concerns are the ones that count in the classroom. This knowledge encourages ongoing interaction between writer and tutor by establishing an open and accepting role for the tutor. Tutors can also rest assured in the knowledge that they will have ample opportunity to address higher-order concerns either later within the fifty-minute class period or during the additional office hours they are required to hold outside of class.

## AUTHORITY IN ENGLISH 100PLUS TUTORING

The time limitations of the classroom context also usually prohibit tutors from engaging in the kind of Socratic dialogue recommended in the writing center. As Gillespie and Lerner note, "in a good tutorial, the tutor asks questions, and the writer decides what to do with the draft" (2000, 27). Good writing center tutors then are learners, questioners, and listeners, not experts, teachers, or authorities. However, this role structure cannot always be adapted to the classroom-based tutoring context. As we have noted above, it is not always appropriate for an English 100Plus tutor to answer a student's question with another question. The student wants an immediate authoritative answer, so that he can continue writing. Because the student wants an authority at those moments, the tutor becomes one.

However, the student is not the only one who confers authority on the classroom-based tutor. The instructor and the writing program do as well. Since tutors are part of the curricular structure of English 100Plus, and since the primary authority figure in the classroom—the instructor—introduces tutors to the students, tutors do, in essence, receive a "stamp of approval" as an expert. Ideally, student writers should not see tutors as authority figures, as teachers. The context of the writing center, a context student writers *choose* to enter, Christina Murphy notes, "places those students in a different type of relationship with the tutor than with the instructor in a traditional classroom setting. . . . the tutor's role often is primarily supportive and affective, secondarily instructional, and always directed to each student as an individual in a unique, one-to-one personal relationship" (2001, 296). Gillespie and Lerner also emphasize an affective, nonauthoritarian tutor/student relationship in their discussion of trust and tutoring. "As a writing center tutor, you'll create an atmosphere of trust for the writers who seek your help. In that environment, you and the writers with whom you meet can accomplish truly important work.

. . . You're not going to give a grade to a writer's essay, you have great insight into what it means to be a student, and you'll have many things in common with many of the writers you meet. . . . the rapport that you can create with writers is one of your best assets as a tutor" (2000, 8).

For English 100Plus tutors, there are impediments to the kind of non-authoritarian, affective working relationship Murphy and Gillespie and Lerner describe. Again, their presence in the classroom is not a matter of student choice, and their authority is automatically conferred on them by the endorsement of the instructor.

While this authority may give tutors certain kinds of credibility in the eyes of the students, it may also hinder the building of the more peer-based relationship that their training has led them to expect. Some students may feel, for example, that they cannot express their frustration with an assignment or an instructor with a tutor they perceive as the instructor's proxy. They may be more reluctant (than they would be with a writing center tutor) to disagree with or ignore a classroom-based tutor's advice. In effect, they might not see the tutor as a supportive peer; they may not trust their tutor. Therefore, many tutors find themselves sometimes calling on, sometimes resisting their authority.

In resisting their authority, tutors sometimes fall into the role of classmate (rather than tutor) by getting wrapped up in conversations with groups of students about other classes, the latest basketball game, the residence hall scandal of the moment, or their personal lives. We have noted that some tutors find that a friendly approach is the best way to make initial connections with students; however, the productive motive for their friendliness is subverted when tutors forget their sanctioned role in the classroom and become friends and fellows with the students, spending too much time in off-topic social conversation. Therefore, tutors like Holly have found that the best way to establish a friendly working relationship with a student is to focus their conversations on that student's writing, rather than on other topics. The most appropriate way to be friendly, and to reinforce their supportive role, is to offer consistent encouragement and judicious praise. Since they get glimpses of students' work at various moments throughout the writing process, it is relatively easy for tutors to find appropriate moments for comments such as "You've really been productive today; is that two new pages of writing I see?" or "Your new introduction really grabs my attention!" Such comments reinforce for students that the tutor is there to talk about writing, but that their role is more in the way of encouragement than policing.

## IMPLICATIONS FOR TRAINING

The examples we've shared here show a number of ways in which our tutors have revised the writing center(ed) tutorial model in which they were trained in order to create and maintain productive working relationships in the context of the English 100Plus classroom. They have learned to take the initiative and act as catalysts, not waiting for motivated students to come to them. They have learned that there are times when higher-order concerns should take a back seat to immediate questions about correctness and effectiveness. And they have learned that their role in the writing curriculum confers authority on them that they must sometimes invoke and sometimes resist in order provide a foundation of trust on which a productive relationship can be built.

As a result, we have also learned that we need to adapt our training to better prepare our tutors for classroom-based tutoring. We need to update our handbook (revising it for this essay has helped a great deal in that endeavor) and incorporate the revised handbook more fully into the training curriculum.[2] But we also need to find voices in writing center theory that, as Linda K. Shamoon and Deborah H. Burns put it, provide alternatives to the "orthodoxy of current practice" (2001, 226). In considering for this chapter the classroom-based context of tutoring in 100Plus and the adjustments our tutors have had to make to work productively in those classes, we have sought out such alternatives in the published discourse of writing center theory. We feel that given the preponderance of theory that maintains the dominance of the nonintrusive, writing center(ed) model, tutors might see the exceptions we suggest they make to these rules as ethically, professionally, and theoretically suspect. Certainly many tutors—such as those whose experiences we have cited here—make the necessary adjustments as they move into the classroom and the reality of the situation reveals different demands. But if in their training they were acquainted with other models that have received some sanction and recognition in the field (through publication in its journals and books), they might make those adjustments with greater ease and efficiency. They might not spend the first several weeks of the semester standing awkwardly at the front of the classroom, hoping that a student will be motivated to ask for their help. They might not then ask every student who finally does request their help to read his or her paper out loud in its entirety. And they might more quickly find ways to connect with students and build productive working relationships so that they can fill their office hours with the more in-depth and nonintrusive kinds of work typical of the writing center.

Therefore, when she next trains tutors, Barbara is planning on going beyond the orthodoxy expressed in the current training materials and expose new tutors to a variety of alternative models of tutoring. One source of alternatives will be Clark and Healy's article "Are Writing Centers Ethical?" Clark and Healy question the prevailing orthodoxy of nonintrusive tutoring (or, as they put it, *textual noninterventionism*) on two fronts. First, they note the basis of this approach in the need to "assure colleagues in the English department that the help students receive in writing centers does not constitute a form of plagiarism." Their response is to argue that "such a philosophy perpetuates a limited and limiting understanding of authorship in the academy" and misunderstandings about the importance and nature of collaborative conversation in much important writing (1996, 36). Next, they argue against the dominant writing center model on pedagogical grounds: "Textual noninterventionism is suspect not only on theoretical grounds . . . ; it also overlooks the possibility that for some students, an interventionist, directive, and appropriative pedagogy might be more effective—as well as ethically defensible" (37). Clark and Healy share examples of writers who have profited from more directive forms of tutoring, then make a parallel between such tutoring methods and Vygotsky's concept of "the zone of proximal development," which they say, quoting Vygotsky, "suggests that tutors should work on 'functions that have not yet matured, but are in the process of maturation, functions that will mature tomorrow, but are currently in an embryonic state.' Such functions might require the tutor to assume a more directive role until the student can assume the function alone" (38).

Vygotsky leads Clark and Healy to validate other models of tutoring, especially the models offered by Shamoon and Burns in "A Critique of Pure Tutoring." Clark and Healy draw examples of successful directive tutoring from Shamoon and Burns, who note that the frequency of such stories makes them "seriously question whether one tutoring approach fits all students and situations" (2001, 230). As a result, Shamoon and Burns turn to master classes in music as one model of beneficial and productive directive tutoring. They offer this description of the elements of the master class:

> What strikes us as important about master classes is that they feature characteristics exactly opposite current tutoring orthodoxy. They are hierarchical:

there is an open admission that some individuals have more knowledge and skill than others, and that the knowledge and skills are being "handed down." This handing down is directive and public; during tutoring the expert provides the student with communally and historically tested options for performance and technical improvement. Also, a good deal of effort during tutoring is spent on imitation or, at its best, upon emulation. Rather than assuming that this imitation will prevent authentic self-expression, the tutor and the student assume imitation will lead to improved technique, which will enable freedom of expression. (232)

It seems to us that there is much in this example that speaks to the situation in the English 100Plus classroom. Just as the musician conducting the master class is not the students' regular instructor (he does not have the power of the grade over them), so our tutors are not instructors. And just as the master still has authority based on his greater experience and expertise, our tutors have the authority of their greater experience in academic writing—in fact, they are often more experienced in the specific writing required in that class, since many (like Mandee) are recruited after taking English 100Plus and work with the same instructor for multiple semesters.

Shamoon and Burns provide examples of other contexts in which alternative tutoring models are practiced: studio seminars in the fine arts and "clinicals" in nursing training. Their point is that through modeling their own "widely-valued repertoires" of skills and strategies and allowing students to "practice similar solutions and try out others," directive tutors provide "a particularly efficient transmission of domain-specific repertoires, far more efficient and often less frustrating than expecting students to reinvent these established practices" (2001, 234).

Finally, Shamoon and Burns find examples of such directive tutoring in Muriel Harris's description of "Modeling: A Process Method of Teaching" (1983) and various writing centers around the country that are designed to enhance writing across the curriculum programs and, hence, take as part of their mission the handing down of discipline-specific expertise (Shamoon and Burns 2001, 238). The plethora of examples Shamoon and Burns provide can offer tutors in training insight into a variety of tutoring models. Just as good writers need a broad repertoire of skills to address a variety of writing situations, tutors will see that they need a broad repertoire of approaches to address a variety of student needs. As Clark and Healy put it, "Leveling its clientele through rigid policy statements—e.g., 'Refuse to proofread,' or 'Don't even hold a pencil when you're tutoring'—denies the diversity found in any [writing] center and stifles the creativity of writing center consultants. Writing centers need to be creative in opening up the world of discourse to their clients and their clients to that world" (1996, 44).

Shamoon and Burns and Clark and Healy are not the only authors who are questioning nonintrusive writing center orthodoxy, suggesting alternatives, and emphasizing the need to match the pedagogy to the writer, context, and situation. Others include Muriel Harris (1983), John Trimbur (1998), and Christina Murphy (2001). These authors provide ample fodder for a revised reading and discussion list in our tutor-training course at Eastern, an institution without a writing center, so that tutors will be more fully prepared for the realities of where and how they will be tutoring—the classrooms of English 100Plus. While we still will present our novice tutors with writing center orthodoxy (after all, with all these well-trained tutors, we hope to found a center soon), we will balance and complicate that orthodoxy with an awareness that it may not always make sense in the class, or with a particular student, or at a particular moment. We hope that with a less exclusive vision of writing tutoring, our tutors will be more willing and able to adapt to their job in the classroom and that their idea of a writing center will not limit their ability to work productively within the reality of classroom-based tutoring.

# 7

# BRINGING THE NOISE
## *Peer Power and Authority, On Location*

Steven J. Corbett


*It launched forth filament, filament, filament, out of itself.*
*Ever unreeling them, ever tirelessly speeding them.*
Walt Whitman, "A Noiseless Patient Spider"


*The writing center is wide and long, stretching everywhere the conversa-*
*tion will take it . . . expanding to immense girth without wearing out.*
Mike, Noise from the Writing Center


A few years ago we started getting serious about the idea of sending tutors into classrooms for peer group response facilitation, presentations, and what became special writing workshops here at the University of Washington's English Department Writing Center (EWC; a semiautonomous center staffed mostly by undergraduates). The excitement and critical pedagogical issues that emerged from our experimentation led me to write a short article in the *Writing Lab Newsletter*, "The Role of the Emissary: Helping to Bridge the Communication Canyon between Instructors and Students" (2002). In that essay I talk about how writing center tutors, as writing coaches, can expand into classrooms as representatives of writing center theory and practice for peer response facilitation and brief informational visits—with full confidence. My conclusions urge that we try our best to send tutors into classrooms in order to share the powerful message of peer-talk and to shake up the teacher-centered authority of the conventional classroom. I try to show how, and hint at why, tutors should interact with full faith in their own ability to act as a communication bridge between instructors and students. In other words, I encourage a directive, interventionist (I use these terms interchangeably) attitude and methodology to be carried into the classroom visits by writing center emissaries.

I still believe strongly in the interventionist idea behind that essay. Fortunately, in my multiple roles as a graduate student, writing center tutor, quasi-assistant director, and first-year composition instructor, I am not alone in this belief. A noteworthy trend in writing center research, theory, and practice on the debate between the directive and nondirective tutor points to reasons why we should reconsider the importance of the directive tutor, both ideologically and epistemologically (Clark 1988, 1999; Shamoon and Burns 1999, 2001; Grimm 1999; Wingate 2000; Latterell 2000; Boquet 2000, 2002; Carino 2003). As the opening quotes imply, great ideas can be expressed and shared—authoritatively—by the well known (Walt Whitman) as well as by the not so well known (Mike). But the opening quotes also juxtapose, suggestively, the idea of the (supposedly) noiseless, patient nondirective tutorial approach advocated by such scholars as Brooks (1991) and Harris (1986, 69–71), and the (supposedly) noisy, urgent directive approach, most recently argued by Carino (2003) and Boquet (2000, 2002).

Since, with the help of scholars like Dave Healy (1993), Thomas Hemmeter (1990), Harvey Kail and John Trimbur (1987), and Mary Soliday (1995), my fellow contributors to this collection have done an ample job rationalizing why tutors belong in the classroom, I will turn the focus of this essay to the issues of power and authority that must be negotiated with every decentralizing visit writing center tutors make.[1] If the trend for classroom-based writing tutoring has been established, we must now ask about the types of tutoring style emissaries should carry into the classroom. In this essay, I will illustrate why more directive forms of tutoring are not only acceptable but also quite useful, as long as we remember that there are also beneficial aspects of nondirective tutoring as well. The first part of this essay theoretically links classroom-based tutoring to interventionist tutoring practices in writing centers. The second part offers a classroom-based snapshot that illustrates ways directive, along with nondirective, tutoring philosophies may be played out simultaneously in the classroom. Finally, I offer a discussion of what is at stake in balancing the role of minimalist tutor with interventionist tutor.

## THE CALL FOR CONNECTIONS: POSITIONING THE DIRECTIVE TUTOR IN THE CLASSROOM

In his essay "Power and Authority in Peer Tutoring" (2003), Peter Carino urges writing center personnel to reconsider the importance of the too-often vilified directive tutor. He points to two recent essays in the *Writing Lab Newsletter* that deal specifically with issues of what it means to be a "peer" tutor: one by Jason Palermi (2000), in which the author realizes the importance of tutor authority when he is unable to show a student how to incorporate source material from her discipline; the other by Julie Bokser (2000), in which a new director comes to a writing center from the corporate world, where hierarchical power relationships are the norm (96–97). These examples lead Carino to assert that nondirective tutoring is a grassroots problem in writing centers. Carino suggests that because Palermi and Bokser are fairly new to writing center theory and practice, they can more closely identify with the types of power and authority issues tutors must face. From his claim that "to pretend that there is no hierarchical relationship between tutor and student is a fallacy," Carino moves on to explain how "except for a few notable exceptions, writing center discourse, in both published scholarship and conference talk, often represents direct instruction as a form of plunder rather than help, while adherence to nondirective principles remain the pedagogy *du jour*" (98). Carino sets up for critique the idea of interventionist tutoring as anathema to the strict Rogerian questioning style advocated by Brooks (1991).

Carino then discusses Shamoon and Burns's "A Critique of Pure Tutoring" (2001), in which the authors explain how master-apprentice relationships function in fruitful and directive ways for art and music students (2003, 99). In the master-apprentice relationship, the master models and the apprentice learns by imitation, from the authority of the master artist, the tricks of the trade. Reflecting on Clark and Healy's essay (1996), Carino argues that nondirective approaches are defense mechanisms resulting from the marginalized history of writing centers within the university and their subsequent paranoia over plagiarism.[2] Further, Carino reports that Nancy Grimm (1999) advocates the directive approach so that traditionally marginalized or underprepared students are not barred from access to mainstream academic culture (99–100).

Conclusively, Carino suggests a dialectic approach to the directive/nondirective dilemma, implying that directive tutoring and hierarchical tutoring *are not* synonymous: "In short, a nonhierarchical environment does not depend on blind commitment to nondirective tutoring methods. Instead, tutors should be taught to recognize where the power and authority lie in any given tutorial, when and to what degree they have them, when and to what degree the student has them, and when and to what degree they are absent in any given tutorial" (2003, 109).

He offers a seemingly simple equation for when to be direct and when to be nondirect: the more knowledge the student holds, the more nondirective we should be; the less knowledge the student holds, the

more directive we should be. He wisely affectively qualifies this suggestion, however, by stating that shyer but more knowledgeable students
might need a combination of directive prodding to urge them to take
responsibility for their work and nondirective questioning to encourage
them to share their knowledge, while chattier but less knowledgeable
students could benefit from nondirective questions to help curb hasty,
misdirected enthusiasm and directive warnings when they are making
obviously disastrous moves (2003, 110–11). Interestingly, Carino points
to the dichotomy of power and authority that has historically existed
between the classroom and the center. Because centers have a "safe
house" image compared to the hierarchical, grade-crazed image of the
classroom, writing center practitioners feel the need to promote a nondirective approach, which they view as sharply contrasting to the directive,
dominating, imposing nature of the classroom (100–2).

Along with Carino, Catherine Latterell (2000), Elizabeth Boquet
(2000, 2002), and Molly Wingate (2000) have recently confronted the
issue of tutor power and authority, advocating a more flexible approach
to the directive/nondirective issue. In her essay "Decentering Student-
Centeredness: Rethinking Tutor Authority in Writing Centers," Latterell
uses feminist theory to question the assumptions we make when we
confine ourselves to minimalist tutoring or nondirective teaching.
Informed by the work of Madeleine Grumet (1988), Latterell's essay
urges us to consider the contradictory nature of power: how we must
be cautious, but not too cautious, with our authority. Part of realizing
this contradiction involves admitting that we, as teachers and tutors, *do*
have knowledge and if we continually deny or withhold that knowledge
(by adopting a strict minimalist approach), we are robbing ourselves
of the ability to empower students by sharing our insights with them
(115–16).

In *Noise from the Writing Center* (2002), Boquet argues for performative excess, play, and freedom from the fear of nondirective tutoring.
Notably, she uses the example of legendary musical artist Jimi Hendrix
to urge tutors to explore and inhabit the noise-saturated realm of the
creative, uninhibited genius. In an earlier essay (2000), Boquet hints at
why she advocates such a performative, directive approach: "I don't want
students to perceive me as having all the answers, yet very often I do have
the answers they are looking for, and the students themselves know it. . . .
What sort of message are we sending to the students we tutor if they perceive us as withholding information vital to their academic success?" (19).

Similarly, Molly Wingate (2000) warns us that "being too cautious results in sessions that are dull and unproductive. Writers come to the writing center to move their projects along; what a shame to lose them because the tutors try too hard to stay on safe ground" (14).

Moreover, research shows that a minimalist philosophy may sometimes actually cause tutors to (un)intentionally withhold valuable knowledge from students. Muriel Harris recounts how a student rated her as "not very effective" on a tutor evaluation because she was trying to be a good minimalist tutor; the student viewed her as ineffective, explaining, "she just sat there while I had to find my own answers" (1992a, 379). Although we could certainly question the student's perceptions, the fact that writing centers' most valuable player admittedly sometimes drops the ball prompts us to question the writing center's dualized directive/nondirective philosophies. Applying these insights to classroom settings, I want to pose the same "higher-risk/higher-yield" question that Boquet asks of any tutor: "How might I encourage this tutor to operate on the edge of his or her expertise?" (2002, 81).

Arguments for negotiated, shared power and authority between tutors and teachers in classrooms should likewise guide our use of directive and nondirective strategies:[3] Louise Z. Smith (2003) hints at these power negotiations in urging writing center directors and faculty across the curriculum to observe the "choreography" of one model writing center/classroom collaboration. Hemmeter asserts that group instruction does not solely "belong to the classroom" (1990, 43), suggesting that classrooms and center can share teaching authority; and Soliday (1995) shows that the roles of the classroom-based writing tutor must be flexible enough to move between what are traditionally considered more teacherly (interventionist) and more tutorly (noninterventionist) approaches during any given visit.

Recent examinations of classroom-based tutoring likewise suggest more active positions for tutors. At the IWCA/NCPTW 2003 Joint Conference in Hershey, Pennsylvania, four presentations focused on the rationales and methodologies—both directive and nondirective—that may be employed when tutors are assigned to classrooms on a regular basis (Nicolas et al. 2003; Spigelman et al. 2003; Ackerman et al. 2003; Ryan, Zimmerelli, and Wright 2003). In Nicolas et al.'s sessions, for example, I joined a mock peer group facilitation subtitled, "The 'Just-Fix-It' or 'We-Just-Want to-Work-on-Grammar' Group," in which the problem of the uncooperative group member was acted out with authoritative style. Two "students" basically ganged up on a volunteer tutor, pushing and prodding him to "just edit" the papers. But the volunteer was obviously an experienced tutor and led them toward a dialogue and, at least, some progress. Afterward, as a group, we critiqued the volunteer tutor's efforts. The two "bullies" lauded the tutor's effectiveness, acknowledging how rough they had been on him for dramatic effect. They liked that he explained "the difference between a tutor and an editor," emphasized "the importance of writers learning how to edit their own papers," and explained "the purpose of the group" with authority *and* patience.

Meanwhile, all around me, other groups worked on "the apathetic group" and "the 'we-don't-trust-the-writing-fellow' group." The way these last two groups dealt with issues of power and authority is reminiscent of Smulyan and Bolton's 1989 essay, "Classroom and Writing Center Collaborations: Peers as Authorities." In that essay, the authors show that peer tutors can communicate aspects of the writing process that teachers cannot because of the teacher's role as ultimate authority, especially over grades. Smulyan and Bolton conclude by suggesting how tutors negotiate issues of power and authority with every visit they make. Like Nicolas's groups above, Smulyan and Bolton's tutors had to deal with students who were "afraid to share their writing" or "took everything I said as law" or "didn't take [them] seriously" (48).[4]

More directly, Barbara Little Liu and Holly Mandes, in chapter 6 of this volume, present a rationale and working model of interventionist tutoring during classroom writing workshops. Taking their lead from tutors in writing classrooms, Liu and Mandes discuss effective strategies for interventionist tutoring that do not seem overly intrusive to the students and then theorize these strategies by turning to recent writing center scholarship.

## HIGH-WIRE WALKING: BALANCING AUTHORITATIVE (NOT AUTHORITARIAN) AND MINIMALIST TUTOR ROLES IN WRITING CLASSROOMS

In her essay "Collaboration Is Not Collaboration Is Not Collaboration: Writing Center Tutorials vs. Peer-Response Groups" (1992a), Muriel Harris compares and contrasts peer response and peer tutoring. She explains how tutoring offers the kind of individualized, nonjudgmental focus lacking in the classroom, and how peer response is done "in the context of course guidelines" with practice in working with a variety of reviewers (381). But she also raises some concerns. One problem involves how students might evaluate each other's writing with a different set of standards than their teachers: "[S]tudents may likely be reinforcing each other's abilities to write discourse for their peers, not for the academy—a sticky problem indeed, especially when teachers suggest that an appropriate audience for a particular paper might be the class itself" (379). Obviously, the issue here is student authority. Since students have not been trained in the arts of peer response, how, then, can they be expected to give adequate response when put into groups, especially if the student is a first-year or an otherwise inexperienced academic writer? How can we help "our students experience and reap the benefits of both forms of collaboration?" (381).

The answer lies, as practitioners and theorists have found out, in a marriage of the two processes. Wendy Bishop made a call to be "willing to experiment" (1988, 124) with peer response group work over fifteen years ago. Laurie Grobman's chapter 3, "Building Bridges to Academic Discourse" answers that call by illustrating the pivotal role of the group leader in peer response. In "The Ethics of Appropriation in Peer Writing Groups," Spigelman addresses the issue of plagiarism and the active group member: "we might address the problematic of the student writer as individual, as primary author, and as active group member, by raising questions about autonomous originality and cooperative textual production and about public and intellectual property" (1999, 240). Spigelman suggests that students need to know how the collaborative generation of ideas differs from plagiarism. If students can understand how and why authors appropriate ideas, they will be more willing to experiment with collaborative writing. It follows, then, that tutors, who are adept at these collaborative writing negotiations, can direct fellow students toward understanding the difference. Programs like Spigelman's and ours here at the UW continue to experiment, willingly, encouraging the deployment of both directive and nondirective methodologies during these group negotiations.

An opportunity to try out these dual tutoring methods occurred recently, when Kimberly, an academic advisor/composition instructor, invited me, in my role as a writing center tutor, to visit her Advanced Expository Writing class to facilitate a peer response workshop. Although she would not be present during the workshop, she offered a detailed account of her students' progress on the assignment and furnished her assignment sheet, which asked students to write persuasively on any controversial topic they chose, and her guidelines for peer review. Her students had been asked to read each other's papers and supply comments.

The two-hour session involved twelve English majors. In addition to me, three additional tutors from the writing center were available for the session, one tutor for each group.

Taking full advantage of the two hours, I decided to lead a brief overall discussion at the beginning of the class. I encouraged the students to talk as much as they could about what they should look for in each other's essays—by asking an open-ended series of questions—and I wrote our plenary brainstorm on the board. To my delight, the class came up with most of the salient issues concerning peer review: clarity, focus, claim, warrant, tone, support, and so on. After the class brainstorm, I joined my group. They were in mid-dialogue over one student's paper. I heard constructive comments, so I tried not to be too invasive. Usually in such situations I just sit back and listen, playing the good minimalist tutor. If I hear good suggestions, I simply acknowledge with nods and umhms; if I hear something really crucial, I might extend the conversation. Glancing around the room, I saw my fellow tutors taking the same nondirective approach.

This time, however, while listening to one group member comment on her peer's paper (arguing that Asians should not undergo cosmetic eye surgery just to look Western), I started to think about the student's need for counterclaims. The critiquing student had advised her peer to try to empathize with someone who feels so out of place that they would resort to cosmetic surgery. Instead of simply encouraging a good suggestion, I went one step further, taking a more directive role. I gathered the whole class' attention and gave a brief speech regarding counterclaim. I emphasized how important it is to consider the opposition's point of view in order to make one's own case more sound. After my announcement, the room erupted into fresh, almost urgent, conversation. I watched as tutors sometimes held back, listening to the stream of student utterances, or sometimes let loose, offering their own brainstorms regarding counterclaim.

The overall results of this session were positive, and all of the writing center tutors gained from knowing that we helped this class gain a better understanding of what it means to review a peer's work. We entered this class as a nonjudging group of (near)peers with the attitude of listeners and facilitators. We did not rush here and there trying to get every student to some magical place of readiness for (re)writing; instead, we sat and listened and offered advice when we could and praised smart comments when we heard them; we did it with laughs and jokes. But we were also not afraid to provide direct suggestions when we felt it appropriate, modeling how the appropriation of ideas is negotiated. We found that the best way to model peer response is by becoming a "meta-tutor" employing meta-talk. As Decker explains in chapter one of this volume, the role of the meta-tutor is "encouraging students to tutor each other. In this capacity, tutors are not doing what they would be doing in a one-on-one conference in the writing center—they are showing students how to do it."

Any time tutors venture into classrooms, they inherently bring their more sophisticated level of meta-talk with them: they model for students and teachers how to talk about what they're learning, exploring—and they concurrently learn how to become better models. They rehearse, rehearse, rehearse—and students, then, *imitate* their tutors' actions. Edward P. J. Corbett argues: "Classical rhetoric books are filled with testimonies about the value of imitation for the refinement of the many skills involved in effective speaking or writing" (1990, 461). He further illustrates the importance of imitation with more recent testimonies from Malcolm X, Benjamin Franklin, and Winston S. Churchill (462–64). Corbett, as well as Carino, show how as artists/writers, we empower and we become empowered when we rehearse and imitate—students, tutors, and teachers—together. We learn to negotiate how much authoritative knowledge student, tutor, and teacher hold in any given moment.

In *Collaborative Learning: Higher Education, Interdependence, and the Authority of Knowledge,* Kenneth Bruffee asserts that peer tutors can bring about "changes in the prevailing understanding of the nature and authority of knowledge and the authority of teachers" (1999, 110). Boquet, likewise, asks if writing centers should be places "where people seek out the genuine information that might otherwise be suppressed or eliminated" and whether they can be places "powerful enough to allow for the mutation and potential reorganization of our system of education." She goes on to assert, "These are not rhetorical questions. I really believe the writing center is that place. And if you are working in a writing center, if you are 'supporting' the writing center at your own institution (however you might define that support), then you had better believe it too" 2002, 51–52). Writing centers, and by extension tutor trainers of all stripes, can help classroom-based tutors to understand just how authoritative they can be, and how, with just enough minimalist in them, they can avoid being authoritarian.

## TOWARD A CLASSROOM WRITING COACH HYBRID (ONLY IF . . .)

When Bob Dylan (1969) sings "whatever colors you have in your mind, I'll show them to you, and you'll see them shine," he captures and reflects how part of any artist's (or educator's) job is to capture his or her impression of a given event and reflect that image back to participants and audience as poetically and clearly (and, perhaps, educationally) as possible. The epistemological and ideological stride that marks the postmodern movement in education is the view that knowledge is constructed, negotiable, and mutable. Such postmodern thinkers as Foucault, Fish, Rorty, Bakhtin, and Barthes have exposed complicated notions of power and authority in communicative situations. However, if students do not receive much modeling of effective academic communication, they will not experience what Bruffee deems "iterated social imbrication" (1999, 45), or the gradual layering it takes in order for a student to learn how to negotiate a specific academic discipline. This layering is learned much quicker in an environment that places peers in Vygotsky's (1978) zones of proximal development. When tutors enter classrooms, they can bring profound knowledge of how to maneuver within disciplinary discourses. As Bruffee's early work on collaboration and peer tutoring explained, peer tutors can act as models of the kind of academic communication that is valued by the university, which fellow students can rehearse or imitate (1984). But it takes a directive, confident tutor to be able to share valuable information with students *and* teachers. A tutor satisfied with playing a strictly minimalist role may learn a lot but may lose out on important opportunities to also teach.

Tutors and tutoring program directors are immersed in collaborative learning and collaborative teaching theory and practice every day. The collaborative games tutors learn to play can be shared with others who are interested in learning more about issues of communicative interdependence and the writing process as collaborative rather than individual. In classrooms, tutors will learn a lot also, about the dynamics of situations in which they have to interact, with some authority, with many students. These close collaborations allow tutors a glimpse of just how hard a job classroom teachers have and help to blur "us" and "them" power and authority issues.

The idea of learning as collaborative and negotiable rather than individual and prescribed motivates my praxis, whether in the classroom or in the center. As a first-year writing instructor, it has spilled over into my teaching as well as with my work with other tutors. In "Tutoring and Teaching: Continuum, Dichotomy, or Dialectic?" Helon Howell Raines argues for tutors and teachers to explore the "Hegelian dialectical process, in which opposing forces conflict, but in their meeting they also mix, each altering the other until ultimately both transcend the interaction to become something new" (1994, 153). I believe this transcendental notion can be shared with teachers and students visibly in the classroom, but *only if* tutors approach these teachers with a Freirean authoritative, but not authoritarian, willingness to learn as well as teach, as so many WAC (official and de facto) scholars have urged (see Graham 1992, 125–26; Haviland et al. 1999). Only then will all who offer instruction be able to help teachers revise their roles as authority figures and help tutors (re)consider their roles as teachers, as Soliday suggests (1995, 64). When tutors and teachers enter classrooms together, they are participating in a two-way dialectical street involving listening as well as talking, directive questioning as well as nondirective questioning. If they offer themselves as partners in a dance in which the choreography is shared and negotiated, then they will truly enjoy the fruits of their labors with a clear conscience, and with the deeper respect of their classroom colleagues. They will be able to better model, thereby allowing students to better rehearse and imitate, how academic communication works.

Recently, I invited a group of tutors to aid with peer response in my first-year composition class. The first half of the class, though, I just had Anna, a senior and new tutor, visit to talk about her writing class experiences as a first-year and to offer any words of wisdom she could. I invited her because I have noticed her charisma when she tutors or talks about tutoring (or anything else for that matter). But I didn't expect her to act with the authority and confidence she did. I was amazed at how earnestly she talked about her shyness as a first-year, how she was afraid to talk to her teachers, how she didn't talk that much in class. This confession stood in stark contrast to the confident, assertive student I saw before me. She articulated the importance of making oneself stand out in the classroom, how it helps students learn more and do better in the class. She talked about how she wished she'd heard of writing centers when she was a first-year—how she studied, wrote, and researched *alone*. Finally, she segued into peer response workshopping by urging my students to utilize writing centers—to take advantage of them before it's too late. She stressed that help writing—quality, authoritative, informed help—is available. I've had classes with instructors and professors who could learn a good lesson on delivery from powerful, effulgent undergraduates like Anna.

# 8

# A CAUTIONARY TALE ABOUT "TUTORING" PEER RESPONSE GROUPS

Melissa Nicolas

In this (post?) postmodern era, it has become de rigueur to question definitions that fix meaning and create rigid categories. Even a cursory review of the current literature in rhetoric and composition shows scholars "questioning," "troubling," "refining," "refiguring," and/or "redrawing" conventional definitions and categorical boundaries. One of the ways compositionists have challenged traditional ways of thinking about the teaching and learning of writing, for example, is by developing pedagogies that decenter teacher authority and privilege collaborative learning. Indeed, in the last two decades or so, writing center tutoring and peer group work have come to play an increasingly central role in the teaching of composition. As teachers seek ways to facilitate collaboration in order to collapse the boundaries of traditional classroom walls, innovative approaches have been developed; composition and writing center programs have brought students into nursing homes, retirement communities, prisons, elementary and middle schools, and many other locations.

Even within the institution, composition teachers are working to refigure traditional teacher-centered pedagogies. The peer consulting program at my former school, Ohio State University, for example, brought together students from basic writing courses with students from an upper-division English class to form writing groups. This program enabled students of different institutional ranks (first-quarter first-year students to graduating seniors) with varying degrees of writing experience to work together on improving their writing. As the peer tutoring director of this program for two years, I had close contact with all the program's constituents—teachers, students, and administrators—and I was able to observe the program from various angles: in the classroom, in peer group sessions, and in administrative meetings. I supported the program's goal of creating an environment where students in different classes, who normally would not come in contact with each other, were able to meet and discuss their writing. However, the more time I spent in the program, the more concerned I became that even though, in theory, the type of collaboration we were promoting made sense, something was just not "clicking" in the program. This uneasiness was caused by what I eventually regarded as the program's conflation of two related collaborative learning models: peer response and tutoring, and even within the category of tutoring, there was an uncritical collapsing of the boundaries between curriculum-based tutoring and writing center tutoring.

While I am an advocate for peer tutoring and have firsthand knowledge of the asset peer tutors can be to a writing center staff, what follows is a cautionary tale about the problems that can arise when peer tutoring programs, like the one I will describe below, do not align their theory with their practice. In this essay, I suggest that it is important to keep the divisions between peer response and tutoring, as well as distinctions among types of tutoring, firmly in mind as we train our writing consultants because, while these activities are all collaborative, the nature of the collaboration in each model is fundamentally different. Instead of trying to elide these differences, as we did in our program, tutor trainers need to be acutely aware of the distinctions between peer response groups and tutorials and, within tutoring itself, between curriculum-based tutoring and writing center tutoring, in order to clearly present these different models to our tutors.

To begin this tale, I first describe the structure of the peer consulting program that I directed and provide a comparison of peer response groups and tutorials. Then, I explore the role confusion of the peer writing consultants at my former school and end with a description of the ways I have altered my tutor-training pedagogy as a result of this experience. While this essay focuses on the undergraduate consulting program at a particular institution, the issues that surface are relevant to any program using tutors to facilitate peer response groups. My hope is that the critical eye I turn on this program will aid others as they begin to reexamine similar programs at their own institutions, just as this experience caused me to make some fundamental changes to my presentation of this collaborative model when I was given a chance to try it again at a different institution.

My goal in this essay is to continue the conversation Muriel Harris began in "Collaboration Is Not Collaboration Is Not Collaboration" about the merits of keeping the lines between peer response and tutoring clearly drawn (1992a). I realize it may appear strange at this historical moment to argue for a definition of more discrete categories, but I believe that, pedagogically and ethically, tutor trainers need to be able to clearly

articulate the position(s) they want their tutors to occupy. To put it another way, while I see nothing wrong with the combining of writing center
tutoring and peer response groups, I also want tutor trainers to be able to
define and explain the roles we ask our students to play and to be able to
create training scenarios that more closely align what we ask students to
do both theoretically and practically.

## THE NUTS AND BOLTS: THE PEER WRITING CONSULTANT PROGRAM

The Peer Writing Consultant Program (PWCP) at Ohio State University
evolved out of a complex set of institutional circumstances. In the 1990–
91 academic year, the Writing Workshop piloted ten sections of English
110W—a seven-hour course that counted as students' first-year writing
requirement. English 110W replaced English 060, a three-hour course
that was developmental and did not count toward students' first-year
writing requirements. According to Suellyn Duffey and Donna LeCourt
(1991), two of the creators of the PWCP, the most obvious goal for the
program was "to prepare undergraduate students of all majors to meet a
growing need for tutors as a result of several curricular changes at Ohio
State in general and the Writing Workshop in particular."

The PWCP at Ohio State University combined students and resources
from the university's basic writing program, English department, and
writing center. Two primary groups of students were involved: those
enrolled in the first-year basic writing class, English 110W, and those
taking English 467, an upper-division writing theory and practice class.
Both of these classes were taught by faculty in the English department,
yet part of the administrative funding came from the Center for the
Study and Teaching of Writing (CSTW), which housed the university
writing center. Together, English 110W and English 467 formed the
PWCP and worked in the following way. Students enrolled in 110W reg-
istered for class four days a week. For three of these days, students met
in a traditional writing classroom with a professor. On the fourth class
day, 110W students met in peer groups (two to five students per group)
with one or two students from English 467. Students in English 467, or
peer writing consultants (PWCs), met with their English professor two
days a week. In addition to these traditional class meetings, each PWC
worked with two separate groups of 110W students throughout the ten-
week quarter. These weekly peer tutoring sessions were required for
both the 110W and 467 students, but there were no faculty present at
the group sessions.

## MISTAKEN IDENTITY: ROLE CONFUSION IN THE PEER CONSULTING PROGRAM

While peer group work and both writing center and classroom-based tutoring are predicated on notions of students directing their own learning and using each other as resources, the chart below summarizing the major differences between peer response groups, writing center tutorials, and classroom-based peer group tutoring illustrates the significant differences among the activities. Both peer response and peer group tutoring are largely influenced by the teacher, while writing center tutoring is student initiated and student led; peer response groups and peer group tutoring are also closely tied to the classroom, while writing center tutoring (usually) is completely separate from the classroom. Peer response groups do not (usually) have a "writing authority" as a member, while both writing center and peer group tutoring rely, to some extent, on a tutor's expertise. Because all the collaborative models have different foci and because each model allows students to learn from each other in a different way, there are sound reasons for creating opportunities for all forms of collaboration in a writing curriculum.

|  | Peer response groups | Writing center tutorials | Peer group tutoring |
|---|---|---|---|
| Location | Meet in class during class time. | Occur in the writing center outside of class time. | Usually meet in class during class time, sometimes outside of class. |
| Attendance | Required for class. Participation is usually factored into course grade. | Voluntary and does not factor into course grade. | Required during class time and outside of class. |
| Structure | Made up of two or more students from the same class. Teacher decides how to set up groups and when groups will meet. | One-to-one. Client decides how often he/she will have a tutorial. | One-to-one and/or small groups. Teacher decides how and when tutors will work with students. |
| Focus | Product | Process | Product and/or process |
| Use of time | Must negotiate how to get to all members' work in allotted time. | Entire time devoted to one writer. | How time is spent is (partially) determined by the teacher. |
| Authority | May have group leader, but all members are from the same class and have similar levels of writing expertise. | Tutor is (usually) more experienced writer than client. Tutor has received special training. Tutor and client are probably not in the same writing class. | Tutor is (usually) more experienced than students in the class. Tutor has received special training. Tutor and student are not in the same writing class. |

However, the very reasons students benefit from each model—the different foci and the different types of collaboration—are the same reasons why it is imperative for tutor trainers to make the distinctions among each activity clear, even when a program, like the PWCP, brings these models together.

In English 467, Theories of Writing and Learning, PWCs were introduced to the ideas of writing as process, social constructionism, and writing center tutoring theory and practice. Some of the tutoring handbooks required in recent years include *The St. Martin's Sourcebook for Writing Tutors* (Murphy and Sherwood 1995), *The Practical Tutor* (Meyer and Smith 1987), *The Harcourt Brace Guide to Peer Tutoring* (Caposella 1998), and *The Allyn and Bacon Guide to Peer Tutoring* (Gillespie and Lerner 2000). These texts share the assumption that the tutors in training reading them will be working in one-to-one situations. None of these books, however, address tutoring in a group situation, nor do these manuals discuss how to work with a teacher as a classroom tutor, so PWCs were not introduced to the theoretical or practical issues that could arise in their particular situation. Even though 467 instructors, from time to time, would engage PWCs in conversations about how they could adapt what they were reading to their particular group situation, it seemed difficult for PWCs to grasp the nuances of the differences since this was (for most of them) their first exposure to this kind of literature.

The training portion of the PWCP was based on a writing center model that stresses personalized attention. As a short excerpt from the *St. Martin's Sourcebook for Writing Tutors* illustrates, focusing on individual clients and their needs is germane to tutoring practice. "Students vary in levels of autonomy, sensitivity to criticism, ego strength, personal maturity, motivation, and perseverance. Relating to the student as an *individual* and empathizing with his or her particular personality and character traits will go a long way toward forming a special trust, one that provides the motivation, energy, and direction for the tutorial itself" (Murphy and Sherwood 1995, 6–7; emphasis added).

Being able to meet writers where they are is central to productive tutorials. This kind of empathetic connection between tutors and students is enabled by the intimacy of the one-to-one tutorial situation. When the PWCs were sent out to work with their students, however, they were asked to work with groups of two to five students. In order for peer consultants to create personalized relationships with their students in the peer groups, the consultants had to think about, empathize with, and build trust with several students simultaneously, a formidable task even for the most experienced tutors and teachers.

Additionally, our PWCs had responsibilities not typical of writing center tutors. As Muriel Harris explains, "tutors don't need to take attendance, make assignments, set deadlines, deliver negative comments, give tests or issue grades" (1995a, 28). While consultants did not give tests or grade 110W students, and they (hopefully) did not give writers negative comments, when 110W students came to sessions without work, PWCs were asked to facilitate activities and set agendas for future meetings, thus functioning more as teachers than peer group members. Also, consultants were required to take attendance; PWCs, in essence, then, had to monitor and report on their groups, a responsibility that writing center tutors and peer group members do not have. This responsibility for setting agendas, monitoring, and reporting conflicted with information PWCs were given about their roles as tutors and sufficiently afforded them more "authority" than the other members of the group, further altering the consultant's status as peer and also complicating the idea of tutor.

This confusion was furthered by the program's investment in peer group autonomy, following Anne Ruggles Gere's description of semiautonomous writing groups. In semiautonomous groups, teachers relinquish some authority by allowing students to make decisions about what to work on and how to use their time. While semiautonomous groups are institutionally mandated and group participation is usually required for a satisfactory grade in the course, the ultimate purpose of convening these groups is to empower students to take control of their own writing and learning (1987, 101–3). Unlike peer response groups that meet in class with the teacher present, in order to push our groups toward semiautonomy, 110W groups met without their teachers. Although the 110W and 467 faculty did ask their students to report on what happened in their groups, teachers were almost never invited to sessions. Indeed, oftentimes 110W and 467 professors did not even know where peer groups were meeting because groups chose their own locale: a coffee shop, the student union, a library, a dorm, and so on. Also, in order to stress the autonomy of the groups, the PWCP strongly discouraged teachers from assigning work to be done during the peer group meetings; the program's ideal was for the 110W students, with help from the PWCs, to decide what to work on, how to work on it, and how group time should be budgeted.

Even though 110W students were required to attend these sessions, by meeting with a peer consultant (not the teacher) outside the classroom,

a central program goal was to simulate a low-risk environment similar to
that of the writing center. In theory, because the PWCs and 110W students
were all undergraduates and approximately the same age,[1] they could
share a relationship that was more relaxed and less restrained by the rules
of classroom decorum than in-class groups that met under the gaze of the
teacher. As leaders of these groups, PWCs "inhabit[ed] a middle ground
where their role [was] that of translator or interpreter, turning teacher
language into student language" (M. Harris 1995a, 37). Indeed, consultants helped 110W students interpret writing prompts, decode teachers'
written comments, and aided students in incorporating those comments
in their revisions. Also, because Ohio State is a large university and most
110W students were in their first year of college, PWCs often served as
unofficial guides, helping 110W students negotiate their way around that
(sometimes) impersonal institution.

All in all, PWCs were asked to perform some of the functions of peer
group members, writing center tutors, and curriculum-based tutors,
and the results, for the most part, were a combination of confusion and
frustration. They were involved in the multiple tasks we find typical of
writing center tutors—helping students figure out school, providing
emotional/psychological support, addressing local and global writing
concerns—but, as I have shown, PWCs did not work in a tutorial situation.
And as Michelle, a senior PWC, explained, the conflicts resulting from
this situation affected even the 110W students. According to Michelle,
110W students "knew they were supposed to be in [the] group, but they
really didn't know the purpose behind it [or] what they're supposed to
get out of our session. . . . I don't think a lot of the students in any of the
groups know the purpose behind the [peer group sessions]."

In our program, then, many contradictions emerged. One of the main
reasons writing centers are low-risk environments is precisely because students are not forced to visit and tutors are not affiliated with the client's
course. In the case of the PWCP, however, students had to attend the
sessions, and tutors not only were affiliated with the course but they were
also supposed to have at least some direct contact with the 110W teachers. This is an area in which I think the PWCP failed the students because
we did not make room in the program for the PWCs, or the basic writing
students, to address these very real tensions. The theoretical language we
gave PWCs about writing center tutoring and peer response groups did
not adequately describe what they were actually doing, so, being novices,
they may not have been able to adapt the theoretical constructs we gave

them to their situations or even articulate for themselves how these constructs may or may not have applied to them and their experiences.

Another source of confusion for the peer consultants was that they interacted with the peer groups they were asked to tutor only on a limited basis. PWCs were not active participants in 110W classes and therefore were at a disadvantage when it came to understanding what 110W instructors were asking of their students. And, perhaps more important, consultants joined the peer groups on a limited basis while the group members interacted regularly in the 110W class without them. While PWCs were encouraged to attend as many classes as their schedules permitted, the reality was that most PWCs observed only one or two classes per quarter. Since the idea behind a peer response group is to have students in the same class with similar writing expertise work together, adding a consultant—already marked as more of a writing authority than the other group members—who was not a classmate to the group significantly altered group dynamics and marked the PWCs as outsiders to the group process (Soliday 1995). As outsiders, consultants were not privy to 110W class discussions, lectures, or in-class peer group work even though all these classroom activities impacted the dynamics of the peer group. PWCs had to find ways to insert themselves in the middle of relationships and conversations already in process.

Michelle described her frustration with this situation: "Last week . . . they [the 110W students] had papers due, and I e-mailed them all and told them to `bring your papers, bring copies for everybody so we can talk about it' . . . and they came to class [the peer consulting session] and they had already done it [shared their papers] in their regular class." Michelle was justifiably confused because, as she admitted, she had understood that facilitating peer groups "was supposed to be our role," yet the teacher had given students time in class to meet as a response group without Michelle. At this point, both Michelle and her group were unsure about how exactly they were expected to spend their time together.

Because the PWCs were not really group members nor were they writing center tutors, it was difficult for PWCs and 110W students to understand exactly what role the PWC should play. For example, 110W students had the guidance of their instructor during their traditional class time, so when the peer groups met in class the teacher took an active role in assuring that each group was on task. When these same groups met with their PWCs, however, the burden of providing guidance inevitably shifted to the consultant. Since PWCs lacked the training required to effectively work with these groups in nondirective ways and because the 110W students worked in teacher-directed peer groups in class, when these constituents met each other, they readily adopted the only model of academic interaction they were familiar with: teachers teaching students. I observed sessions where the roles of "teacher" and "student" were enacted so dramatically that the PWC actually stood in front of the 110W students and lectured them. I point this out not to criticize the work of the PWCs. On the contrary, I think they did a good job given the inadequate training we provided. Rather, I am interested in the paradox of the situation: we wanted so much to provide students with an empowering experience that we allowed them to meet on their own, without a teacher, as part of their course requirement. However, most of the 110W and 467 students were unsure of what to do with this freedom, with this refiguring of roles, so they chose a default position they were comfortable with—the PWC became the substitute teacher. Karen, a junior PWC, expressed this role confusion also. She constantly had to tell her group: "'I'm not your teacher. I'm not a TA. I don't get paid to be here. I'm a student like you.' But I don't know. Sometimes they just always seem to look at me or toward me. . . . They like to be told what to do. . . . It's kind of confusing. It's sort of like a balancing act where you try not to be in it too much but try to be there, but it's like you're just not there. It's hard."

The 110W teachers, on the other hand, saw the PWCs' role differently. Michelle said the message she received from the 110W teachers was that "we're [the PWCs] there to kind of make sure they [the 110W students] are working. They [the 110W teachers] don't really want us to teach them anything, and we're just there to help." In other words, while 110W students expected PWCs to teach them, 110W teachers expected PWCs to take a hands-off approach to the group process.

In retrospect, it is obvious to me that the 110W teachers, 467 instructors, and PWCP administrators were sending mixed signals that ultimately confused and frustrated many of the people involved with the program. The situation that the peer consulting program put peer consultants in asked too much of these talented undergraduates because we did not provide them with the tools to succeed: we wanted them to be part of a peer group even though they were really outsiders; we trained them in one-to-one writing center tutoring methods when they were in fact working with peer groups; and we expected them not to become substitute teachers when, in reality, assuming this authoritarian role was the only option visible to them. During my observations, I saw consultants struggling to balance this series of contradictions, and I witnessed the "tutoring a peer group" dynamic perplex even the most skilled PWCs. While I did occasionally see a consultant—usually an advanced undergraduate who had previous exposure to tutoring, peer group work, and/or composition theory—who was able to negotiate these contradictions in a meaningful way, ultimately most PWCs (and 110W students) were confused about their role. When students are not well equipped to handle the collaborative situations they are placed in, the activity itself becomes a secondary concern, and participants begin to view the exercise as a waste of time.

## THE SAME BUT DIFFERENT: GIVING IT A SECOND CHANCE

Mary Soliday, writing about a similar peer consulting program at her school, sees the situation I just described as a positive "blurring [of] the traditional tutoring role" (1995, 60). She believes this "blurring" of boundaries is a fruitful site for "imagining different ways of collaborating and thinking about the differences in roles" (70) between the classroom and the writing center. I agree with Soliday that programs like the PWCP push on the boundaries between the classroom and the writing center, but I do not see this blurring as necessarily good or productive when tutor trainers cannot articulate *how* they are blurring these boundaries and, subsequently, do not provide adequate instruction for tutors about what their role(s) should be.

Challenging traditional notions of writing centers and the roles writing centers play in the academy is a worthy goal, and this collection, *On Location*, provides examples of the productive ways this is happening in programs across the country. However, if we wish to collapse the boundaries among peer response, writing center tutoring, and curriculum-based tutoring to create more fluid roles for our tutors, we need to also be especially vigilant about articulating these moves to the tutors we are training. As compositionists and writing center professionals work to create new models of collaboration among our students, we must remember that we approach these collaborative arrangements from a position of educational privilege; we are well versed in the theories and pedagogies that guide our practices. We have a firm understanding of how different models of collaboration can and should work, so, for us, breaking down these models and putting them together in novel ways may be an exciting challenge, full of theoretical and pedagogical possibilities. But our novice students do not have this rich background knowledge, so when we shift the foundations, they may have no place to ground themselves.

I have recently been given the opportunity to start a similar PWCP at another school, Penn State Lehigh Valley, but before I agreed to participate in classroom-based peer group tutoring again, I had to decide if I really believed in the possibilities this type of collaboration holds. Ultimately, my decision boiled down to one key question: Do tutors and peer group members gain something from this experience that they could not gain from more traditional writing center tutoring or peer response groups? In the course of answering this question and revisiting this essay, I have come to realize that there is enough promise in using consultants to facilitate peer groups that I want to try to redress at least some of the problems with implementing this collaborative model that I have talked about in this essay. Hindsight has helped me see that what I first thought of as an inherently flawed model (tutors facilitating peer groups) is not so.

By utilizing this model of peer collaboration, writing consultants and peer group members have opportunities to participate in a sustained collaboration with a group in ways that even individuals using the writing center on a regular basis cannot experience. Because the model I discuss in this essay mandates both consultant and peer group attendance, many students who would not otherwise meet a writing tutor have the opportunity to build trust and community with a writing consultant and their group mates at predictable and regular intervals. Additionally, since this model is an integral part of the first-year writing course, over time, students may begin to view what they may have initially thought of as "fluff" or a "waste of time" as an important component of the writing process.

Tutors benefit from this model, too, because meeting with the same group of students week in and week out allows tutors to build rapport with their group, which in turn can help tutors be more at ease with the new role of "tutor" they are trying on. Also, tutors in this model get to see multiple drafts of the same essay, follow an assignment from prompt to final revision, and see how their tutees are growing as writers. Unlike in many "one-and-done" writing center tutorials, both tutors and peer group members can become invested in the writing process for an extended period of time.

Almost paradoxically, I have decided that to enable the kind of free and open exchange this model presupposes, I need to become more directive and prescriptive in my approach to teaching this model. This assertion may make advocates of any form of peer tutoring uncomfortable because, as Peter Carino reminds us, writing center scholarship (at least since the late 1970s) has emphasized the nurturing, nonauthoritarian, nonhierarchical nature of peer tutoring (2003, 96–97). In our quest to model this type of environment for our tutors in training, many tutor trainers, like me, have adopted a kind of egalitarian pedagogy in our tutor-training classes or workshops, but I now think this decentering of authority and power was at the heart of many of the problems I saw in the PWCP at Ohio State. No one person, neither among the 110W teachers nor the 467 teachers, had the definitive say on how the peer groups should work. Indeed, a large part of my job as the peer consultant director was to be an intermediary between these parties because neither group was supposed to act as a sole authority. While I was initially drawn to this idea of shared authority, in reimagining how to set up a program in light of the concerns I have raised throughout this essay, I have decided that the program needs to mark a clear authority figure, and this authority figure needs, as much as possible, to provide clear definitions to all the participants about their roles.

To start this process, I have decided that it is vitally important for the writing teacher and the tutor trainer to have a firm understanding of what roles they expect tutors to assume in the peer groups, in addition to having specific criteria for what the groups should be striving for. Because I am now at a small institution where the logistics of this arrangement are possible, I am both the tutor trainer and the first-year instructor involved with this program. In other words, I am training peer tutors to work with peer groups in a first-year writing course I am teaching. This move hopefully eliminates many of the mixed messages that were so confusing in my old program and provides me with the opportunity to gain firsthand knowledge of the types of issues I will need to call to the attention of first-year writing teachers who may want to use this model in the future.

For example, one issue I am already aware of is the need for the peer groups to meet during regularly scheduled class time with me present. My hope is that my presence, both figuratively in the structure of the program and literally in the room as peer groups are meeting, helps to deflect some of the authority novice writers want to invest the tutor with while relieving tutors of the burden of having to take attendance, provide discipline, or otherwise "be in charge." Keeping the groups in the classroom may make this activity seem more formal than when students could meet anywhere, but it also suggests that the peer group time is important and serious enough to take place in the classroom, and, hopefully, the familiar setting makes a positive contribution to the comfort level of the groups. As an added bonus, questions or problems are addressed immediately and, therefore, groups do not reach an impasse where they cannot go on with their work until they find the answer, as often happened in my former program.

Another critical difference in the way I am (re)constructing this program is that I am introducing my tutors to the literature on both one-to-one tutoring and peer response groups. For the former I have chosen Donald McAndrew and Thomas Reigstad's *Tutoring Writing: A Practical Guide for Conferences* (2001) and for the latter Karen Spear's *Sharing Writing: Peer Response Groups in English Classes* (1988). While neither text addresses the specific model of tutors tutoring peer response groups that my students are participating in, including conversations about the nature of peer group work in the structure of the tutor-training course gives the PWCs a broader understanding of the different ways collaboration can happen. I am hopeful, too, that as texts like *On Location* and Moss, Highberg, and Nicolas's *By Any Other Name: Writing Groups Inside and Outside the Classroom* (2004) become available, I will be able to incorporate reading that does concern itself with the specific nature of the work my PWCs are doing.

Besides providing PWCs with information about their roles, I am able to train my first-year writing students about how their groups should work. To address this goal, I place my students in "permanent" peer groups at the beginning of the semester, and I construct classroom activities that require them to work together throughout the semester at times other than just during peer group sessions with their PWC. This set up is, of course, similar to the one in my former program; however, the crucial difference this time is that the first-year writing students do not use their peer group time away from the PWC to work on their papers. Instead, they use that time to perform other writing-related tasks, like discussing readings, responding to in-class writing prompts, or reviewing homework. Additionally, while my syllabus calls for several single-authored papers, the final paper for the course is a collaborative paper that requires the group to work together to collect data, do research, draft a paper, and present an oral report. Since the first-year students know that this group project is a course requirement, they (hopefully?) have a vested interest in making their group functional, and they have assignments they do without the PWCs so that the time the PWC is present is reserved for discussion of and work on specific writing assignments.

I have also built this focus on group work into my tutor-training course, as I think it is important for tutors who are facilitating peer groups to also have the experience of being in a peer group. My PWCs worked together to create a conference presentation for the National Conference on Peer Tutoring in Writing, and the assigned final project for the course will be completely designed and carried out by the class. In both cases, the PWCs need to negotiate authority and workload as well as balance individual personalities, strengths, and weaknesses in order to help keep the group moving forward. An integral piece of both projects is a reflective essay the PWCs write at the completion of each project in which they think about their participation in the process, identify key issues that arose during the collaboration, and draw connections among the theory they have read, the work they are doing with their peer groups, and their own experience as a peer group member.

The changes I have made to the way I present this program to both the tutors and the first-year writers certainly do not address all the issues I have highlighted in this essay, and, as such, I am sure I will continue to alter my pedagogy as I continue to learn from each class. Importantly, though, I am learning to work with/in the ambiguity. Although I still believe it is important not to conflate tutoring and peer response groups, I also believe there is much promise in figuring out how to bring these models into productive coexistence.

# 9

## ACTIVE REVISION IN A PEER GROUP
### The Role of the Peer Group Leader

Kelly Giger

Typically, college composition students receive responses to their writing in the form of margin and end comments written by their professors. These comments are filled with suggestions, praise, criticism, and reactions. It is then the students' responsibility to take these comments and incorporate them into their papers. Because understanding response and revision is often difficult for basic writers, it is common practice for their teachers to organize them into peer writing groups (Bruffee 1998; Spear 1988; Willis 1993; Brooke, Mirtz, and Evans 1994a). However, if students are going to make the best use of their writing groups, peer readers will need to know how to offer useful responses, and writers will need to know how to use their group's suggestions to revise their papers.

As part of a research project on peer writing groups, I was chosen to be an undergraduate peer group leader in a basic writing class at Penn State Berks. My purpose was to act as a facilitator in a group of three students, Zach, Ryan, and Kristin,[1] and to model how a peer writing group should work. My goal was to help students improve their writing abilities and to become comfortable with the writing process as they offered and accepted suggestions for revising their essays.

In the early weeks of the semester, I thought that I was effectively guiding my group to make substantive changes when they revised. A week after what seemed to be a most successful peer group session, I discovered to my great disappointment that my group members were making no real conceptual changes to their papers. On examining drafts they'd handed in to their professor, I saw that there were a few grammatical corrections, some rewording, but that they had not touched the major problems that we had discussed in the peer group the week before. In fact, the professor's comments and suggestions were the same ones that they had given to each other at our meeting. This made me realize that, as the peer group leader, I needed to reinforce revision in my group, to give my developmental writers an understanding of what revision actually meant. Without such reinforcement, the students could not revise because they did not know how.

Experienced writers know that revision involves reshaping the paper to make sense of it. It is a time-consuming process that requires the writer to redesign the work, making it fuller, more interesting, and more expressive (Murray 1978; Willis 1993). Even when we tell college students that they need to revise, at the basic writing level they will quite often skip this process. Either they don't know how to revise effectively or they cannot imagine the degree of change required for "real" revision.

In her seminal article, Nancy Sommers (1980) found that an experienced writer will throw out an entire draft without even thinking about it, but when I asked my group if they had ever thrown away a draft and started over from scratch, all three told me "No!" and looked quite horrified at the thought. Zach told me, "If I write it down, I am going to keep it there. I will just make it sound better." This mindset was part of the difficulty I confronted in trying to teach my peer group how to successfully revise their essays through writing group conversations. In this chapter, I will describe the strategies I implemented as a peer group leader to encourage revision by training group members to respond more productively and by teaching my student writers to position themselves to use their peers' suggestions.

## HELPING BASIC WRITERS TO RESPOND IN PEER GROUPS

If my writing group members were going to be good readers and responders, they needed to know how to give the right kinds of response, and they also needed to know what kinds of issues to address at our meetings. Initially, the peer group could not distinguish between surface-level changes and deep revisions. Like the students in Sommers's case study (1980), my group members thought of the revision process as similar to the editing process. As Sommers also observed, when my students defined the revision process, their common definition involved scratching out words and rewriting them to make them sound better. When I asked members about the difference between revising and editing, they seemed perplexed by the question itself. There was a moment of silence after I asked the question while they tried to find an answer. Zach guessed that editing and revising were the same thing, which meant to "fix the paper up" and make grammatical changes. In fact, during my first peer group meeting, Zach told us that he was a C student in writing in high school because "I didn't know my grammar rules." Like the other members, he seemed convinced that if he better understood grammatical principles, his writing would improve.

This fixation on having a grammatically perfect paper took much attention away from our peer group's tackling the more important issues in a paper. For example, Kristin came to one peer group meeting saying that she had already started to revise her paper. She stated that she had only one paragraph that she was unsure of. As she began to read the paper, I found problems with organization, confused duplication of ideas, and quotes that did not relate to her argument. I could tell by Ryan's and Zach's expressions that they were also confused. After Kristin finished reading her draft, Zach looked at her and said, "Um, I don't get it." However, when I asked Zach what he didn't understand, he couldn't tell me. Rather, he suggested changing a single word. Similarly, when I asked Ryan what he thought, he told me the essay was confusing, and then he began to point out grammatical errors. Like her peers, Kristin's attempt at revising showed that she did not understand what the revision process entailed. At the end of our session, I asked Kristin if I could see where she had started to make her corrections. I discovered that all of her corrections and revisions were at the surface level. She hadn't even attempted to address global issues.

Why is it that students focus on grammatical issues versus substantive issues? Karen Spear says that in first-year composition writing groups, students often lack the confidence to focus on broader issues. In a peer group setting, the students want to be helpful contributors, so they will focus on those problems where they are confident they can offer a correct or helpful solution (1988, 41). Zach and Ryan both saw something wrong with Kristin's paper, but they didn't know exactly what it was or how to approach it. Instead of attempting to tackle the bigger problems, it was easier for them to point out where a comma was missing because they knew that they would be right.

Helping my group to distinguish between surface-level errors and the substantive needs of the paper and to respond primarily to the substantive issues was my first challenge. I knew that in order to get students to focus on global issues, they needed to understand more about the revision process (Murray 1978; Spear 1988; Sommers 1980; Willis 1993). Therefore, during our sessions I repeatedly told my group that we needed to focus on the ideas and organization of the paper, and I stressed that taking care of their commas should be the last thing that they do. When one of the peer group members pointed out a grammatical error, I told them that they were right, but I quickly asked that student a question dealing with the main ideas in the paper. Since according to Mina Shaughnessy, in order for basic writers to conquer their problems, they need to develop self-esteem, (1977, 127), I never flat out told my group members that they were wrong to say where a comma should be placed. I always let them know that they were correct and then encouraged tackling a bigger issue.

According to Robert Brooke, response is "the third essential element of a writer's life," directly following after "time" and "ownership" (1994, 23). Brooke, Ruth Mirtz, and Rick Evans say that "response helps writers develop the feelings of social approval necessary to continue writing, an understanding of audience reactions and their own writing processes, and the ability to revise particular pieces effectively" (23). Feedback gives writers a sense of social approval and the feeling that their writing has value. This feeling of social approval boosts their self-esteem and confidence in their writing, which in turn will improve their writing skills because they will be more willing to try. A peer group's response to writing is or should be a kind of conversation, which Bruffee views as the key to writing improvement. The writer must be able to express him- or herself orally before his or her thoughts are written down (1998, 130–31). Therefore, the peer group should be responding to the writer in a form that will engage the writer in a conversation, similar to the way that the writer should be writing.

In the peer group, it is important that the conversation between members is concrete and directed toward the problems in the paper. Often I found that my group could not provide this kind of feedback to their peers, as is illustrated in the transcript of one of our early sessions. Ryan had started out his paper by explaining that animals react instantly on instinct. By the end of the paper, however, he'd changed his focus to argue that humans have boundaries in life that animals do not have, thus inhibiting potentially instinctive reactions. After Ryan had read his paper, I gave the group a few minutes to collect their thoughts. Then Ryan asked the group, "Does this paper make sense?" Here are the responses that followed:

| | |
|---|---|
| *Zach:* | Yeah, you gotta keep going. Finish it up. |
| *Kristin:* | Yeah, keep going. |
| *Ryan:* | How do I elaborate more? |

> *[Group is silent.]*
>
> *Kelly:*      What is your main point? What are you trying to say in the paper?
>
> *Ryan* [somewhat unsure]: Animals react on instinct. About the introduction and—
>
> *Zach and Kristin* [cutting in]: It's good.
>
> *Zach:*      Make it into a question.
>
> *Ryan:*      How should I start that?
>
> *Zach:*      You need a transition between these two paragraphs.

Kristin and Zach knew that Ryan's focus was not consistent in his paper, but they didn't know how to explain what was wrong or how to give suggestions to clarify it. Instead, Zach suggested introducing the argument in the form of a question, but that really didn't solve Ryan's problem of clarity. He then jumped to telling Ryan that he needed a transitional paragraph before the second paragraph. It was a suggestion that might have been helpful if Ryan had been ready for it, or if Zach had been able to explain why it was needed.

At that point, I interrupted and tried to work on getting Ryan to establish one main point. I didn't like having to cut in, but clearly the peer group was not giving Ryan what he needed to know. I wanted Ryan to explain what he wanted to say in his paper first, so we could talk about how he was going to express his main idea and stay focused on that one idea. In order to guide the group to give concrete suggestions, I urged them with questions, a strategy I adopted from Meredith Sue Willis. In *Deep Revision* (1993), Willis suggests asking writers questions like "Could you tell me more here?" in order to get the writer to figure out the essay's central point by expressing it orally.

While Willis offers this suggestion as a strategy for working with writers individually or in peer groups, I redirected the strategy to peer readers by asking Zach and Kristin what they thought Ryan' s main point was. They both told me that Ryan was arguing that animals react on instinct, while humans act by choice. When I asked for suggestions about how Ryan could make his focus clearer, Zach told Ryan that he needed more examples of instinctive animal behavior. Although I agreed with Zach's suggestion, I knew that more elaboration was needed, so I engaged Ryan in a conversation about his assertions by simply asking him to explain his thoughts in different words. He told the group about an experience that he'd had with a deer, an incident he had mentioned in his essay. In talking out his thoughts, he offered much more detail about the differences in the reactions of deer and humans. I turned back to the group and asked them to explain the significance of Ryan's story. This led to a discussion of the boundaries humans construct that deflect their natural instinctive responses. The group gave Ryan several suggestions about developing his paper to create a more meaningful and consistent argument. My strategy of directing specific questions drove the peer group to offer concrete suggestions for Ryan to use.

Another strategy that I used to encourage group communication was breaking down the paper paragraph by paragraph, as suggested in "Revision: Nine Ways to Achieve a Disinterested Perspective" (1978). According to George J. Thompson, by focusing on each paragraph separately and stating the purpose for each paragraph, student writers can begin to discover their essays' intentions and meanings. Again, I redirected Thompson's strategy to the group by asking group members to explain the significance of each paragraph in their peers' essays. During a session in which Zach was having trouble determining what he wanted to say in his paper, I had the group look at each paragraph and find its importance. Zach had written about the relationship between language and culture. His main point was that a person's language reflected his or her culture and determined how the speaker or writer was perceived by society. To argue his point, he used examples from the movie *Rush Hour*, but his paper seemed more like a movie review than an academic argument.

During the session, I asked Ryan to look at Zach's second paragraph and come up with a reason why Zach would have placed it in his paper. Ryan told me that the paragraph portrayed how the two main characters (one Chinese and the other African American) perceived each other based on their culture and how they talked. I then asked Zach if that was the purpose of the paragraph and if he could explain its importance. Zach agreed with Ryan's explanation and was able to express the importance to me in his own words. We continued to work our way through his essay, breaking down each paragraph as we had done with the second paragraph. For each section, Zach wrote down what his peers said. As he was writing, I could tell he was getting a better grasp of the paper and knew how to express his point from his examples. He then explained to me that what he really wanted to say in his paper was that people judge each other based on their race and language, and he explained how his examples proved this point. What he said made complete sense.

## APPLYING PEER GROUP FEEDBACK TO THE PAPER

Although a class may be set up to help students with the revision process, there is no guarantee that students will actively revise their paper once they leave the classroom. In private, Zach confided, "When I try to revise, I just stare at my computer screen not knowing what to do with the suggestions that were made." This was a major problem with my group. They knew that changes needed to be made with their papers, they had heard the suggestions, but as the following scenario illustrates, when it came to making those changes after the group meeting, they didn't know what to do with them.

During one peer group meeting, we spent a lot of the time discussing Ryan's ending paragraph for his essay on the ways media influence society. In his conclusion, Ryan had written,

> Are we the people influenced by the media? I am influenced by the commercials for apparel. Whenever I see a commercial for a new pair of shoes or a commercial for a new style of clothing, I feel like I have to have it, even if I don't need it. Many people are influence by this form of media. Media is shown in many different ways. There are commercials for advances in technology or new apparel arriving in stores. Other types of media are the news and movies. Some people can be influenced by movies. I went to the movie *Gone in 60 Seconds* with a friend. It is a movie full of suspense with a group of artists who steal rare or extremely expensive cars. After the movie was over he said to me, "I feel like stealing a Mercedes." I said, "What?" I couldn't believe the movie had that affect [*sic*] on him. I just thought that it was an excellent movie with lots of suspense. That's all! But again we are all different people. We are all affected by things differently.

It was obvious there were several ideas operating in this one-paragraph conclusion, ranging from an example of how Ryan had been swayed by advertising to a listing of influential forms of media to discussion of how his friend had responded to a violent film. Since everyone, including Ryan himself, was confused about the essay's argument, we spent a great deal of time talking about how media influences our beliefs and opinions. Everyone was offering examples: Kristin told Ryan that she, along with many other women, wanted to change her hairstyle after watching the television show *Friends* and seeing Jennifer Aniston's hairstyle; Zach talked about how television commercials had convinced him to buy a certain pair of sneakers. As Ryan began to tell the group what influenced him when he watched television, I could tell he was starting to understand what he wanted to say. We continued to provide concrete feedback and examples so that at the end of our session, Ryan was able to state his argument out loud to all of us. He had been taking notes during the revision session and honestly seemed ready and prepared to revise.

A week later, when I saw Ryan's paper after he had handed it into the professor, I discovered that Ryan hadn't used any of the suggestions developed during the peer group meeting. Although I was terribly disappointed at the time, in retrospect, I realize that Ryan came into the session confused. In the fifteen minutes, we threw a lot of information and suggestions at him. He listened to everything we said, but he was not ready to deal with all of that feedback, nor was he capable of taking the examples and suggestions and writing them down in his own words. Ryan felt overwhelmed after the peer group session. Now I realize how much need there is to reinforce revision strategies during the session. This reinforcement is necessary not because students are lazy or don't have time to revise, but because they are truly not able to accomplish successful revisions on their own.

In the first place, if writers like Ryan don't really know how they feel about their argument or aren't really sure about what they are trying to say, they won't be able to use their peers' suggestions because they will be trying to work on their own meanings. In order to help writers to tackle their revisions using suggestions made during the peer group meeting, I had to first help them to clarify the central point of their draft. To do this, I borrowed a teaching strategy from Karen Pepper at the University of Maine (2001). In Pepper's classes, students hand in their essays at the beginning of a class. After she teaches the lesson for the day, she asks her students to spend a few minutes writing about the essays they have just submitted. This exercise helps students to reinforce their main focus or central argument because they have spent time away from thinking about their papers. When they are asked to write down their main point, their statements come straight from their immediate reactions without any deep thinking. Following my confrontation with Ryan's (non)revision, I adapted this idea into my peer writing group. After we finished commenting on everyone's papers, I asked each writer to tell me the main idea in his or her essay and to offer examples of how he or she was going to back up the main idea. I did not let them look down at their drafts when they talked to me, and this restriction forced writers to restate their point without rereading it. It also showed me whether the student understood what was being suggested to him or her during the group meeting. If they couldn't state what the paper was about, then obviously they didn't know what the focus of the paper was, nor did they comprehend what had been discussed in the group.

Over time, I also realized that the group actually made real revisions on their papers. In one of the later classes, their professor had assigned the class to write a short reflective essay explaining the revisions that they made on their papers following a peer group meeting. When my group met a week later to discuss the same paper, I saw that my students had attempted to address conceptual issues, not just their grammatical errors. Without having to write the reflective statement, those changes most likely would have not been made. Therefore, I introduced end-of-writing-group reflections by asking the students to turn over their papers and to write out what they learned from the group that day and what changes they were going to make on their papers. I found this strategy useful because it helped writers to formulate their strategies for making changes while we were still together in the peer group. Also, I could then tell who wasn't going to be able to tackle his or her revisions. If the student couldn't write out what he or she needed to do, then I knew that I needed to spend more time with that student figuring out the essay's meaning so that he or she would be ready to revise.

Throughout the semester I noticed that students would readily make the changes suggested by the professor but not by their peer groups. Ironically, often the peer group had given the same suggestion as the professor. Clearly, the writer would have saved time if he or she had listened to the peer group in the first place. When I asked Zach if he listened to suggestions that the peer group gave him, he told me, "Yes." But when I asked if he generally used the suggestions to make changes, he said, "No." In contrast, when I asked if he always made changes from the professor's comments, he answered, "Yes," but he could not explain why this was the case. Gerry Sultan's research in peer writing groups found peer group members' willingness to revise in response to teacher comments and their reluctance to revise on the basis of their peers' comments resulted from a desire for artistic freedom. One student interviewee explained: "When a teacher tells you, you need to change something, you have to, whether you want to or not; but when one of your friends says it, you say, 'I don't want to'" (1998, 67). In "Beyond the Red Pen: Clarifying Our Role in the Response Process" (2000), Bryan Bardine, Molly Schmitz Bardine, and Elizabeth Deegan recognize that students are willing to revise from teacher response because they know that their actions will ultimately give them a better grade. In contrast, students cannot be sure that their peer group's feedback is accurate.

These studies, as well as my own experiences with my group, suggest that teachers and peer group leaders need to collaborate to find ways to work with students to revise by reinforcing the work that a peer group puts into a paper. Teachers can show developing writers that if they use the suggestions given by the peer group, it will improve their grade and save some of their time. For example, the reflective statement that the students wrote for the professor was beneficial to their understanding of revision. Although it helped greatly, requiring students to write reflective statements for every revision that they made following their peer group meetings would become tedious. Students would find revision even more of a burden because of the extra workload. However, I do feel that students need some kind of required reinforcement to revise from peer feedback. Peer group leaders need to collaborate with the course instructor to insist on "proof" that revisions were made. Students could write a short paragraph of explanation or attach a copy of their rough drafts with their revisions written in and with a brief explanation as to how or why they made them. In any case, peer group leaders and teachers must reinforce the use of peer group suggestions and hold student writers responsible for using this feedback as they revise. Without the strong demand for peer-generated changes, students will not attempt deep revisions because they will think that it is not that important to do so.

## WHAT A PEER GROUP LEADER SHOULD EXPECT

When I discovered that members of my peer group were not revising their papers, I was upset. I felt like all of the work and time spent in the group meetings was for nothing. Then I came across something that Ryan had written on his end-of-semester reflective essay about his writing and the peer group. Ryan had talked about how the peer group was a big help to him and how his writing had improved because of it. Most significantly, he had written about an incident in which the peer group helped him add detail and explain ideas in his essay dealing with the influence of language on culture. He wrote, "My peer group helped me to find my lack of detail and elaborate on [my friend] Larry and what he had to do with my essay." After reading this statement, I checked my journal entry, where I'd noted that the group had spent time helping Ryan elaborate on the relationship between his central argument and Larry's role in his paper. But when I checked the essay Ryan had turned in to the professor, it showed no changes from the draft we had talked about during our session. Ryan had not revised the paper according to his group's suggestions; in fact, no changes on clarifying Larry had been made.

However, instead of being discouraged, I was impressed that Ryan even wrote about the incident. It showed me that he did learn something, that he knew that the changes to the Larry segment were necessary and he even thought he'd made them; therefore, the peer group was accomplishing something important. Similarly, in an interview with Zach in the middle of the semester, he told me that the peer group was a big help because the group showed him what needed to be changed that he didn't see himself. Realizing what needs to be changed is the first step in revising. Although this may seem like a small step, it really isn't. Like anything that one learns to do, it takes time and practice. The peer group forced the student writers to see their writing from a different perspective. They were learning about revision because they were hearing suggestions to improve their papers by other readers and they were thinking about how other writers might change their own papers. The recognition of what revision is and the realization of what needed to be changed in their papers were huge steps toward improving and developing their writing abilities.

As Shaughnessy (1977) reminded composition teachers long ago, a basic writer is a student who is a beginner in writing. I now understand that the members of my peer group came into the class with little knowledge of college-level writing. Therefore, it was unrealistic to think they would leave the peer group and rewrite their papers to realize their full potential. They did not have enough experience to do so. But working in a peer group is a significant step forward in aiding basic writers to understand the complexities of writing as a process. The peer group taught the peer group members how the writing process worked and what is involved in revision.

A peer group leader cannot expect perfection from the group and should not feel discouraged if drastic improvements are not made. The peer group leader is essential in the peer group to guide basic writers. As Donald Murray says, "It is the job of the writing teacher to find what is on the page, which may be hidden from the student" (1978, 58). The peer group leader takes on a similar role in the group by guiding the whole group into seeing the meaning of the paper and assisting the student to make the paper say what the student means. Getting students to revise their papers in peer groups is often a perplexing problem. With a peer group leader reinforcing and facilitating the revision process, revision is made easier for the group members. This leads to a better understanding of the writing process and greater improvements in developing students' writing.

# PART THREE

## Addressing Issues of Authority and Role Definition in Classroom-based Writing Tutoring

Perhaps even more than practical concerns, for those involved in classroom-based writing tutoring, issues of authority and role definition reveal the colliding theoretical perspectives emerging out of this hybrid instructional genre. In various ways, the essays in this section expose the rich and complex theoretical under-girding of on-location tutoring projects. Oppositions like tutoring sovereignty versus institutional dependence, nonintrusive versus directive tutoring methods, traditional process-oriented strategies versus writing group pragmatics, tutors as peers versus tutors as specialists, and tutors as students versus tutors as "teachers" appear again and again in the many configurations discussed in these chapters. We see that, among participants, inherent contradictions in viewpoints may not be easily resolved or reconciled; at the same time, our contributors demonstrate the potential for on-location tutoring to intervene in traditional institutional power structures.

Marti Singer, Robin Breault, and Jennifer Wing look closely at communicative and material conditions in a peer tutoring program attached to their institution's WAC program. Telling stories of tutors and classrooms, the authors infuse their critique with Marxist perspectives relating to authority and privilege and discuss their ongoing efforts to successfully manage power issues through consultant training and faculty workshops. Lack of authority is likewise the subject of David Martins and Thia Wolf's work on a "Partnership Program" that sends writing center tutors into classes across the disciplines. They describe the clash between tutors' training in writing center literacy theory and teachers' adherence to a skills-based writing paradigm. Tensions and conflicts arise when classroom tutors lose authority and flexibility with regard to pedagogical approaches. Taking their lead from the tutors, Martins and Wolf argue for a more complex position of shared authority required in the classroom-based setting.

Conflicts in authority also result when a writing center administrator, even for very good reasons, appropriates control of tutor activities in the classroom setting. Discussing her writing center's tutor-led classroom workshops, Susan Georgecink critiques her efforts with respect to Andrea Lunsford's notions of authority. She argues, finally, that if tutors are to assume successful mentoring roles in classrooms, they must not be asked to perform as "marionettes," merely enacting the program administrator's script. In a study of her efforts to democratize tutors' and teachers' roles, Candace Spigelman confirms that institutional hierarchies perpetuate traditional role definitions. In her project, education majors enrolled in a peer tutoring seminar and led weekly peer group sessions with students in basic writing. Spigelman examines tutors' positionings within classroom peer writing groups, their group members' constructions of their authority, and their conflicted status in the seminar class. She illustrates that in these democratic classroom settings, power was repeatedly resisted, negotiated, and recentered.

Finally, Jennifer Corroy argues that small inroads and local conversations can produce positive large-scale changes in attitudes toward writing and the authority of writing instruction, as they did at the University of Wisconsin–Madison. Corroy discovers the positive impact of a writing fellows program on traditional faculty and institutional notions of literacy.

**10**

# CONTEXTUALIZING ISSUES OF POWER AND PROMISE
## *Classroom-Based Tutoring in Writing across the Curriculum*

Marti Singer
Robin Breault
Jennifer Wing

This chapter begins with the true tale of two tutors, Jessica and Julie. The names and departmental affiliations have been changed to protect the innocent. Both tutors worked for the writing across the curriculum program at our institution as writing consultants for writing-intensive (WI) courses during spring semester 2002. Our WAC writing consultants function mainly as classroom-based tutors who conference with students on writing assignments for the courses; however, they are also expected to attend approximately 50 percent of the class meetings and work with instructors to develop WAC exercises and support materials. In addition, they collect student writing samples and write end-of-semester reflective reports. Here are their stories.

Jessica, who worked with an instructor in the economics department, had a good relationship with her WI course instructor. He communicated clearly with her from their initial meeting. He asked her to participate fully in the instruction of writing in the course. Jessica was responsible for teaching minilessons related to writing in the discipline. Together she and the professor developed assignments and split the reading of student drafts. She held student writing conferences, which she noted students attended fairly regularly. Jessica and the professor held office hours concurrently once a week. The professor gave her access to use his office because, as a graduate student in his department, she wasn't entitled to an office. He allowed her to use his computer to draft handouts for the course. Jessica and the professor reported that "the WAC assignments and handouts helped the students to understand the importance of writing as a tool to reinforce learning as well as learning to write in ways appropriate to our discipline" (end-of-semester report). Both professor and tutor noted that from their perspectives the WI component of the course was effective. Jessica truly served as a consultant.

Julie, who worked with an instructor from the marketing department, also had a good relationship with her WI course instructor. The professor communicated with her on a regular basis, but rarely took her suggestions into account until the end of the semester. The professor asked her only to be available to students for conferencing and to assist in the grading of student writing. She wasn't asked to participate in any course writing instruction until the semester was nearly over. She suggested and developed supplemental handouts and short lessons on writing to help the students grasp the assignments they were being asked to complete. However, the professor did not seem to consider Julie's contributions. Although the department provides office space for graduate students, several teaching assistants share each office. Therefore, Julie held office hours in various places on campus in order not to disturb her office mates. She arranged conferences with students, many of whom did not attend, and she read initial drafts of all WAC assignments. Julie reported that for most of the semester the students did not utilize the conferencing services she offered. She and the professor noted that they did not feel the students' writing was as advanced as they had expected it to be nor did it improve in ways they had hoped. In a private conference with one of the authors, Julie noted that if she were teaching a WAC course, she would do it differently so that the students would have better opportunities to learn about writing.

Although these stories are the isolated accounts of just two writing consultants, their experiences are similar to others in our WAC program. Writing consultants, both graduate and undergraduate, are an integral part of most WAC programs, but they are the least defined in terms of the various roles that are assigned to them. In this chapter, we assert that the lack of clear definition for their roles may stem from various power issues inherent in the postsecondary community. Foucault writes that power is the problem of our time, arguing that "no situation is excluded from the strategies of power" (1988, 99). In other words, in every context the distribution and balance of power, or control, affect the ways in which we act and react. Who dominates our discourse determines what work we are able to accomplish and how and controls our ability to access resources and information. For WAC consultants, instructors, and students, the ways in which power is distributed among the players in the classroom is inseparable from the effectiveness of classroom-based tutoring.

These power issues manifest themselves through the kinds of support graduate assistants in our program receive from individual professors, their departments, and the university as a whole. In our experience, power becomes most evident in the consultant/professor relationship in the areas of communication and discourse—symbolic and real—between the professor and the consultants and access to resources and support, material conditions that relate directly to the work of the writing consultant.

Both symbolically and materially, writing consultants are empowered to facilitate writing and learning in WI courses. At times the communication and material support for writing consultants are successfully provided; at other times these support systems are inadequate, consciously or not. When the symbolic and material supports are evident, writing consultants report success with their students. As we will see from the tales related below and from other examples from our program, power plays an integral role in writing consultant effectiveness and student learning. As the director of training for writing consultants, the administrative assistant for the WAC program, and a graduate student who has served as a graduate research assistant for the WAC program, we provide a critical approach to addressing issues of power and promise by presenting a brief history and our current stance on consultant training and workshops for professors at our university. In addition, through a Marxist perspective, this chapter considers ways power impacts the teaching and tutoring of writing in WAC programs. We define and contextualize power in classroom-based WAC tutoring, looking closely at forms of communication and material indications of power.

## BACKGROUND

Writing across the curriculum at our university began in 1996 with a mandate and a budget from the provost. Initially, the program was headed by the director of composition, who established an interdisciplinary, ad hoc committee of full-time faculty from several colleges within the university. The director of composition and the committee established a mission and began promoting the teaching of WI courses throughout the colleges. In 1998, the university, through the English department, hired an assistant professor to serve as full-time director and teach at least two courses per academic year for the English department. The new director expanded the program in several ways. She established faculty grants for course development, which included faculty workshops on writing to learn and learning to write. The workshops emphasized constructing syllabi with sequenced writing assignments and writing instruction and assessment. She brought in experts to work with faculty: Art Young, Cynthia Selfe,

Kathleen Yancey, and others. In addition, the program funded writing consultants to work with faculty.

Although hiring writing consultants seemed like an advantage for the faculty, it sometimes complicated their academic lives as well. Not only did professors have to learn to think differently about writing within their content areas, they were expected to manage a graduate or under-graduate consultant. The first writing consultants had little training, and many were English majors who were unfamiliar with the writing in the discipline they consulted for. The role of consultants in our program was fashioned after Mary Soliday's classroom-based tutors at CUNY and the Brown University model for WAC writing consultants. Our consultants were (and are) expected to work with individual classes to provide additional writing expertise in various forms both in and out of the classroom itself. However, as the WAC program was new and understaffed, and the consultant facet of the program was in its beginning stages, there was no formal training for consultants, no written guidelines or requirements that helped professors utilize the expertise of their consultants in ways that might enhance student learning in the classroom. Therefore, most of the writing consultants spent much of their time grading papers. Many of the consultants, who were initially hired as classroom-based, on-site writing assistants for students in WI courses, became alienated from the courses they were assisting, existing only in the background behind the red pen and the professor's final comments. This was not the case for all consultants, of course, but the frustration experienced by both the professors and the assistants was evident.

During the next two years, the WAC program developed more effective consultant guidelines, consultants' training seminars, and workshops. And eventually, the program incorporated an administrative coordinator, research assistantships, and a director for training for WAC writing consultants. Focusing workshops with and beyond the professor not only provided the necessary training for writing consultants, it also communicated to departments and instructors that the writing consultant was an integral part of the WAC program at our institution.

## ALIENATION, IDENTITY, AND SYMBOLIC MANIFESTATIONS OF POWER

"Alienated" is a word that several writing consultants use to describe their experiences working with professors who seem to resent their presence in the classroom. Unfortunately, some instructors appear to view consultants as a threat to their own authority in the classroom and, consequently, fail to communicate with them. Consultants like Julie, for example, encounter professors who deny them inclusion in the way of contributions to the course pedagogy, and in the case of other consultants, professors fail to provide access to a job description or list of expectations, as well as pedagogical materials such as detailed lesson plans, handouts, and assessment guidelines. We are not suggesting here that professors consciously feel threatened or intentionally withhold communication or materials from consultants, though some may. Rather, we are more interested in the ways that the consultant's perception of alienation may affect the outcome of classroom-based tutoring. The alienation many consultants experience when occupying the position of middle management (between students and the instructor) can be directly addressed and analyzed by looking at power relationships.

In Madan Sarup's book *Marxism and Education,* he notes that "an individual cannot escape his dependence on society even when he acts on his own: the materials; skills; language itself, with which he operates; are social products" (1978, 134). In her essay "Marxist Feminism," Rosemarie Tong concludes: "[I]t is not the consciousness of men that determines their existence, but their social existence that determines their consciousness" (1989, 40). Tong, like Marx, suggests that our economic or social existence determines our sense of identity or consciousness. As writing consultants become an integral part of the university's social existence, their knowledge of themselves, their identities, and their power to affect student writing become clear as well.

Considerations of power relations in this context must include dialogue and communication, more symbolic manifestations of power that occur between the professor and the consultant and between the consultant and the students she works with. It is within this symbolic realm that issues of alienation become most powerful for writing consultants. They are acutely aware of their "identities" as middle managers in the classroom. But what must be accomplished in this dynamic is the enhancement of their identities as people of knowledge, people of experience, and people who care to share the talk and text of their discipline while encouraging students to engage in the conversation.

Much of the research that has been conducted on Marxism and education focuses on the relationship between the instructor, who functions as a manager, and the students, who fulfill the role of the workers. The introduction of a consultant into this already tenuous dynamic dramatically alters the power structure of the classroom. Sarup claims that "the monopoly of knowledge by management is used to control the steps of the labour process and its mode of execution; conceptualization is separated from execution" (1978, 159). In Julie's case, the writing consultant works directly under the instructor, often grading papers and maybe designing a writing assignment that does not get incorporated into the class. In this scenario the consultant is alienated from the conceptual design of the course and occupies a space on the periphery of the classroom psychologically and physically. In *Karl Marx: Selected Writings*, Marx concludes that alienated labor alienates "(1) nature from man, and (2) man from himself . . . (3) species-life and individual life . . . (4) man from man" (2000, 81–83). If the consultant is not allowed into the discourse of the instructor's class, the work becomes just that—work, a means to a meager monetary end.

As a result of denied access to knowledge, the consultant also enters the classroom with very little status. Sarup notes that status "can be seen as a form of profit" (1978, 141). The instructor serves as the authority figure because he has the well-earned title of "professor," backed by years of hard work and experience. Yet, the writing consultant occupies the liminal space of being a student as well as a teaching assistant. Students sometimes disregard conferences with consultants because they view them as powerless and consider the professor to be the sole authority figure—the one holding the almighty power of assigning grades. In addition to this, some instructors might resent a graduate student in their classroom suggesting ways to improve their students' writing—and in essence, the professor's teaching. Thus, the middle-management role and identity of the writing consultant remain static.

Identity is a theme found not only in Marxist theories discussed by Foucault and Freire, but also explored on a more practical level in Black's discussion of student-teacher conferences (*Between Talk and Teaching*, 1998). In her chapter "Power and Talk," Black writes that "one concern of critical discourse analysis is access to and participation in discursive events, particularly those events which have the power to affect lives in important ways" (40). Whether the discourse involves the sharing of course information and writing instruction between a writing consultant and a professor, or whether it centers around conferences among writing consultants and students in the class, participation in the construction of knowledge creates identity for all participants in the discourse community. In addition, Black quotes Peter Mortenson, P.L.: (1989) Analyzing Talk

About Writing. In G. Kirsh ND p. Sullivan, EDS. Method and Methodolgy in Composition Research. 105-129 Carbopdale: Southern Illinoise UP. in her discussion of social construction: "Since talk involves both consensus and conflict, to document this is to document negotiation of both consensus and conflict that constitute communities. These negotiations determine nothing less than who is allowed to say what to whom, when, how, and why—the social construction of texts" (120). When a writing consultant is denied the power of negotiation with the professor, to agree or disagree or suggest methods to enhance student writing, her identity as a writing consultant for the students in the class is thus shaped. She will struggle throughout the semester to identify herself for the students as one who has the knowledge and power to help them with the writing required in the discipline.

In his introduction to Freire's *Pedagogy of the Oppressed,* Macedo relates the importance of blending theory and practice, the "unity" of the two in dialogue. One without the other results in disconnection and reduction and "leaves identity and experience removed from the problematics of power, agency, and history" (Freire 1970, 17). Jessica's experience indicates that she not only had the support of her professor in terms of material power, she also had the communication and dialogue with her professor that empowered her to share content knowledge as well as writing knowledge within the discipline. As an active participant in developing pedagogy for the class, she was empowered to share both theory and practice, which then enabled students to "transform their lived experiences into knowledge and to use the already acquired knowledge as a process to unveil new knowledge" (Freire 1970, 129) It seems to us that Jessica—and her students—benefited greatly from her professor giving up power in order for her to gain identity in the classroom and in the conferencing situations. Julie, on the other hand, lacked the dialogue with the professor that would empower her to the position she needed—initially at least. Because she found ways to develop the dialogue with the students, she was eventually somewhat successful in her position. But one must wonder how much more might have been accomplished had she been empowered from the beginning. People benefit from others giving up power in order for them to gain "position" or access, but as Julie's experience demonstrates, some will find the power within themselves to get the job done.

Bakhtin's theory of the dialogic may help us to understand issues of power among WAC consultants, faculty members, and students. In *Speech Genres,* Bakhtin states that thought itself "is born and shaped in the process of interaction and struggle with others' thoughts" (1986, 92). Adding Foucault's assertion that power is an integral part of the control and production of knowledge, it becomes clear that the consultant must not only address the notion of dialogue as a struggle with others' thoughts, but as a struggle with an authority figure or faculty member. However, students in the classroom may be at an advantage because the consultant is not often perceived as an authority figure or gatekeeper, but rather as a coach who is part of a level playing field. Bakhtin's solution to the constant struggle between speaker and listener involves the idea that "in order to understand, it is immensely important for the person who understands to be located outside the object of his or her creative understanding in time, in space, in culture" (xiii). Thus, improved communication between the professor and the writing consultant can be achieved if both parties are willing to abandon any preconceptions they may have about the other and re-create identities for each. For faculty members this may mean becoming more open to the suggestions of the consultant, and more conscious of whether or not they perceive discussions as a threat to position. Writing consultants must also be willing to embrace the power to offer ideas about improving students' writing while remaining willing to accept constructive criticism and suggestions that, hopefully, result in effective teaching strategies for the course. Language is a reflective process that allows the listener to respond to another's ideas and attempt to reveal a layer of meaning or understanding about a given subject. In this case, dialogue becomes the construction of knowledge and, indirectly, a construction of identity. If the consultant and the professor are unable to communicate effectively and share a dialogue of knowledge, then how can we expect students to benefit from and understand the concepts involved in writing to learn?

Professors need to empower consultants on at least two levels: first, they need to include and draw them into the conversation, the dialogue of their discipline and teaching within that discipline; second, they need to empower writing consultants to do the same with the students in the classroom. This means that not only are they to serve as "graders" and "reviewers" of material for courses in their respective disciplines, but they become the "object" of knowledge empowering students to engage in learning and knowing as well. As long as writing consultants remain alienated from the knowledge and communications inherent in the workplace, their identities will remain separate from the classroom. As professors model the kind of interaction that empowers students to identify themselves as knowledgeable in their discipline and as social agents of change for students they tutor, the consultant is more likely to mirror that approach to empower the student toward shaping an identity as a writer in a particular discipline.

## POWER AND ALIENATION: MATERIAL CONDITIONS FOR WRITING CONSULTANTS

The materials and other resources we have access to are dependant upon our social positioning. The more social power we wield, the more material power we hold. As we apply Sarup's idea of dependence on society to the classroom, it becomes clear that in order for consultants to function effectively, they must be able to depend on the instructor and the program to meet their material needs. When the professor or program is unwilling to offer the material support the consultant needs to conduct his job (or even merely negligent in doing so), unfortunate results often occur. The consultant denied access will be unable to understand or perform his job well. Consequently, the writing consultant is alienated, outside the social "loop." As Sarup and Marx would argue, in order for the consultant to avoid alienation, he must gain some personal satisfaction from the labor, and he must see how his work fits into the instructor's and program's plan. Providing access to the materials required to conduct that work is essential for consultants—for all productive people actually. If the consultant understands his work and has access to the materials he needs, he will find value and satisfaction in his labor. He will more likely be an effective tutor. Jessica, who fully understood the professor's goals for the course and had full access to all pedagogical materials, was able to devise assignments that meshed with the professor's pedagogy and tutor students effectively. However, Julie, whose professor did not share many course materials and expectations, ended up generating unused materials for the class and felt her tutoring wasn't very effective.

Access to space may also complicate the job of writing consultants. In their introduction to *The Power of Geography: How Territory Shapes Social Life*, Jennifer Wolch and Michael Dear assert that "social practices are inherently spatial, at every scale and all sites of human behavior" (1989, 9). What this means for writing consultants is that their access to tutoring or office space is most often equivalent to their access to agency or power. As Foucault asserts, "space is fundamental in any exercise of power" (Driver 1994, 116). Therefore, writing consultants who have been granted no space, no place to work, conference, assess, or prepare, have no power. In the case of Jessica, the professor allowed the consultant to meet with students in his office. However, Julie had to hold office hours in various places so that she would not disturb her office mates. Office space is a practical, material need, yet it also functions as a status symbol as well. Students are acutely aware of the difference in authority between a consultant who has no office and a faculty member who does. Space becomes representative of the consultants' place within the social hierarchy between instructor and student. If the consultant has no space, she becomes alienated, hovering between students and instructor, office and classroom, no place to sit down and claim her authority. Having a designated space to work and tutor within the department or in a WAC facility helps consultants, instructors, and students to realize that consultants are a vital component of the success of the university.

Additionally, space facilitates student learning by providing a "safe" environment where students can meet one-to-one with the consultant to discuss writing. While the consultant still serves as an authority figure to the students, the power dynamic is less rigid than that between instructor and student. Hence, a consultant's office space fosters the informal atmosphere of a tutorial, rather than a formal conference with the instructor or leading authority figure.

Finally, along with course materials and space, consultants must have access to the physical, temporal, and monetary support their job requires. Without the supplies, time, and money consultants need, they again become alienated and unsatisfied with their work. In chapter 1 of *Capital*, Marx and Engels note that commodities become valuable once an exchange value is placed upon them (2001, 777). They add: "[T]he social character of labour appears to us to be an objective character of the products themselves" (778). Consequently, when defining pay or wages, value is placed upon the object instead of the amount of work/labor that went into producing the commodity. While we would disparage the idea of attaching a price tag to knowledge (the product the consultant produces), we cannot ignore the amount of labor writing consultants expend tutoring, preparing writing exercises, giving lectures, responding and assessing, and so on. All of this work takes time and requires supplies. Consultants' work must be assessed and valued for the time they expend. They must be provided the monetary and material support for all of the tasks that they complete. Again, Jessica's experience provides a good example.

At the beginning of the semester Jessica did not have an access code to the copier in her department. Nevertheless, she was responsible for providing students with instructional handouts and assignments. A few weeks into class, she came to one of us and asked if she could have access to the WAC copy code in our department. She informed us that her professor had asked his department to provide her with a code, but the code was refused and the instructor was told not to share his code with her or face consequences. In the interim she had been paying for the copies with her own money. Making copies for a class of fifty students several times a week would surely not be economically feasible for her to continue on a writing consultant's stipend. Fortunately, the professor and the WAC program were able to work out a reasonable way for Jessica to have access to a copy machine. The lack of access to supplies potentially alienated her from her work, denied her the agency to provide the students with the knowledge they needed to complete the course successfully.

Marx's concepts of the division of labor and alienation provide us with a theoretical lens through which we can examine the writing consultants' isolation when occupying the awkward role of someone in middle management. Only when the professor and the program meet the material needs of the consultants and effectively empower them within the community of the university can the writing consultants work successfully as a vital part of the community and social structure.

## MODELING A PROGRAM OF PROMISE

When we started looking at the difficulties our classroom-based writing consultants were having and how these problems might impact student learning, we did not initially notice that many of our concerns were power related. In positions of administration (those with power), power is easy to overlook or ignore. As Black writes, "When we are in our culture, firmly a part of it, it is invisible to us" (1998, 90). But as we stepped back to analyze and document what we observed, and as we began to listen and dialogue with the writing consultants, power relations manifested more than we had ever expected. In the previous sections we have demonstrated how issues of power are meshed with the work of writing consultants tutoring in our program. In this section we outline the ways we have developed/ designed our program to address the problem of power in our consultant training and WI course workshops.

### Program Development: Faculty Workshops and Seminars

Early in the development of our WAC program, neither the consultants nor the WI instructors had any idea how the consultants should be working. Some were exclusively tutors and had little or no real interaction with the instructor, although they attended the class periodically. Others were merely graders who held office hours that students rarely utilized. However, there were a few exceptions in which writing consultants and instructors communicated clearly, and one example wherein the writing consultant developed an online feedback/tutorial through e-mail.

During the first year of her appointment, the WAC program director initiated a faculty grant that awarded faculty a stipend for attending a spring workshop and several follow-up seminars. The first several workshops focused on Art Young's learning to write and writing to learn concepts, emphasized WI course development, included guest lecturers and workshop hosts that incorporated technology and assessment, as well as specific activities that professors could incorporate into their syllabi. In addition, a document for professors and instructors of WI courses suggested ways in which instructors might collaborate with their consultants (see appendix). None of the models suggested using the consultant as a grader exclusively, but rather encouraged collaboration for developing course materials, assisting in the assessment of student work, participating in writing instruction and tutoring—face-to-face and/or through an online system. The professor or instructor was encouraged to view the writing consultant as a classroom-based tutor as well. Once or twice a year, the consultants might meet to share experiences, but the first years of our program focused mostly on faculty and program development.

### The Identity of the Writing Consultant

Early in the development of the program at Georgia State University, the writing consultants came from the English department. During these first few years, issues of communication and space were most apparent. The writing consultant was sometimes unaware of the expectations of the professor and/or the discipline for which she tutored, and communication between them was sometimes strained. In addition, because the consultant was not working for the English department, or specifically for the particular discipline in which she consulted, space was not provided in either place. Fortunately, at that time, the director of the learning center, through the Learning Support Program, offered the location of that center as space for the writing consultants to meet with students. Providing space solved only some of the problems the consultants experienced, however. Many writing consultants expressed frustration and confusion about how to tutor the students from the disciplines, where to find the information they needed, how to talk with the students about their writing rather than edit their papers for them. So, the director of WAC and the director of the learning center collaborated to offer training workshops specifically for the writing consultants. In addition, the director of the learning center invited the writing consultants to join the training sessions she designed for the tutors in the learning center, generally more generic sessions on tutoring and communicating with students who came to the center for help.

During the first semester that we worked with consultants, we primarily listened to their concerns. We noticed that some consultants were very happy with their positions; these consultants worked with both the students and the instructor, functioning as a true consultant to both. But as a whole, the majority of the consultants seemed a little confused about their role in and out of the classroom—were they tutors? Graders?

The first couple of spring workshops for faculty addressed only briefly the role of the consultants, but faculty were encouraged to initiate dialogue with the writing consultants about workload and student learning issues that the consultants were ideally there to help with. By the third year, faculty seeking WAC grants were asked to include a request for a writing consultant that outlined ways the instructor might work with the consultant to facilitate student learning in the WI course. We also asked that before submitting a proposal, the grant applicants identify the consultants they would like to work with and strongly encouraged professors to find a consultant who was a graduate student or undergraduate from the department designing the WI course. These changes were designed to emphasize the participation of writing consultants in the conception and implementation of WI courses. In addition, including writing consultants in the initial proposal addresses the ambiguity about the consultants' role and their alienation from the knowledge generation associated with the course development.

With three years behind us, we had gathered enough material and confidence in our program to develop a handbook for the consultants. The handbook contained writing samples and writing to learn/learning to write assignments from a number of disciplines. It included some writing theory, a history of the program—at our university and generally throughout the country—and several tutor-training guidelines. We hoped that this handbook would provide solid ground for the work we were beginning. We added workshops designed specifically for the consultant, a time to share both frustrations and successes, teaching ideas, assessment ideas, and suggestions for future workshops.

To further develop the interaction between the consultant and the instructor at the early stages of course development, we now invite the consultants to attend the spring seminar. Fortunately, the program is able to provide the consultants with a small stipend for attending the workshop. We feel that the addition of consultants to the seminar makes a significant difference in the consultant/instructor relationship and consequently the student/consultant relationship as well. We want to provide the consultants with greater access to the resources (both discourse and material based) that they need to do their job.

The addition of the consultants to the spring workshop implemented at the end of the fourth year has been wonderfully successful. The seminar addresses the role and positioning of writing consultants, making instructors and consultants aware of how access to the discourse and materials they need would empower consultants and instructors alike and ideally increase student learning. Workshop participants work in collaborative sessions that address ways to implement access and then begin the process through collaborating on the development of assessment rubrics, revised WI course syllabi, WAC assignments and exercises, and classroom activities to enhance student learning. Instructors and consultants are also asked to develop a list of expected duties and requirements of the consultant. The collaborative aspect of the spring seminar truly facilitated the changes we hoped to see.

In the past year and a half, we have seen a significant difference in the consultant program. This semester not one consultant is used only as a grader. Consultants and instructors have attended workshops and luncheon roundtables together, and all but one pair seem satisfied with their relationship. Although we have not "fixed" all the problems inherent in the complex role of the WAC writing consultant, empowering the consultants through programmatic support of various kinds has helped everyone involved begin to understand the complexity of power dynamics at work in the writing consultant (middle-management) position. Consequently, our consultants are now better equipped to help.

## CONCLUSION

As writing consultants on our campus move from alienation to identity, and as our program grows—not only in numbers, but also in advocacy for professors, writing consultants, and students—the issues of power continually shift. And the tales of tutors shift and emerge as well. Toward the end of the semester that Julie worked as a writing consultant, she and her professor began to communicate more effectively. Julie tells us that she had to learn ways to talk with her professor about the needs of students that made "sense" to him. As Black reminds us, the amount and direction of "talk" matters (1998, 40). Julie reports that she also encouraged the students individually to come see her during her office hours, and we provided space in the WAC office. At this time, Julie is teaching her own class as a TA in her department. She tells us informally and with great enthusiasm that she uses many writing to learn activities to enhance content and to understand what students know and still need to know. And her sequenced assignments are proving effective for writing in her discipline. So perhaps one of the most rewarding outcomes for writing consultants is their empowerment in their own classrooms. Their experiences as writing consultants may indeed enhance their teaching as they join the professorate. But that's another story.

# *APPENDIX*

## WORKING WITH WAC CONSULTANTS AT
## GEORGIA STATE UNIVERSITY

As the purpose for writing-intensive courses in the various disciplines is to offer sequenced writing experiences with feedback, finding ways to work with graduate assistants that are appropriate and effective in particular disciplines is essential. Following are three "models" to consider as the professor and the writing consultant work together to meet the needs of the students in writing-intensive courses. Ideally, the writing consultant could incorporate all three models during the semester.

Students in writing-intensive classes need to know not only that writing is an important part of the learning process in a course, but also that someone is there to help the professor help them with the writing aspects of the subject. Early in the semester, within the first week preferably, the professor should introduce the writing consultant to the class. The professor and the writing consultant should explain the kinds of writing tasks that will occur during the semester and the role that the writing consultant will play in guiding students toward meeting the expectations of the professor (and the discipline).

### SUGGESTED MODELS

### Writing Consultant as Participant/Guide

In some situations, and especially the first semester a graduate student works with the writing-intensive course for a professor, an effective method for communication and for meeting the needs of students is to have the writing consultant observe the class as a participant for much of the semester. This model serves many purposes. The consultant is available to the students in the course who are then more likely to seek help and advice on their writing; it gives the graduate student an opportunity to observe the professor and to understand more clearly the expectations for the writing experiences in the class; it keeps the graduate student up-to-date about the content issues in the course; it builds community among the writing consultant, the students, and the professor. Some writing consultants and professors may want to include observation for only certain parts of the course, and others may want to involve the graduate student more consistently during the semester. Also, as the consultant is present and becomes comfortable with the classroom setting, the professor may choose to ask the consultant for short presentations about the writing process and assignments as they emerge during the semester.

## WAC Consultant as Guide

The professor and the writing consultant may choose to hold specific office hours, during which the writing consultant is available to students for face-to-face feedback on writing assignments. The place for these office hours should be arranged through the professor's department, or the WAC director may be able to arrange some time for these meetings in the writing center. In addition, writing consultants may choose to create a handout for students to inform them of these hours and to explain what students should bring to the feedback sessions. The consultants will focus on writing issues defined by the professor and guide students toward the kinds of writing valued in the discipline. Once a week or so the professor and the writing consultant should meet to review expectations, assignments, and to look at models of "good" writing appropriate for the assignment. The consultant will share concerns and successes, and together the consultant and professor can monitor progress.

Some professors may choose to conduct some feedback sessions along with the writing consultant (especially during the first part of the semester). These collaborative sessions are helpful to both the students and the writing consultants as they hear directly from the professor issues regarding content and writing pertinent to the course.

## Writing Consultant as Cyber Guide

Along with the office hours for face-to-face feedback, some writing consultants and their professors may choose to work with students online. During the introduction to the consultant, students may be given an e-mail address to which they may send drafts and questions concerning the writing process and assignments. The writing consultant would reply over e-mail, providing feedback and answering questions. This e-mail address may be available through the Web site of the course, or the consultant may choose to obtain a special e-mail address through the university for this purpose. During the regular meetings between the writing consultant and the professor, the process and progress of this model of feedback should be carefully monitored.

These suggestions are meant to provide professors and writing consultants with a few ways to think about working together in writing-intensive courses. We would welcome any feedback regarding successes and pitfalls of these options, as well as other ways to work with students and their writing.

# 11

## CLASSROOM-BASED TUTORING AND THE "PROBLEM" OF TUTOR IDENTITY
### Highlighting the Shift from Writing Center to Classroom-Based Tutoring

David Martins and Thia Wolf

In academic year 2000–01, the institutional support for writing across the curriculum at California State University–Chico solidified in the form of a tenure-track hire. Although WAC workshops for faculty in the disciplines had a long history at our campus, the hire of a new WAC coordinator made it possible to broaden the outreach and establish new programs for faculty. Based upon work begun by Judith Rodby and further developed by Tom Fox, a "Partnership Program" that joined faculty with WAC specialists and brought experienced and novice writing tutors into classrooms throughout the university became the principle means of support for faculty teaching writing-intensive courses.

By the time David Martins was hired to be WAC coordinator, there was already significant demand for assistance from faculty teaching writing-intensive courses. At the same time, Thia Wolf became the new director of the writing center. Together, Wolf and Martins, the authors of this chapter, attempted to merge the WAC program into the writing center, offering nineteen partnerships in Martins's first year on campus. During that year, the tutors in the program provided well over fifty in-class writing workshops for classes in agriculture, health and community service, education, sociology, political science, civil engineering, geography, English, history, philosophy, mathematics, and religious studies. In addition to the workshops, tutors regularly observed classes and met with students individually and in small groups during out-of-class appointments. Depending upon their schedules, tutors occasionally attended faculty consultations among the writing center director, WAC coordinator, and participating faculty.

Making the Partnership Program a success meant providing good support for faculty in the disciplines while simultaneously complicating their understanding of literacy and literacy instruction. We knew that in order to do that, we needed to create an interdependent, interactive structure between our tutor-training program and the structure of the Partnership Program itself. Overall, we aimed to introduce faculty to some of the ideas from literacy theory and writing center research that our tutors had encountered in our tutor-training seminar. Relying heavily on work by Nancy Grimm (1999), Laurel Black (1998), and David Russell (1991, 1995), tutors in the seminar learned to think about ways that writing assignments and expectations situated students in the academy; they learned to consider how literacy standards sort and rank students, selecting some for academic success and marking others (especially those from lower socioeconomic, nonacademic, or foreign backgrounds) as failures; and they learned to think of writing not as a single, invariable set of skills requiring mastery, but as a term for an array of socially meaningful practices used by a community in order to achieve shared goals.

Because the idea of literacy as practices rather than skills runs counter to widely held cultural beliefs and teaching approaches, we assumed at the outset that our work with faculty would be complicated and time consuming. David Russell, in his excellent history of writing in the academy, notes that ideas about the teaching of writing involve a "conceptual split between 'content' and 'expression,' learning and writing. . . . Knowledge and its expression could be conceived of as separate activities, with written expression of the 'material' of the course a kind of adjunct to the 'real' business of education, the teaching of factual knowledge" (1991, 5). It was this conceptual split we hoped to address and to mend.

Given this goal, we initially saw writing tutors situated in disciplinary classrooms as anything but "adjuncts." We had faith in our tutors' training and in their abilities to work with students from varied contexts, and we assumed our own work with faculty would be improved by the insights that tutors could bring to us from their classroom-based work. Thus we initially imagined a program structure that would begin with faculty-writing program administrators consultations, resulting in in-class work on writing assisted by program tutors, who would then report to us on their work and their concerns, allowing us to revise our work with faculty appropriately. The context-rich classroom setting would, simultaneously, allow us to revise and refine our approaches to tutor training as we attempted to complicate tutors' understanding of how best to work with peers in disciplinary writing situations.

Through our semester-end survey, both faculty and students participating in partnerships indicated that there were writing practices they had learned that they would use in other classes. Many students wrote that they would spend more time on prewriting activities. Other students listed citation, critical thinking, peer response, and proofreading as the kinds of practices they would take with them as they wrote papers in other classes. Faculty indicated the use of peer groups, assignment sequences, and the use of models for writing as the practices they would permanently integrate into their teaching. One promising success was demonstrated by the sense from faculty that their expectations to learn from the coordinators and the writing assistants about how to improve their writing instruction were satisfied "very well."

Within the contexts of a classroom-based program, however, the possibility of ongoing revision is limited by the demands of each faculty member's syllabus and his or her expectations of tutor work negotiated during the initial consultations with administrators. Thus, while the tutors who worked in the Partnership Program had a semester's worth of experience working in one-to-one situations in the writing center, which offered them overt authority to make decisions about the focus of each writing session and the flexibility to change pedagogical approaches when needed, the partnerships offered tutors neither the same kind of authority nor flexibility. Tensions arose when tutors' sense of identity, based on writing center training in literacy theory, clashed with teachers' authority to construct writing assignments and classroom activities using a skills-based model of literacy. In the writing center, tutors experienced themselves as agents in writing sessions, while in Partnership classrooms tutors lost their sense of identity as agent when they encountered institutional pressure to comply with faculty agendas and instructions. Under this pressure, tutors sometimes engaged in critiques of teachers' pedagogy, abdicated responsibility for Partnership work, or complained to one another about their confusions and difficulties. This chapter examines these responses to the shift in tutors' roles. By viewing tutors' reactions to their work as an invitation to revise tutor training, we argue for the importance of moving tutors from a position of individual authority in a one-to-one writing session to a more complex position of shared authority required in the classroom-based setting. Our work with tutors in a classroom-based WAC program points to some difficulties with and possible approaches to training tutors who do situated literacy work.

## IDENTITY FORMATION: TUTORS AS NEW PROFESSIONALS

In her visionary work, *Good Intentions*, Nancy Grimm argues that writing center workers "*can* be held responsible for changing the habits and attitudes that contribute to oppression" (1999, 107–8) and describes her hope that *Good Intentions* will be read as "an invitation to reconsider the work of writing centers in higher education, to imagine a practice where social justice replaces pale versions of fairness" (120). Tutors in the Partnership Program emerged from an administrative model that stressed their role as agents for change in the university setting. They worked with the writing center administrator in training meetings, one-to-one conversations, and classroom discussions to name and address writing center problems, review and reconsider tutoring practices, and write critiques of program structures. This approach uses Grimm's *Good Intentions* as a guide to reimagining the writing center, not as a site for the remediation and correction of students-in-the-wrong, but as a site for the inclusion and support of students who might previously have been excluded from the university,

For many students working as tutors in the CSU–Chico Writing Center, the role of tutor is the first professional role of their career. The administrative and training model they encounter in the center encourages them to question, to reflect, to make changes in their own teaching practices, and to suggest program changes to the center's administrator. While many find this role unexpectedly demanding, most come to regard it as an engaging opportunity. Many tutors see the writing center as a site for future research and some see it as a possible career home beyond graduate school. Their sense of themselves as developing professionals helps them to construct self-definitions that place them centrally in conversations about literacy practices, instructional strategies, and administrative structures. The role definitions that emerge from their training include a strong sense of purpose, a belief in conversation and negotiation, and a belief in their right to participate in work-related conversations, negotiations, and structural change.

## TEACHERS, TUTORS, AND WPAS: SHARED AUTHORITY AND ROLE CHANGES

As we look back at our WAC experiences and our work with tutors in the Partnership Program, we clearly see the strong institutional demand—on us, on program faculty, and on tutors—for the effective, efficient use of time and resources and for verifiable positive outcomes. The professional culture at our university is, we assume, similar to that of many other teaching institutions, where faculty must demonstrate regular improvement in teaching evaluations and progress/work on teaching. Every year, for example, tenure-track faculty are evaluated by department, college, and university committees that review letters, teaching evaluations, a personal narrative, and any other demonstration of contributions to teaching, professional development, and service.

Because the majority of the faculty we worked with in partnerships were not yet tenured, they often expressed concerns about the Partnership Program's role in their retention, promotion, and tenure review. More than one teacher, for instance, expressed a fear that modifying teaching practices would result in poor student evaluations at the end of the term. Newer faculty also noted that there was no clear indication of the kind of "value" that participation in such a program might have in department, college, and university review committees. These faculty concerns certainly influenced our own identity construction as administrators relative to the WAC work. We heard faculty concerns, felt a need to respond to them, and believed we were positioned to do so. Given the pressures on the tenure-track faculty to continually produce strong teaching evaluations, our interest in placing trained tutors in their classes asked faculty, in effect, to relinquish some of their authority and to open up their classrooms for experimentation. For untenured faculty especially, our request for teachers to experiment with their pedagogy amounted to significant professional risk.

Mindful that faculty needed encouragement and support as they revised class plans, we poured our energies into faculty consultations and into the creation of writing workshops based on the faculty's stated needs. The result was that we thought of classroom-based tutoring as a response to faculty concerns more than as a site for tutor training. Our response to faculty concerns placed us more on the "side" of faculty than on the "side" of tutors, limiting our ability at the time to see faculty development and tutor training as mutually dependent, dialectical activities. Thus we were more likely to respond to faculty worries than to tutors' worries, and more apt to regard well-received classroom workshops as information about the program's success than to place emphasis on tutors' critical commentary.[1]

The cultural capital of WAC in the university setting was not sufficient to encourage change in most teachers' approaches to writing instruction. As a result, though many teachers participated in the program, for some that "participation" involved little more than scheduling classroom periods for tutor-led workshops. During these workshops, teachers sometimes absented themselves or sat in the back of the classroom doing paperwork. Such behaviors clearly indicated that the teachers understood writing to be separate from disciplinary content. That teachers felt it reasonable to hand their classes over to tutors, some of whom were undergraduates, indicated as well that they saw the writing component of the course as basic, a low-level skill that could be handled by individuals with far less training than their own.

Another kind of teacher emerged in the context of the program, however. These professionals developed and maintained some level of interest in literacy theory, especially in the idea that disciplinary genres "evolved to meet [disciplinary] objectives" (Russell 1995, 66) and that writing in a discipline cannot be adequately taught while the myth of a single, "universal educated discourse" (60) remains in place. Teachers intrigued by this view of writing in the disciplines often spent significant amounts of time revising writing assignments with an aim to demystify for their students the reasons why certain kinds of writing were valued in a given field. This shift in understanding did not, however, necessarily result in major pedagogical changes. Rather, the changes we saw repeatedly had more to do with assignment design and making room within their calendar for WAC-designed writing workshops than with discipline-specific ways of discussing and teaching writing.

In the program's busiest year, as we said, the demand for these in-class workshops was so high that tutors gave over fifty workshops in twelve different disciplines. While this indicates WAC popularity, it does not indicate, or necessarily lead to, a change in how faculty understand literacy instruction. That is, WAC-lead workshops may be viewed by faculty as a way "to teach students to write better in general," rather than as a way to "improv[e] the uses of the tool of writing" in a particular disciplinary setting or undertaking (Russell 1995, 69). The necessary guiding involvement of the faculty member, who was, after all, the expert in disciplinary genres, remained elusive in most partnerships. Even when faculty remained present in classroom workshops, moved among groups, and answered questions, their announcement that writing center personnel would "handle" or "lead" the class session signaled to students that writing existed in some way apart from the central work of the course, the part directly controlled by the teacher.

Because we wanted to assist faculty with the work they identified as important for their teaching, and at the same time needed to demonstrate the program's effectiveness to both the administration and the faculty, in the end we accepted and acted on faculty requests for individual workshops that focused on teachers' biggest worries about student writing: research, plagiarism, organization, and editing. At the same time, we engaged faculty in ongoing conversations about literacy theory and its application to future classes they might teach. This way of working encouraged many faculty to make repeat requests for WAC support across semesters, allowing us, we hoped, to encourage further development over time. In some cases, though, depending on the extent of faculty involvement in providing disciplinary reasons for each workshop's focus, the effect of this approach was to continue breaking writing down into separate parts that seemed to exist on their own, as skills to be mastered without reference to disciplinary values or aims.

This situation created a crucial point of conflict for several program tutors because, as a result of our strong focus on faculty, we came to employ classroom-based tutoring more and more as a response to faculty concerns, with less emphasis than we had originally intended on simultaneously developing the program as a site for tutors' strong participation and training. In this way, while tutors had developed their sense of identity and authority within the center as made up of continual negotiation and discussion, the Partnership Program began to mirror more typical institutional structures that distributed authority to individuals in particular positions—namely the teacher and the WAC administrator. These changes resulted in identity crises for several tutors and in a rejection of Partnership work by some.

## TUTORS' IDENTITY VERSUS INSTITUTIONAL VIEWS OF LITERACY

This crisis in identity was most clearly manifest in training meetings, especially those in which partnerships in technical disciplines were discussed. Often, when Martins discussed plans for potential future classroom activities, tutors repeatedly expressed high levels of anxiety about their lack of disciplinary knowledge. During one Partnership meeting, for example, after tutors had experienced a particularly contentious class visit, tutors requested that Martins step in to become the primary initiator of all future discussions with the faculty member. Although he had not wanted to play such a directive role, Martins believed that his expertise and experience, and the institutional authority that supported him, would save time and frustration for the tutors, the teacher, and the students in the class.

This mode of operation, however, signaled a shift in how the program was administered; tutors' reflections for this partnership changed from engaged questions about the role of writing in the field and its pedagogical uses to more rote descriptions of classroom activity and its discussion.

After an extended conversation about a student's draft, for example, one tutor who had previously taken a leadership role in the partnership simply recapped the key points that the students had made about the paper.

By the end of the course, Martins felt that the tutors had helped the students do the work of the assignments, and that he had helped the faculty member think differently about how to structure assignments and scaffold students in their work. The end-of-semester survey, however, suggested something different. When asked what they had learned about the discipline-specific expectations of writing, the students all responded that they knew they were expected to write with clarity and precision. They knew that they needed to pay attention to the audience of a text, and to use "clear examples" and "not make too many assumptions about the readers." But the student comments did not address the discipline-specific aspects of the writing assignments. The faculty member himself indicated that he had learned a lot about writing instruction as a result of the partnership, but was skeptical about how much he might do in the future to integrate writing into his math classes because of the amount of time involved.

In terms of professional identity, such responses from tutors, students, and faculty indicate an ambivalence toward effective writing instruction when that instruction could interfere with what might be seen as managerial expectations for smooth, effective, effortless work. The participants in this particular Partnership session continued to see writing as a surface device for encoding knowledge; its roles in shaping knowledge in a field, revealing values among professionals, and supporting learning remained obscured. In spite of "successes" one might point to, this partnership may have actually reinforced notions of literacy that we had hoped to challenge.

## TUTORS' NEGOTIATION OF IDENTITY CONFLICTS

When we hired experienced tutors from the writing center to work in the Partnership Program, some reacted strongly to the shift in administrative structures. In postprogram interviews, some tutors noted that they had felt literally constrained during Partnership work, unable to ask questions, propose changes, or negotiate their roles with students, faculty, and administrators. For example, two of the program tutors reported that, while they saw their roles in the writing center as "work" in the sense of "a commitment," "a passion," "my work," they saw their involvement in the Partnership Program as "a job." One tutor went on to say, "I hardly recognized myself when I was a Partnership tutor. I missed meetings. I avoided responsibilities. I was like my teenaged self."

But, upon reflection, postprogram interviews were not the only moments when tutors gave us indications of their struggles. Tutors in the Partnership Program also revealed concerns about identity issues in tutor-to-tutor conversations, small-group training sessions, and in e-mail exchanges and written reports. In these other arenas, the questions tutors frequently asked included: What is my role? What is my work (what is expected of me)? How am I perceived in this role? What change/plans can I make to ease my discomfort or confusions about my role? How am I positioned in my team? How do I feel about what is happening to/around me? How can I express to others (teachers and students) my understanding of literacy practices and literacy instruction? Though we mistook these as personal or individual issues at the time, we now see that these concerns can all be viewed as a set of questions pertaining to tutor's sense of agency, revealing information about inevitable tensions tutors must face when making the transition from one-to-one work in the writing center to classroom-based tutoring work in a WAC program.

In 693 lines of printed e-mail exchanges and individual reports, the concerns listed above account for 49 percent of tutors' conversations and reflections about the Partnership Program. In what follows, we examine the written e-mail exchanges and postprogram responses of three tutors who participated together in three Partnership classes. They repeatedly describe the tensions caused by their roles in the program—roles that they felt prohibited them from intervening when they recognized teachers using skills-based notions of literacy—and seek to imagine themselves and their work in ways consonant with their training and their sense of their professional identities.

Studies of individuals in workplace and other institutional settings (e.g., mental hospitals and prisons) by sociologist Erving Goffman (1959) reveal the many ways that hierarchy, work expectations, and social rules affect each individual's self-definitions, behaviors, and in-group/out-group identifications. One's "front," the aspects of self made visible to others in social interactions, "tends to become institutionalized," according to Goffman, "in terms of abstract stereotyped expectations to which it gives rise, and tends to take on . . . meaning and stability. . . . The front becomes a 'collective representation' and a fact in its own right" (27). Tutors' sensitivity to being "typed" and thereby trapped in roles that will render them ineffective is evident in e-mail exchanges from early in the term. For instance, writing about a class meeting tutors attended in a social sciences class, Liselle describes a growing sense of unease:

> He [the teacher] introduced Margret and me as "the tutors who are going to help with the second writing assignment." From what I understand, the goal of Partnerships is that we complicate the thinking of the students and professor on what writing is, and find ways to make writing in the discipline more clear, its function in the field more understandable, and come together with the students and professor to find ways of explaining that writing more fully. I get the feeling that Professor L. thinks that we are here to help edit these second writing assignments. I have met him and discussed at some length his views on this Partnership, and I know that he is extremely willing to learn about writing in the field . . . and he is open to new ideas, so I am a little confused with regard to how he defined our role in the class. Any thoughts? (e-mail, 9 September 2001).

Nowhere does Liselle suggest that the tutoring team should continue to negotiate with the teacher about its classroom role. In spite of her strong belief that the teacher is "open to new ideas," she cannot find room in the program structure to address the teacher directly with her concerns or to propose new ideas. Another tutor, Margret, admits in the same e-mail exchange that she has been avoiding Professor L's class, skipping a session she was supposed to attend because the construction of her role in the classroom made her uncomfortable (e-mail, 9 September 2001). Thom, on the other hand, responds with a strategy for analyzing the dilemma: "I think that our feelings of awkwardness are due in part to others' ideas of `writing assistants.' These are my own thoughts here so take them as such. I try to imagine how I am being seen through others' eyes so that I can more readily be prepared for those moments when we `don't seem to fit.' I am thinking that [the students] think that we are `experts' and that we are there to evaluate them in some fashion."

All of the tutors indicate that something is amiss, but they have no ready ideas for addressing their concern about being misidentified and assigned unacceptable roles and work. Yet all of them had previous experiences of interacting with students in the center who saw them as editors, and each had strategies for helping student users of the center to see them as offering a wider array of support strategies for writers. At the heart of their dilemma, then, is not their lack of familiarity with responding to faulty role identification, but their lack of experience with addressing that misidentification in their new, low-status role.

In reviewing this exchange, we see Liselle's statement of program goals as consonant with our intentions. Indeed, we also had hoped that through interactions with us and with program tutors, teachers would find themselves invited into an ongoing dialogue about writing, a dialogue that would shift teaching practices because it would shift understanding. Russell argues that this is a "crucial step" in WAC work because "unless disciplines first understand the rhetorical nature of their work and make conscious and visible what was transparent, the teaching of writing in the disciplines will continue to reinforce the myth of transience" (1991, 300). This myth of transience, a term Russell borrows from Mike Rose, describes a widely held belief that a simple, formulaic solution to solve all writing problems exists. In objecting to being handed only an editing job, Liselle responds with appropriate alarm, for the cost of "reinforcing the myth of transience," according to Russell, is to "[mask] the complexities" of writing instruction (7).

Because we thought that we were mindful of this myth as we worked with faculty in consultations, we failed to see the significance of the tutors' concern when they believed the myth was reasserting itself. For us, faculty development could take place over a number of semesters as teachers worked in the program and/or availed themselves of consulting services; for tutors, on the other hand, the problem felt urgent. Working in the Partnership Program episodically, sometimes for only one semester, they hoped for rapid, visible change in literacy instruction. In retrospect, the difference between our perspective and tutors' experience seems so great as to suggest that the administrators and the tutors worked in separate programs. While writing administrators expected slow change and frequent reassertions of literacy myths, tutors' frequent confrontations with those myths created a sense of emergency; the tutors, of course, had to *do something* in classrooms tomorrow or the day after, while administrators could look forward to conversations with faculty next week or next term.

While Liselle deals with that sense of emergency by asking her tutoring team for suggestions to solve the problem and Margret avoids going to class, Thom analyzes the dilemma by imagining that "[the students] think that we are experts and that we are there to evaluate them in some fashion" (e-mail, 16 September 2001). He offers, however, no evidence for this claim, nor does he suggest why the insight might be useful to the group. Each tutor, then, employs a strategy to counteract the stress of this situation; further, Liselle and Thom appear to use strategies aimed at addressing the situation in some way.

Their inability to reach a decision about what to do in response to their dilemma is particularly telling, as all of them had extensive previous experiences of interacting with students in the center who saw them as editors, and each had strategies for helping student users of the center see them as offering a wider array of support strategies for writers. In complicating students' views of tutoring, the tutors also intended to complicate students' views of writing. While Liselle and Margret would not hesitate to negotiate a shared understanding of their role with a student in the writing center, they apparently fear that such negotiation would amount to a "faux pas" in the classroom setting. In the center, the tutors excelled in part because they were perceived by students either as equals or as superiors.[2] In the Partnership Program, tutors saw themselves as called in after the "real" work of negotiating the classroom plan had already taken place; the perceived lack of control in the situation translated for tutors into a loss of agency and professional status.

The problem of tutors' feeling disempowered to assert their authority over their own role when confronted with a teacher's authority to assign that role strikes us now as predictable, but we did not consider it deeply at the time. One goal of our pre-semester consultations with faculty was to establish the kinds of work tutors would undertake in classes; this work most frequently took the form of participation in writing workshops, where tutors could circulate among peer groups to assist students by providing feedback. That this work was often changed, simplified, or reduced to skills work later by faculty indicates how entrenched a skills-based view of literacy is in the academy and how comfortable faculty are employing it.

In our effort to provide effective, efficient support for faculty, we had unwittingly made the tutors technicians, much like the carpenters who have the skill to follow a vision created by an architect, but who are rarely called upon for their opinions about the plans. While we valued their role in the classroom because they could lead workshops that demonstrated that "writing" is a term for socially meaningful practices, to be discussed and reviewed according to the goals and standards of a discipline, we did not explicitly engage tutors in a dialogue about these changes in their roles and practices. Such a dialogue could have helped tutors to describe their concerns in more detail and might have challenged us to involve them differently in consultations with faculty. In other words, foregrounding tutors' concerns might have led to long-term revisions, both in tutor training and in work with faculty.

## ROLE CONFLICT AND TEAM IDENTIFICATION

One way to encourage such dialogue is to notice and respect more fully the tutors' conversations among themselves. When the meeting space failed to yield a means for dealing with the dissonance tutors felt between their writing center training and their Partnership work, they relied on their membership in a tutoring team to help define their professional roles. Most e-mail exchanges among Liselle, Margret, and Thom end with queries about other team members' perspectives on whatever issue the group has chosen to discuss. Team members frequently praise each other, signaling their interest in being supportive ("Wow! That was a great reflection!") (Thom, e-mail, 8 November 2001) and hasten to correct any possible misimpression, even before other team members had a chance to respond in an e-mail exchange ("I am not saying that's what you meant, but I am definitely saying that I feel more comfortable, less tense, in the dominant [power role]") (Liselle, e-mail, 8 November 2001). Liselle in particular frequently asks her team members to provide information, opinions, and ideas and lets team members know she cannot do Partnership work without thoughtful, ongoing team interaction.

As evidence of their sense of responsibility to and dependence on each other, all of the tutors write in self-derogatory ways when they worry they have not lived up to their team members' expectations or fear they are about to disappoint team members in some way. For instance, Liselle writes that she is a "loser" when she cannot open a team member's attached document through her e-mail (Liselle, e-mail, 20 October 2001), Margret writes a lengthy apology one day when she is out sick, and Thom ends some transmissions with regrets that he has not handled his schedule properly and is therefore unable to write as much in his e-mail response as he would like.

These strategies for communicating with team members, establishing themselves as belonging to the team and trying to imagine the impressions other members might have of them, provide important areas for reflection and pedagogical intervention. In the problem with Professor L described earlier, when Liselle felt confused about her role in the classroom, the team might have decided to voice their concerns as a collective, either to the WAC coordinators or to the teacher. This suggestion did not arise, however, perhaps because when left to their own devices, team members who must perform activities together develop an in-group/out-group mentality, learning to rely on each other in stressful situations and to downplay outsider perspectives that challenge the team's self-concept. Goffman notes that the very act of collaborative performing requires that team members maintain an impression for their audience that they cannot maintain before one another. Because team members are "[a]ccomplices in the maintenance of a particular appearance of things, they are forced to define one another as persons 'in the know,' as persons before whom a particular front cannot be maintained" (1959, 83).

This pressure to develop and maintain a shared public "front" is inevitably part of team activities; Goffman points out that public teamwork can be viewed as a kind of performance. In managing the performance before an audience (in this case, students and teachers), team members want to avoid embarrassment and therefore often move self-consciously through unfamiliar interactions. While tutors in the writing center use questions to address gaps between the student writer's knowledge and the tutor's familiarity with genre and course expectations, in Partnership classrooms tutors did not feel as free to resort to questioning as an instructional strategy. A question in the classroom might be misread as an undermining of teacher authority or as a sign that the team lacked expertise. The pressure to avoid making a mistake multiplies when one works with others in a team effort because "[e]ach teammate is forced to rely on the good conduct and behavior of his fellows, and they, in turn, are forced to rely on him" (Goffman 1959, 82).

Another manifestation of role conflict and team negotiation we eventually noticed was tutors' negative critique of the faculty they were working with. In effect, tutors had a different orientation toward Partnership faculty than we did, often feeling as though these instructors lacked key information that would enable tutors to do their work. Though we attempted to bring the tutors into the loop by repeating the plans made between WAC administrators and faculty, our secondhand accounts about our exchanges with faculty rarely affected tutors' understanding of their own classroom roles. They had no felt personal or professional relationships with the program's teachers; those relationships seemed confined to authority figures only: WAC administrators and program faculty. Finding themselves situated outside of the conversations they most needed to enter, tutors challenged our accounts of faculty development with accounts of their own, using the evidence they had at hand to level critiques at the teachers they had been assigned to assist.

Tutors' critique of teachers and surprise at students' successes may be attributable in part to their way of working with each other, of team building. If the group begins to self-define as "in the know" about literacy, about pedagogy, or about student learning, this must contrast with those "not in the know." In other words, the dynamic of team building alters perception, providing strong reasons of mutual dependence, shared experience, and performance stress to develop and maintain a team identity that, in this case, supported particular ways of thinking about teachers and students. For example, of Professor Z, who taught in a technical field, Thom noted: "From the way that Professor Z presented the material I think that maybe the students are afraid of the grammar. I thought . . . that her understanding of writing is stock. . . . I know that our job is not to critique professors' teaching styles, but I just feel that the lack of explanation of the why's is adding to the student's apprehensions about writing."

Liselle responds by noting that she is "really concerned that I don't know anything about technical writing," identifying one possible reason for Thom's critique: fear of the course's subject matter and writing requirements.

While students in Professor Z's class developed a clearer understanding over time about ways that writing functioned in their field—to persuade others that their plans are sound, to provide instructions for those carrying out physical work, and to work through possible problems with design in advance of a project's being implemented—and while Liselle in particular would come to admire this teacher's ability to describe writing in ways that mattered in the field, working with Professor Z brought many insecurities to the fore for the tutors in our program. Tutors' own lack of expertise in technical writing made them deeply uncomfortable, and except where they reflected on the meanings of that discomfort, they moved fairly automatically to assuming that the teacher's authority gave her the power to teach badly. In the absence of crucial conversation among Partnership participants, tutors often adopted blaming and complaining strategies, which Goffman notes are predictable "defensive" behaviors arising among members of a team (1959, 174–75). "Derogation" helps team members to save face, alleviate fears, and build team solidarity. The tutors did not appear to recognize their blaming responses in this context as defenses, and the program administrators tended to see the blaming as "bad behavior" rather than as indicators that tutors—along with student writers in classes—felt "out of their depth" when faced with certain writing assignments.

The tutors' way of working together—collaboratively, through ongoing negotiation with colleagues—is, in fact, a crucial part of professional development and should be highlighted as a positive, if sometimes difficult, part of literacy work in the academy. We have no evidence, however, that tutors in our program consciously valued the team experience or saw the Partnership Program as a place where they could develop collaborative approaches to institutional difficulties. Our own wish now is that we had drawn their attention to the ways they tried to work together. While we believed in the importance of tutors' relationships to one another, we took those relationships for granted, thus missing an opportunity to review e-mail transcripts among team members in training meetings and to discuss how collaborative work (between administrators and faculty, between WPAs and tutors, and among tutors, faculty, and students) provides opportunities for negotiating *shared* authority among all team members.

## CONCLUSION

As David Russell notes in his history of writing in the American academy, "on an institutional basis, WAC exists in a structure that fundamentally resists it" (1991, 295). A WAC program that works toward real change will encounter opposition. Because we aim to educate colleagues and administrators about current literacy theory and research, we must expect to encounter significant resistance—some intentional, some the result of normalized notions of literacy as a set of skills. Our view, then, is that if the central goal of writing across the curriculum programs is faculty development, the opportunities for faculty development and support need significant overhaul. Institutional hierarchy suggests that faculty interact in particular, professional ways, but that faculty interact with students in professorial, teacherly ways. We envision a classroom-based tutoring program that combines the best of both approaches. Faculty, like the students who have learned how to be literacy workers, can benefit from immersion in a literacy curriculum prior to undertaking course reform; the best model of this would be a course in literacy theory and research for faculty, accompanied by the useful incentive of assigned time for course revision. Offering classroom-based tutoring as a support for that revision, rather than as the only available example of it, counters the view of such efforts as "service" and helps to define the tutor's significant role in this process.

A course alone will not, however, necessarily alter the traditional view of tutors as "hired help." Any program using classroom-based tutoring to further any larger WAC goal must recognize the fundamental importance of tutor training and the ways that writing center work differs from classroom-based tutoring. Our experiences suggest that the shift in tutors' roles from individual authority in one-to-one sessions to shared authority in the classroom-based program directly affects their sense of professional identity. As the tutor responses described above suggest, this change in identity can cause significant confusion and frustration, limiting tutors' ability to work effectively with faculty across the disciplines.

During our work in the Partnership Program, we often misrecognized opportunities for continued reflection and learning with and from our tutors because we were most concerned with presenting a "successful workshop." From the perspective of the faculty members and students in the Partnership classes this may not appear to be a problem, but in our minds it reiterates the view that the work tutors do is limited to a specific event or assignment. While any classroom-based tutoring program will likely experience its moments of frantic planning and frenzied preparation, periodic meta-reflection during the semester will surely provide opportunities for adjustments to be made at the level of how faculty, tutors, coordinators, and students interact.

Writing program administrators in charge of classroom-based tutoring programs must then become responsible for highlighting the difficulties and opportunities inherent in the shift from writing center to classroom-based work. Tutors' work in classroom teams provides an important site for the construction of new, more complex professional identities, identities that may enable tutors to express concerns and contribute to programmatic changes through productive critiques of class plans, tutors' roles, and training activities. Increasing tutor participation in the program in this way should provide better access to and more information about faculty perceptions of literacy instruction, thus enabling WPAs to work more effectively with faculty in WAC programs.

## 12

## "I'VE GOT NO STRINGS ON ME"
### Avoiding Marionette Theater with Peer Consultants in the Classroom

Susan Hrach Georgecink

Our writing center's first forays into classroom work began unceremoniously, without any conscious thought given to the philosophical ramifications of going "on location." A faculty member from the education department called one day during the writing center's (and my) first year on campus and asked if I might be able to send a consultant to her evening graduate class to help her students "get off on the right foot" with their research projects. At the time we had on our writing center staff a senior student who was one of the finest all-round English majors the department had seen in years. I mentioned the request to Laurie and she cheerfully accepted the assignment to visit Dr. Templeton's class.

Aside from marking the date on our calendar, I gave the project little further thought. Laurie (and the other three consultants on our staff) had been carefully trained in peer tutoring the previous spring by my compositionist colleague. In that term, Laurie had copresented a prewriting workshop at the student center in front of a large crowd and she was currently in the midst of preparing to give a paper at the 1999 National Conference on Peer Tutoring in Writing. Of her own accord, Laurie decided to demonstrate clustering to the class as a method for generating ideas. Laurie may have discussed her plan with me, but, swamped by the daily operation of the center, I didn't press her about what she planned to do. I received the following note from Nan Templeton the day after Laurie's visit:

Hello Susan,

I wanted to tell you how much we appreciated Laurie coming into my EDUF 7116 Applied Educational Research class last night. She is a knowledgeable young woman who generously shared her gifts with the class members. Laurie elicited questions easily and was fluid and cogent in her delivery. By the time her presentation ended she had given each student the opportunity to map out a topic based on the student's research.

> I know that the class members enjoyed Laurie's facilitation and benefited from her presence. They were effusive in their praise for her work. I hope we can continue to use the Writing Center as such a resource.

In the months following this first successful episode, Laurie visited another classroom to lead a similar presentation. I completely took for granted her ability to carry off such guest spots. I was pleased that we were easily able to meet special faculty requests. What I didn't realize at all was that we had experienced exceptional luck in having Laurie at our dispatch, a peer consultant with aspirations to graduate school and an academic career, and thus an eagerness for classroom experience.

The prospect of bringing peer consultants into the writing classroom holds so much promise: the consultants are excellent models for struggling students; the writing center and its director gain valuable opportunities to demonstrate and promote the kind of crucial assistance we exist to offer. Faculty outside of the English department are often grateful to call upon the "experts" to help with the difficult work of guiding students through paper writing. Nonetheless, my own experience with consultants in the classroom shows that, despite every clear advantage, it's still possible to mangle the enterprise. I'm going to offer my subsequent stories as "what not to do," but I do take comfort in Andrea Lunsford's warning that bringing collaboration to the classroom isn't the simple proposal it seems: "[W]e shouldn't fool ourselves that creating new models of authority, new spaces for students and teachers to experience nonhierarchical, shared authority, is a goal we can hope to reach in any sort of straightforward way" (2000, 71).

Lunsford's consideration of authority is central to my own critique of my efforts. I want to argue that the configuration of authority in the writing center is worth very careful examination, and, second, that we must proceed with caution and full awareness of our responsibility to consultants when bringing them into the dynamic arena of the classroom. When the administration of a writing center, even for very good reasons, usurps consultant confidence and control by choreographing classroom activities, the possibility of successful classroom-based tutoring is fundamentally undermined. Consultants become like marionettes asked to perform without betraying that the writing center administrator is holding the strings.

## DESCRIPTION OF CLASSROOM-BASED TUTORING AT COLUMBUS STATE UNIVERSITY

The writing center at Columbus State University is very new (it opened in 1999 as an initiative of the English faculty in the Department of Language and Literature), and our efforts in almost every area of operations are provisional; we are still very much finding our identity within the institution. The writing center plays no formal role within a writing program here, but serves as an undergraduate peer consulting center for student writers at every level and from any major. I choose to call our work *peer consulting* rather than *peer tutoring* because we are engaged in a critical mission here of educating faculty and students about the nature of the assistance we offer, and that terminology seems to more accurately describe what writing centers do. As a junior, tenure-track faculty member holding a partial teaching load, I am also still making an impression on my faculty colleagues and administrators. I inherited two major advantages at the time I was hired to direct the writing center: the conditional goodwill of my colleagues, who had long been troubled by a lack of resources for student writers, and the guarantee of being able to train new consultants annually in a semester-long course of my design, ENGL 3256, Peer Writing Consultation. Only students who earn an A or B in Peer Writing Consultation are eligible to become paid consultants in the writing center.

Workshops and conference presentations, undertaken as part of students' course work, have formed the main basis for consultants' preparation as classroom-based tutors. In Peer Writing Consultation, I introduce students to the composition theory from which the writing center movement has grown, as well as the interpersonal aspects of consulting, working with nonnative English speakers, working with basic writers, working with assignments from across the curriculum, and consulting via e-mail. Mandatory internship hours in the writing center are spent observing, role-playing, and consulting "for real." We keep journals, produce handouts for the center, write papers, and conduct generalized workshops, sometimes for very small audiences and sometimes in first-year composition classrooms. Adapting their research projects as panel proposals, students have presented papers at two major writing center conferences. For both on-campus workshop presentations and conference panels, choosing topics and methods of delivery are integral aspects of the students' work. The development of a group presentation assists tutors in training to more thoroughly understand the principles they are encountering in the course; they are teaching to learn. Secondarily, such workshops help us to promote awareness of the writing center, especially among first-year students. Coming directly to the classroom guarantees us an audience; English faculty are generally solicited by consultants in training to promote or host workshops as gestures of support for our apprentice consultants.

## DIFFERENT SCENARIOS, DIFFERENT OUTCOMES

We had two things working in our favor at the time of our initial class-room-based tutoring foray, neither of which I understood because Laurie's classroom visits had gone well. The first was that Nan Templeton had done the necessary work prior to Laurie's visit of creating a col-laborative classroom climate, one that accommodated shared authority among Nan, her students, and a peer consultant. Instructors who invite writing center consultants to participate in their classrooms generally do value collaborative learning, but we cannot always assume that this com-mon value exists. Nor can we assume that students in any given class are prepared to embrace the authority of anyone other than the instructor of that course. Although an instructor may invite peer consultants to the classroom as part of a continuing effort to extend authority to his or her students and to encourage them to accept it, students sometimes resist the active role that collaboration demands of them because they have little experience in shouldering responsibility for their own learn-ing. "Creating a collaborative environment and truly collaborative tasks is damnably difficult," Lunsford has observed, for reasons far beyond student resistance (1995, 39). The cultural and social weight of institu-tionalized education accounts for much of the difficulty we encounter in striving to create collaborative classroom environments. Institutionalized education thwarts our efforts to share authority in others ways as well: the spaces in which we work usually reinforce a centralized notion of class-room authority (desks rather than tables, seats facing in one direction), the length of the academic term sometimes cuts short the time we need to invest in collaborative relationships, and we are challenged to assign individual grades for shared effort (Lunsford 2000, 75–76). It's a tribute to our committed resolve that we attempt it at all.

The second factor working in our favor at the time of these first class-room ventures was that I was too busy to micromanage Laurie's visit, which left her entirely in control of the material she wanted to share with the class. Not only did Laurie choose an appropriate activity, she wel-comed the opportunity to stand in front of a graduate class and introduce clustering to these students. Laurie's appearance in class that evening was comfortable for her, and it was comfortable for Nan and for Nan's stu-dents. While the class accepted Laurie's bid for authority within that set-ting, her role as presenter did not ask them to radically revise their expec-tations about how learning takes place. She apprehended the theatrical conditions of the classroom and adapted them to her purpose. She commanded the attention of the class; she "elicited questions easily and was fluid and cogent in her delivery." In short, Laurie performed well.

In my second year, two colleagues separately approached me with requests to involve the writing center in their classes; each instructor was looking for a new way to help students through the arduous process of research assignments. Neither instructor had a predetermined idea of what shape the collaboration would take; both were already teaching the research assignment very carefully and with impressive attention to students' needs. On the whole, however, the situations differed greatly: the first class was a junior-level family communications course; the second was a second-semester first-year composition course. The family communications research assignment required students to produce a formalized literature review; the composition course asked students to produce a documented research essay related to literary texts. My reaction to both requests was to confidently suggest classroom-based tutoring. Privately, I imagined that I could expeditiously plan these activities without conferring with the consultants and count on my crack staff to carry them out. The enterprise would be thus largely under my control.

Communications professor Dr. Lang met with me ahead of time at his request and talked about what particular difficulties his students usually had and what kind of classroom activities might meet their needs. We settled on a small-group workshop that would take place after Dr. Lang's students had located secondary materials but before they had written a full first draft. We would address their problems with organization by suggesting techniques for "mapping" the literature review and then follow up our session with a special invitation to bring rough drafts to the writing center for consultation. I did not negotiate any details of this plan with the peer consultants.

I designed a handout/instruction sheet for the workshop and, as a last step, I asked my entire staff of eight to participate in the event. The evening of the workshop, our staff met for half an hour before the class and I ran through the handout with the consultants. I would demonstrate the exercise in front of the whole class first, I explained, and then they would each lead a group of four or five through the exercise described on the handouts. Primarily, their role was to watch and encourage the members of their peer groups as the students "mapped out" the main ideas and supporting materials for their projects. The workshop was a modification of a clustering exercise that I thought reflected the specific vocabulary and conventions of the literature review assignment. I assumed that once I'd explained it to the consultants, no special practice would be required, although none of them (to my knowledge) had ever actually composed a literature review. They were available to monitor the activity, more or less, so I considered the task to be rather straightforward. "The only reason I felt comfortable knowing what we were doing," one consultant confided in retrospect, "was that we had watched Laurie doing something similar as part of our tutor-training class." Though the consultants seemed unusually quiet and anxious, I let them know before we left to walk over to the classroom that I had total confidence in their ability to carry off the workshop.

The room where this survey course met was a midsize auditorium; the students were accustomed to sitting in seats that clearly designated them as the audience of their professor. While Dr. Lang, my very student-focused colleague, had evidently created a classroom atmosphere that reflected informality and approachability (he stood not on the platform, behind a lectern, but on the ground floor and to the side when opening the class meeting), the room itself was intimidating. Not only would it make gathering in small groups a physical challenge, but also its very size contrasted sharply with our intimate writing center surroundings. The seats were half full at best in this auditorium classroom, a factor that seemed only to emphasize the cavernous space. I wondered if class attendance was significantly down for the night and felt slightly defensive on behalf of my consultants and the writing center.

By the time I had been introduced and took to the platform (where the chalkboard was located, center stage), I was determined to win over any skeptics in the room and to launch the workshop with a compelling presentation. I actively solicited input from the students during my demonstration of our exercise. I marshaled all of my energy and enthusiasm toward convincing them that the services of the writing center and its staff were the solution to their research paper woes.

Because we wanted to keep the group size to fewer than six students, when we divided up the class, I jumped in to work as a consultant with one group. While I prodded the members of that group to think through how the materials they had collected related to their topics and to explain to me how they were creating their organizational clusters, I worried about how the other groups were doing. Eventually, I eased away from my on-task students and wandered around the room a bit. Some of the groups were engaged in lively conversations about their topics and their struggles with research; others, however, had clearly given up on the exercise altogether and were killing time with gossip or were simply staring at the ceiling. I ambled over to a couple of bored-looking groups and asked how their work was progressing; everyone was feeling "fine" and apparently completely satisfied with the amount of effort they'd put into the exercise. The consultants who were leading these groups looked slightly pained.

Before his class was dismissed, Dr. Lang asked for any immediate commentary from them about the usefulness of the exercise. One student raised her hand and spoke earnestly about how much better she now felt about the direction of her review; another student seconded her praise of the workshop. Several other heads nodded in support of our work while the majority of students sat quietly. I announced our hours and the location of the writing center and encouraged the students to bring us their drafts in the next few weeks as they worked.

I thanked my staff profusely as we left the building that night, feeling strangely that somehow I'd betrayed them or that I needed to boost their self-confidence even more than had been necessary before we entered the classroom. Over the next week or two in the writing center, we saw one student from the class for multiple sessions, but in general almost no one from this large class came for a follow-up session. Dr. Lang and I suspected that our lack of evening hours at the center might have been the reason. We were both disappointed that the kind of ongoing student collaboration we'd hoped for did not materialize. The consultants expressed a similar disappointment: "I really wish we could have read a few of those papers," one of them related, "or found out whether or not the papers were any better because of our help."

If leading a large upper-level class through a small-group workshop presented certain challenges, I could comfort myself that my next scheduled writing center adventure was a simple "Laurie-style" repeat performance. I was bringing two of my strongest consultants, one at a time, to different sections of an English colleague's first-year composition course. I reworked our clustering handout and explained to the tutors that all they'd need to do was stand in front of the class, read through the handout step-by-step, and draw sample clustering circles and lines on an overhead projector. Their role in the classroom was not only to offer useful help, but also to put a friendly face on the writing center and thereby encourage students from the class to come visit us on future occasions. They seemed willing but scared. I promised I'd be there for moral support.

At both classroom appearances, I was completely surprised by how suddenly artificial and stiff the consultant became as my colleague Dr. Cooper, and then I, relinquished control of the "front and center" space. In each case, the consultant was visibly nervous but working very hard to overcome her stage fright. The students were cooperative and followed the exercise determinedly; while Dr. Cooper remained seated to the front side of the room, I made awkward forays up and down the rows of seats and watched as students scribbled assiduously on their pieces of notebook paper. My movement about the room was hampered by overcrowded rows of desks; the classroom was at full capacity. I was impressed, however, by the work I could see going on; the students had obviously been convinced by Dr. Cooper in advance that the consultant from the writing center would have something valuable to offer them. In each case, though, the person who still needed convincing that something valuable was happening in the room was the peer consultant. After these classes ended, I was effusive in my praise and reassured each consultant that the workshop had gone quite according to plan and that she had done a good job. "I wasn't really nervous," insisted one of these consultants a month or so afterward. "I just wasn't exactly sure what you wanted."

## SORTING IT ALL OUT

This series of classroom visits was not entirely unsuccessful, but something about the experience of performing them troubled me. My first thought was that the physical limitations of the classroom spaces were to blame. I also considered attributing the problem to the lack of time I had allotted for the consultants to practice the exercises. But I knew that the actual classroom activities had been carefully planned, and the more I fretted over my workshop designs, the clearer it became that the tight control I had maintained over them constituted my real mistake.

My introductory demonstration in the upper-level auditorium class backfired, for instance, because my zeal to win over the students focused the students' attention on my own performance, making it more difficult to then diffuse that energy and authority among the tutors and the students at large. My presence at the first-year composition classes, although well intentioned, only put pressure on the consultant and probably confused the students, who may have wondered why they were under the surveillance of the writing center director. Lost was the principle behind all of these appearances—consultants working as models and as advocates for student-centered learning.

The roots of the problem were twofold: I had asked the consultants to lead classroom-based workshops without eliciting from them either a wish to conduct the workshops or a chance to become comfortable with that role. I hadn't allowed the consultants to come up with their own workshop ideas: I had control over the handouts, the structure of the class meetings, and the methods of delivery. They were performing like marionettes for me with no (visible) strings. Naturally, there was anxiety about that performance. If I had allowed enough time prior to our class appearances for the consultants to practice my own preplanned activities, that would have helped. But empowering the consultants to design the workshops would have critically shifted that balance of authority for the whole enterprise. I have no doubt that they would have designed better and more creative workshops than mine, too.

Further, I needed to look at the reasons for my wish to control, especially my desire to promote writing centers in the eyes of the institution. For new writing centers like mine, whose credibility and status within the university are vulnerable, the prospect of sharing responsibility for public duties (outside of the writing center) with fledgling undergraduate tutors can be worrisome. My reputation and the reputation of my staff were on the line, as I saw it, in the eyes of important audiences.

At issue, too, was the need to promote collegiality between tutors and teachers, as Laurie and Dr. Templeton had exemplified. Laurie's relationship as a tutor with the classroom instructor was largely unmediated; I was not even present for the workshop. As Carol Peterson Haviland et al. have written about the ideal relationship between disciplinary faculty and writing center tutors: "Tutors need disciplinary faculty to reimagine the tutor-professor relationship as that of coinquirers, to expect to learn as well as to teach, to risk not knowing everything in front of a student, even a graduate student. Also, tutors need disciplinary faculty to model this regard to students; when they show students that they see tutors not as handmaidens but as collaborators, students will be more likely to follow their lead" (1999, 55).

Nan Templeton modeled this ideal in the very act of requesting an undergraduate peer consultant to visit her graduate classroom. When Laurie arrived, material solely and authoritatively under her own control, the collegial work of coinquiry could begin. Such a model was likewise possible in the later classroom-based tutoring events, but my interference in the program prevented this collaboration from becoming fully realized. Consultants must be able to perform this work with autonomy.

What I'm advocating here is a model of collaboration between director as trainer and consultants in order to foster consultants' autonomy. How can directors expect to serve as trainers/teachers/supervisors *and* collaborators on an equal footing with student consultants? The transition from teacher/trainer to collegial collaborator involves predictable and continual movement back and forth. Tutors in training need directors to guide them in traditionally authoritative ways as they begin their apprenticeships in the writing center. James S. Baumlin and Margaret E. Weaver use psychoanalytic theory to describe the process of relieving students from their dependency on a teacher/trainer's sole authority and inviting them to seek sources of knowledge among themselves: "Transference—students' projections of trust and authority onto their teachers—is an important, even necessary facilitator of learning, but most effective only so long as teachers remain themselves unseduced; teachers must ultimately repudiate the role of inviolate authority and refuse to remain, in Lacanian terms, the 'subject supposed to know'" (2000, 82). Conducting the training period within a conventional for-credit course framework does not mean impeding future collaborative relationships, but it does mean that the teacher/trainer must plan for that relationship to change.

The director should be providing a model of collaboration that tutors can use as they work with directors, classroom teachers, and other students. When consultants-to-be collaborate on serious projects (writing research papers, designing workshops), they learn that negotiation and the shared construction of knowledge are prized values at the writing center. Allowing them to watch or participate with experienced consultants working in classrooms and offering them the chance to practice on-location consulting enables them "to achieve their own knowledge and become their own authorities" (Baumlin and Weaver 2000, 77).

Ultimately, we must keep our responsibility to tutors squarely in mind when preparing to work in the classroom. Directors should be sensitive to tutors' own maturation as learners. We should explicitly examine with them the subjects of collaborative learning and peer tutoring in the writing center and shared authority in the classroom; we can offer them opportunities to reflect on their own development as thinkers and as writers in the academic community. We must be particularly wary of placing tutors in positions of authority for which they are not developmentally ready or adequately prepared; we must consider whether they will be fairly compensated for duties beyond their normal repertoire of writing center skills. Although they may seem of pressing importance, the needs of the classroom students, the interests of the writing center director, and the satisfaction of the classroom instructor must be of secondary concern.

The dynamics of classroom authority are complicated even before we bring consultants onto the scene; my suspicion is that going on location will never work in the ideal (or even effortless) ways we might imagine. Given that we can't reasonably expect things to work smoothly, however, there are good reasons why bringing consultants to the classroom is still worth trying. I do believe that the presence of experienced writers demonstrating an enthusiasm for writing and an interest in other students' academic work can have a profound impact in the classroom. I believe that bringing consultants on location is an excellent way to establish and maintain positive relationships between the writing center and faculty across the curriculum; we deserve the support of many allies on campus. I don't plan to give up on visiting the classroom, but I am resolved to make these events truly collaborative and that will mean allowing my peer consultants to help decide when, where, why, and on what terms we will do it.

## 13

# RECONSTRUCTING AUTHORITY
## Negotiating Power in Democratic Learning Sites

Candace Spigelman

I am greatly attracted to peer relationships in the teaching of writing: I used writing groups in my composition classes before they were popular, I directed a learning center where knowledgeable peers offered various kinds of writing assistance, and several years ago I introduced classroom mentors into my basic writing classes. One reason that I emphasize peer-ship activities has to do with my own discomfort with too much classroom authority. Yet I appear to be in good company, for as Susan M. Hubbuch points out, academics in general and writing instructors in particular tend to feel guilty about assuming power, which to all of us "smells of coercion" (1989–90, 35). Rather, we want to empower our students, often by way of collaborative, community-fostering activities. Furthermore, our knowledge of the history of rhetoric as social action and the cultural critical turn in composition have encouraged writing teachers to model more democratic activities in hopes of training students for participatory democracy. We want to resist authoritarian classroom arrangements because we want students to be active in their education and in their lives. We see that peer relationships are, in Kenneth Bruffee's words, a "powerful educative force" (1984, 638), a force recognized by John Dewey in the general education of children and espoused by compositionists representing a range of pedagogical and political perspectives, including Bruffee, Peter Elbow (1973; 1980), Stephen Fishman and Lucille Parkinson McCarthy (1992), Andrea Lunsford and Lise Ede (1990), John Trimbur (1989, 1998), and Greg Myers (1986).

But what is actually demanded of us or expected of our students when we attempt to decenter the university classroom? Can we truly shed the mantle of authority? According to Hubbuch, instructional authority is necessary for students' academic achievement: students depend on understanding particular teachers' expectations in order to fulfill their roles as learners. When we frustrate or constrain students' dependency role by asking them to share our authority, we tip both the cognitive and the psychological scales, which, ironically, may "render the student incapable of learning . . . [and] render the student powerless" (1989/–90, 40). In a similar vein, Russel K. Durst (1999) addresses the pragmatic needs and expectations of many students attending college today and examines the conflicts that ensue because composition's cultural studies focus often appears at odds with these expectations. In Durst's view, most students want their teachers to assume central authority in the classroom. Furthermore, Lad Tobin (1993) argues that our decentering efforts and methods may exacerbate, rather than resolve, power imbalances by driving them underground. In democratic classroom settings, competition for grades and instructor approval remain unacknowledged forces, which ultimately sustain teacher power. Andrea Lunsford (2000) observes that students usually expect instructors to enact exclusionary, individualistic, judgmental forms of control, and may actively resist less oppressive instructional methods. Recognizing the historical, social, and cultural forces that support traditional views of classroom relationships, Lunsford states: "We shouldn't fool ourselves that creating new models of authority, new spaces for students and teachers to experience nonhierarchical, shared authority, is a goal we can hope to reach in any sort of straightforward way" (71). Indeed, college writing teachers often find that even more circuitous efforts to refigure authority are confounded.

In this chapter, I want to add another layer to the already complicated problem of power relations in democratic classrooms. I will describe my efforts to develop a "new model of authority, a new space," using classroom-based writing tutors as peer group leaders. In the discussion that follows, I will draw upon learning center theory to account for the student mentors' positionings within their groups, their group members' constructions of their authority, and their conflicted status in the seminar class they took with me. I will show that in these democratic classroom settings, power was repeatedly resisted, negotiated, and recentered among students in both groups and between the tutors and me. I will argue that, like traditional models, our newer practices are subject to institutional figurations that continue to concentrate power in teachers and limit students' authority at every level and instructional site. Thus, together with their students, writing teachers must continue to critique and interrogate each new effort to achieve shared authority even as they create more circuitous paths.

## PEER GROUP LEADERS AND BASIC WRITERS

With support from Penn State University's Center on Excellence in Learning and Teaching, I created a set of linked courses, intended to promote peer collaboration in a basic writing class while introducing prospective primary and secondary teachers to writing theory and practice. I had always used peer writing groups, and I believed they served an important function for developing writers, as they did for published writers in various arenas. But even though I carefully orchestrated my classroom writing groups, I recognized the limits of peer group activity: oftentimes, inexperience with group work, insecurity about their own writing skills, or social concerns constrain basic writers' active participation (for analyses of peer writing group problems, see, among others, Spear 1988; Brooke, Mirtz, and Evans 1994b; Roskelly 1999; Berkenkotter 1984; Leverenz 1994; Goodburn and Ina 1994; Spigelman 2000). My first peer group leaders seminar placed five specially selected sophomore education majors in a section of basic writing that I was teaching. During class time each Friday, these classroom-based writing tutors joined the same group of three to four developmental writers to discuss their essay drafts and also to discuss topics or readings relevant to their writing. In addition, they met with me weekly for a seventy-five-minute seminar, in which they learned to facilitate workshops and to conduct group-tutoring sessions. In the seminar, they also assessed their weekly writing group's progress, problem solved, and planned strategies for upcoming group meetings.[1] By introducing peer mentors into my basic writing class, I hoped that my developmental writers would benefit from a more student-centered classroom environment, where textual authority was vested in the student writers and their readers, rather than in me as the writing instructor.

One of the great ironies of democratic classrooms, however, is that few are genuinely student governed. In my basic writing class, writing group participation was a requirement of the course; likewise, I determined the composition of the groups based on my assessment of students' writing abilities.[2] Anne Ruggles Gere points out the decisive difference between autonomous self-sponsored groups that meet outside of schools and those arranged by classroom instructors: members of self-sponsored writing groups have personal motivation for sharing their writing with others; moreover, the writing group exchange is a dialectical process predicated on mutual respect and individual autonomy (1987, 50). In contrast, classroom writing groups may achieve semiautonomy at best, but "the institutional origins of authority prevent them from becoming completely autonomous" (4). In my class, I orchestrated group work, included peer group leaders, constructed discussion topics, and ultimately graded students' performance.

Despite these inconsistencies, I believed that the students in my basic writing class would respond actively and enthusiastically to their group leaders as knowledgeable peers. Developments in classroom-based tutoring helped me to theorize the project, for peer group leaders seem to combine the merits of writing center tutoring and peer group work: in writing centers, peer tutoring is understood to hold advantages for both tutee and tutor; in college classrooms, writing group theory emphasizes active learning and the collaborative construction of knowledge. Although classroom-based tutors are a more recent adaptation, as early as 1984, Kenneth Bruffee united peer response groups and peer tutoring as two subsets of "collaborative learning." In both "Collaborative Learning and the 'Conversation of Mankind'" (1984) and "Peer Tutoring and the 'Conversation of Mankind'" (1998), Bruffee argued for the value of student-centered, cooperative writing activities, stressing that when students collaboratively problem solve about issues relating to writing, they actively contribute to their own learning and to the learning of fellow students.

I also took direction from existing models of classroom-based writing tutoring. At CUNY, for example, writing center tutors attached to first-year writing courses fulfilled a variety of functions, from reading ungraded papers to participating in classroom activities, including occasional peer group meetings (Soliday 1995). At Ohio State, students taking an upper-level course in writing theory and practice were paired with basic writing peer groups, meeting weekly outside of regular class times (for an expanded discussion of this program, see chapter 8 in the present volume by Melissa Nicolas). In my colleague Laurie Grobman's classes, one or two advanced writing students served as roaming peer group assistants during regular class meetings. They contributed to invention and revising activities and to discussions of assigned readings and also functioned as facilitators for weekly online response workshops. As Grobman explains in chapter 3, her project challenged Muriel Harris's distinction between the tutor's primarily global response, focused on helping students to become better writers, and the peer group's more immediate attention to the specific draft at hand. Grobman asserts that the goal of the tutor and of the peer group members is ultimately the same: to improve each participant's writing abilities and understanding of writing principles.

In both my peer group leaders seminar and my basic writing classes, I tried to foster collaboration, shared knowledge, shared textual ownership, and nonhierarchical leadership by modeling these attitudes and behaviors in my own give-and-take with students in both settings. But I found my efforts repeatedly foiled by the expectations of the students themselves. On every level, when I tried to dismantle authority, students reconstructed it, and in similar fashion, the peer group leaders, Allison, Kathy, Anne, Tim, and Casey,[3] found themselves faced with conflicting role definitions in the peer groups and in the seminar.

## PEER GROUP LEADERS ASSUME AUTHORITY

Because their seminar classes stressed democratic approaches to group mentoring, encouraging student collegiality and emphasizing the social features of invention and other meaning-making activities, the peer group leaders had every expectation of integrating themselves into their groups. However, as they began meeting regularly with their group members, the tutors seemed unable to evade their sense of responsibility for their group's organization and processes. In order to promote peer response and to encourage the basic writers to revise based on their peers' suggestions, for example, they found themselves wanting to create specific policies, and they started to modify the group response procedures we had established together in order to fit the needs of their own groups. Anne instructed her students to offer one positive and one negative comment about the draft before engaging in deeper discussion of the content; Kathy designed a check sheet with four questions about the form and content of each essay; both Allison and Casey asked each writer to briefly summarize his or her essay or to state its central point before reading aloud to the group; and Tim told his group members to put their responses in writing before discussing them. Notably, their basic writing students willingly complied.

Why was this the case? Why did the peer group leaders feel compelled to assume responsibility for the structure and progress of their groups, even though I explicitly encouraged a different model of engagement? Investigating the politics inherent in curriculum-based tutoring programs, Harvey Kail and John Trimbur (1987) argue that assigning tutors to classrooms perpetuates a hierarchical transmission-reception model of learning, since the tutor first and foremost represents the instructor and the institution. Unlike tutors in writing centers, who experience with their tutees the social processes of colearning and knowledge making and who are able to detach themselves from the influence and authority of teachers, curriculum-based tutors (which would include peer group leaders) and their students remain tied to institutional power and approval for their learning. The difference, as Kail and Trimbur see it, is that in the learning center setting students are more able to reflect on their "shared status as undergraduates" and to confront—and ultimately to resist—the ways they have been shaped by institutional structures of authority in favor of their own active learning. In contrast, they say, curriculum-based models encourage the dissemination of teacher-generated knowledge, and, as a result, tutors and tutees alike fail to confront the necessary "crises of authority" that will enable them to recognize themselves as cocreators of knowledge (11–12). Building on Kail and Trimbur's theory, Dave Healy argues that writing center tutors are less likely to experience conflicts of allegiance, since their work is predicated on physical and theoretical semiautonomy from classroom power bases and evaluative structures. In contrast, "heightened role conflict " is a significant outcome of curriculum-based tutoring, since curriculum-based tutors must struggle with allegiance to their instructor, "with a responsibility to espouse his/her party line," or to the principles and practices of peer collaboration derived from their training in writing centers (1993, 23).[4]

In Nancy Maloney Grimm's (1999) view, authority inheres hegemonically in the tutoring role. Invoking Louis Althusser's metaphor, Grimm argues that in writing centers, tutors are "hailed" as institutional representatives of white, middle-class cultural values. Internalizing and projecting these norms, tutors sustain the regulatory role of educational discourse in the United States by representing a single, privileged set of literacy practices. When tutors assume that tutees will benefit by imitating the discourse of the dominant culture, they enact instructional roles that bespeak their affiliation with the institution, rather than its diverse array of students and discourses, and their motivations, no matter how lofty, reproduce their tutees as deficient and Other.

Although these theorists are concerned with one-to-one tutoring situations, their critiques are also relevant to peer group leadership in classrooms, underscoring as they do the ubiquity of institutional power arrangements and their alliance with literacy practices at every level. Following their lines of thinking, we could agree that the peer group leaders' seminar and their status as outsiders in the basic writing class "remove[d the] tutors from the student community by installing them a power station or two above their peers, a step away from student culture, a step closer to the faculty" (Kail and Trimbur 1987, 8). Certainly, the classroom-based tutors took an active leadership role in the peer groups, circumscribing the group's process of text exchange and response. They did so in part because the groups seemed to them too amorphous or nonproductive or out of control, and they did indeed feel empowered, by virtue of their view of their role and the expectations of the writing group members. But their authority was more complicated than first meets the eye, since, ultimately, the success of their leadership hinged on their peer relationships within their groups.

## PEER GROUP LEADERS DEFLECT AUTHORITY

Early on, the peer group leaders discovered that if the groups were to function collaboratively, mentors would need to attempt to deflect authority, to guard against being cast in the instructional role noted in Healy's (1993) and Kail and Trimbur's (1987) critique, as opposed to the role of "knowledgeable peer." When group members viewed their leader as "the teacher," they became passive or resistant, they required more and more prompting to respond to each other's essays, and they quickly learned to take advice from the tutor alone instead of seeking feedback from other group members. In contrast, the groups that revealed the greatest collaboration and enthusiasm for writing were those that sustained more nonauthoritarian, nonhierarchical peer arrangements in the face of pressures to establish tutor-led sessions.

For example, although Casey had instituted procedural changes for reading drafts, she found that she could decenter power by fostering a sense of shared responsibility among members. In her journal, she wrote, "My peer group members wanted to transfer all the authority to me. In order to stay away from this role and give responsibility back to the students . . . , I simply accepted every member's initial suggestions and then pushed them to clarify and develop their ideas and suggestions in the workshop." She also asked group members to write comments for each draft, noting that as written responses, "individual feedback was valued because everyone had something to say, and each member's opinion seemed to be valued more because it was personal, not just an extension of someone else's idea" (see chapter 5 in this volume).

Some of the peer group leaders worked to build a feeling of camaraderie and friendship between themselves and their group members. Allison, whose group seemed always engaged and whose members showed notice-able growth in their writing skill, described her experiences this way: "With my peer group, I began by trying to seem like someone they didn't have to be afraid of. I made myself a peer instead of a teacher figure." Indeed, Allison was a peer: she lived in the same residence hall as two of her group members; she was sometimes moody or tired; but she was also extremely interested in her peer group's writing, meeting on her own time with students who needed help and always offering words of encouragement.

Kathy too cast herself in the role of friend and peer as she worked to build a relationship with and among the group members. She allowed conversations to stray "off task"; she encouraged joking, including playful comments about each other's writing; and she openly discussed her dif-ficulties in passing her anatomy course. At one point, when she wanted to try a new response technique, she appealed to her group as fellow students: she asked them to do it as a favor, to help her get a good grade although, in truth, her grade was not contingent on their completing the activity. On the last day of class, the group invited Kathy to join them for lunch at the local Pizza Hut, in her view a sign that they had accepted her as their friend. In her journal, Kathy connected her group's high level of comfort with their "shared authority." Quoting from Wendy Bishop, she noted her group's "'strong group identity and sense of shared communi-ty' (1988, 122)," and she characterized her group's dynamic as "balanced and comfortable." To Kathy, this comfort was bound up with their trust in her as a fellow student as well as their trust in her leadership. She wrote, "I think they trust me much more now than they did when we started this project. I try to only use my authority when I feel that they are not work-ing up to their full potential."

Yet Kathy's comments also dramatize the irony of the tutors' efforts to deflect power. When Kathy admitted to asking her group members for help she really didn't need and invoking her authority at critical moments, she revealed the unacknowledged tension between her view of herself as a trustworthy group member and her restrained but inevitable authority within the group. Likewise, when Casey described herself "giving respon-sibility back" by "pushing" her group members to elaborate, and when Allison "made herself a peer," they were illustrating Lunsford's caution that "collaboration often masquerades as democracy when it in fact prac-tices the same old authoritarian control" (1995, 37). In Lunsford's view, truly collaborative tutoring, like truly collaborative classrooms, is based on social constructionist theories of knowledge making, so that "power and control [are] constantly negotiated and shared" (41). In our seminars, we had emphasized social acts of invention coupled with negotiation of group authority, and it was this approach to tutoring that most of the peer group leaders tried to enact in their workshops. Ultimately, however, embedded in every gesture to *share* authority was a gesture *of* authority.

According to Grimm, writing center tutors will often "respond to institutional hailing by readily assuming the positions constructed by the institution" (1999, 70). Likewise, the peer group leaders' subject position (and, Grimm would say, "subjected" position) in their peer groups seemed to be elective, natural, and normal; they seemed to be choosing to become insiders in the basic writing class in order to limit the authority they exercised, when, in fact, they continued to exercise their (limited) authority. Moreover, their power as students and tutors was actually quite illusory and complicated, being inescapably bound up with the educational discourse(s) that regulate the conscious and unconscious desires of teachers, tutors, and students.

## PEER GROUP LEADERS' CONSTRUCTIONS OF AUTHORITY

As I have tried to suggest, the peer group leaders worked to sustain their peer memberships within their groups not only because my seminar classes continually rehearsed this perspective but also because they saw positive results when the groups operated more democratically. However, these efforts often conflicted with their own preconceptions about classroom authority (as well as with their group members' preconceptions, which I will discuss below).

Thus, despite my reassurances throughout the semester, Kathy, who had characterized her group role as that of a trustworthy friend, felt that she was not handling her group's process effectively, and she repeatedly mentioned not "feeling like a teacher." Kathy believed that effective teachers were autonomous, authoritative, and directive, although she had experienced democratic instructional methods in her own college classes. As a result, she deemed her peer-oriented approach to peer group leadership a shortcoming. She remarked often that she was "not good at motivating" and that she was "not good at being the 'person in charge.'" Early in the semester, she described herself feeling like "an inexperienced substitute teacher because I usually let them take control of me." Only once, when three members were absent and she had worked one-to-one with the remaining student, did she assert that she "felt like a teacher for the first time." In one sense, we might say that the peer group leaders harbored ideas about tutoring characterized by Lunsford as the "Storehouse" and "Garret" models (1995; for application of these terms to composition theory, see Brodkey 1987; Lunsford, 1992). When they talked about "being in charge," they were conjuring writing centers (or previous classroom experiences) where tutors (or teachers) "possess" knowledge or have access to knowledge from external sources, situations where tutors remain in control of the teaching and learning. When they talked about "being good at motivating," they were conjuring instructional support where knowledge, residing "within" the waiting tutee, is drawn into consciousness by the skillful tutor (or teacher) (Lunsford 1995, 38–40).

Of all the student mentors, Anne had the greatest difficulty mediating the tension between her various roles. Like Kathy, Anne held as sacred the teacher's authority; she believed that teachers should transmit knowledge to eager and compliant students. Prior to becoming part of the peer group leaders seminar, Anne had little experience and almost no personal contact with weaker academic achievers, and she repeatedly marveled at her writing group's failure to "appreciate" their opportunities to revise their work and their reluctance to make the suggested changes to their drafts. In her log, she remarked, "Personally, I don't think they realize how important it is for all of them to be there when we peer edit. It boggles my mind that they wouldn't want to take advantage of this, but that's just me. Their attitudes toward the class are a lot different than mine." In addition to what Anne noted as a marked contrast between her group's "work ethic" and her own, gender issues seemed to be more pronounced in her all-male group than in the others.

The conflict between roles and Anne's desire to assume a more instrumental teacher role were reflected in her comments: "Sometimes I feel like I'm showing too much leadership by always having to address questions about their papers. On the other hand, there are some days where I feel like I'm not showing enough leadership or any for that matter. I can't seem to find a happy medium. . . . I realize that the group sessions will never go as *perfectly* as I would like them to" (emphasis added). Quoting Vidya Singh-Gupta and Eileen Troutt-Ervin in her final project, "Why Groups Fail," Anne observed that "'one group leader cannot play all roles effectively, and in well-functioning groups, roles need to be shared so that tasks are accomplished efficiently within a warm group climate' (1996, 132). Because I carried the label of Peer Group Leader, all of the roles that are needed in a successful group were placed on me." I would argue that consistent with her notions of institutional hierarchy and instructional authority, themselves consistent with her cultural values, Anne identified with the role of teacher, rather than peer group member, and could not find a way to imagine an alternative role for herself throughout the semester.

Other compositionists who have used classroom-based tutoring models have likewise noted inherent conflicts among the various roles mentors are asked to assume. In a conference talk anticipating her chapter in this volume, Nicolas describes her experiences at Ohio State, where the upper-division theory course for tutors emphasized long-range, one-to-one support, while the peer response groups that the tutors worked with needed immediate feedback for short-term revision (1999). In this, her initial endeavor into classroom-based writing tutoring, Nicolas found the classroom tutors in her Ohio State study were not necessarily adept at facilitating peer groups and were caught between their desire to function as peers, whose suggestions were part of a body of feedback, and their more familiar teacher/tutor function of offering specific, valued commentary. This confusion of roles led to frustration for both tutors and students, and for this reason, Nicolas believed the project to be at cross-purposes.

In her study at CUNY, Soliday (1995) found that in many classrooms, instructors had difficulty defining their tutors' roles and gave them little or no responsibility for classroom activities. These classroom tutors characterized themselves as "outsiders" and, unsurprisingly, had few students who sought them out for supplementary tutoring in the writing center. In contrast, tutors who worked continually with the teacher to define and extend their classroom participation engaged in greater numbers of peer tutoring appointments. Noting the necessary tension between learning center and teacher-based roles, Soliday believes her most successful tutors "assimilated into classroom culture without losing a sense of their difference" (69). Although Nicolas and Soliday come to opposing conclusions about the degree of integration possible for tutors in writing classrooms,[5] both recognize role conflict as an inevitable feature of such programs.

Notably, in "'Peer Tutoring': A Contradiction in Terms?" Trimbur (1998) argues that the categories "peer" and "tutor" are logically contradictory: the moment a student tutor is recognized as more knowledgeable than the tutees seeking assistance, he or she loses "peer" status. As a result, tutors are naturally caught within a conflict in loyalties to fellow students, on the one hand, and to "the academic hierarchy" that recognizes them as equals on the other (118–20). When tutor training places tutors in the role of "apprentices," Trimbur argues, they never learn to affiliate with their peers as shared learners and become, instead, junior writing teachers.

From a sociocultural perspective, Grimm (1999) explains that the ubiquitous, regulatory role of literacy practices produces for writing center workers "psychic conflict" by sustaining traditional views of tutors and learners in the face of alternative scripts and experiences. Written into the discourses that define teachers, tutors, and students are tacit assumptions about what counts as knowledge. As a central literacy practice, composition is enmeshed in its own contradictory gatekeeping and emancipatory functions, a system of sustaining traditional power relations by perpetuating a particular construction of literacy achievement. Writing tutors are likewise implicated: believing that they have chosen a particular set of literacy practices, they unconsciously advance their singular perspectives. When tutors pretend this is not the case by denying their own social constructions, or when they assume a therapeutic stance and insist that they are offering tutees what they need to succeed in "the real world," they experience anxiety as a result of the "ambivalent psychic effects of social power" (71–72).

As these theorists show, the conflicts experienced by my peer group leaders arose not simply from a personal decision to behave authoritatively or nonauthoritatively, but rather from a complex network of role attributions bound up with their group members' attitudes and behaviors, with their seminar relationship with me, and with the extents and limits of their institutional authorization.

## BASIC WRITERS' CONSTRUCTIONS OF AUTHORITY

If the tutors experienced conflicts arising from their own conscious and unconscious conceptions about teaching and power, they faced even greater pressure from their writing group members. There was no question that the basic writers wanted their peer group leaders to assume the role of surrogate teachers, despite the efforts the leaders made to sustain a peer relationship and despite the group's achievements when the leaders performed as peers. Almost all of the students in my basic writing class attributed their progress as writers to their work in groups and to the guidance of their student mentors. On the end-of-semester assessment questionnaires, sixteen out of seventeen basic writing students indicated their satisfaction with the workshop arrangements. One student wrote,

"My peer group leader was an excellent leader. She helped me greatly with my papers. It always made it much longer and stronger. . . . She showed me what I was doing wrong and how to fix it."[6]

Many comments reflected the tutors' efforts to decenter their authority, although they also reveal that group members repeatedly characterized their leaders as more than peers. One student remarked that his leader "kept the group in check," and another noted that his leader "did a fine job because when we needed to do a little more or if she saw something we didn't she kept going till someone else hit on it." A third student commented: "Sometimes in a small group it is very helpful to have a little teacher to make everything run smooth and help out if your other classmates don't know the answer." The choice of the phrase "little teacher" is telling. Like their peer group leaders, many of the basic writers had "Storehouse" or "Garret" instructional models in mind and most were eager to vest their mentors with authority and to follow their lead.

To my knowledge, the basic writers never attempted to negotiate their group's workshop procedures or alter their practices. In the seminars, I had stressed that peer workshops were an intermediate stage in a longer process of production and urged the tutors to focus on invention and revision of conceptual and organizational issues rather than on end-product mechanics. As a result, a number of basic writing students complained in their end-of-term assessments that their groups had not spent enough workshop time on grammar and mechanics, since writing group advice was generally content centered. Typically, they described their workshop activities in this way: "Our peer group focused on everything. I noticed though [that] I didn't get much help with commas and capital letters and all the grammar." In their practice and comments, the basic writers deemed it appropriate and natural that the peer group leader would set the agenda, emphasizing certain kinds of writing issues while de-emphasizing others. The fact that the group might have pressed for alternative arrangements seemed outside their possible considerations.

Composition theory makes us aware that literacy practices are never ideologically neutral. Beyond the conflict of student power relations, beyond the possibility that students can ever be "written" as something more or less than "student" is the question of how labels like "basic writer" and "peer group leader" construct student identities. Thus, it is not enough to attribute power relations within the writing groups to the tutors' (overdetermined) views of literacy practices and constructions of self and Other. Also at stake are the basic writers' self-constructs, inextricably bound up with their powerlessness to contest their writing class placement, their designation as "developmental" writers, and the university's attendant silencing of "nonacademic" discourses.

In Tim's group, the students' desire to invest authority in the peer group leader was especially evident. Like Kathy and Allison, Tim had assumed for himself a collegial role and never deviated from that path. He did not intervene in his group's process beyond establishing procedures for reading and response. When members did not offer suggestions, he did not prompt them or press them to elaborate. When the group went off task, he went with them. But in the end, his group's comments reflect disappointment. They wanted more direction and extended critique of their writing, and they felt shortchanged. Their apparent desire for leadership suggests how uncomfortable students seem to be with their own authority and how willing they are to recenter power relations in decentered classrooms.

In contrast, Anne's group, whose values Anne had characterized as so different from her own, resisted her authority and, in doing so, resisted too her efforts to generate collaborative intercourse among them. Anne, who had wanted her group to run "perfectly," viewed herself as teacher surrogate and expected her group members to embrace and appreciate her guidance, but her group resisted her at every turn. Generally, they were unresponsive to her questions and promptings, often they brought only partial or hastily written drafts to the workshop, and only one member actually revised any of his essays after their meetings. There were certainly a number of variables that could have affected the group: gender issues, dismay at their basic writing placement, extremes of ability within the group. While I think that all of these contributed to the difficulties Anne faced, her desire to control the group process resulted in her having no control at all. Her group expressed its antagonism to her excessive leadership by resisting peer engagement, leaving Anne to do all the work.

Grimm (1999) observes that by its very nature tutor authority secures the internalization and projection of social regulation, including the subordination of basic writing students to the bottom of the educational hierarchy. Yet, regulatory efforts do not always succeed: the paradox of agency is not simply that we are dependent on the discourses that construct our self-definition but also that these discourses are always in conflict. Within these conflicted discursive spaces are, Grimm suggests, sites of resistance *and* capitulation, sites that appear to concentrate power around student subjects. Still, it is unclear whether these sites are, finally, only illusory or temporary respites from the forces that will ultimately restore authority to traditional institutional structures.

## POWER RELATIONS IN THE SEMINAR

Just as the basic writing workshops challenged students and tutors to negotiate and reconceptualize issues of power and authority, the seminar class brought similar challenges home to roost, throwing into confusion my plans for decentered teaching and learning. From the start, I had intended to have the peer group leaders set the agenda for the seminars, leading discussions of the readings, determining topics of concern or interest, deciding what was to occur in their basic writing workshops, and generally taking on greater agency and authority as the course progressed. Because of their active leadership role in their groups and their qualifications, I expected that authority and power would be shared among us, and I viewed these students, if not as my peers, certainly as junior colleagues, like the relationship between some graduate students and graduate faculty. To this end, in their syllabus I wrote: "This is your course. You will learn more and be a stronger peer group leader by actively investing in the dynamics of this course. Please let me know how things are going for you and how you want things done. I would like you to be the decision-makers, especially in terms of how you orchestrate your writing groups."

As I explained earlier, my desire to share power was motivated in part by my commitment to decentered educational processes. In the small seminar of education majors, I wanted to model what I believe is the best kind of learning experience: one in which students actively participate in all phases of their own learning process. But I also saw in this select group of students a kinship associated with their gaining "insider" knowledge about teaching writing and about the discipline of composition. Each Friday, they confronted the problems we all face when we work with developmental writers; group members became their "students" as well as mine, and we shared a common interest in their progress.

However, the peer group leaders did not seem to want to accept the kind of authority I was offering. When I asked them what issues they wanted to discuss, they lowered their eyes. When I asked them whether they had problems relating to the assigned readings, they didn't respond. After the fourth seminar, I wrote in my log: "I am disappointed in the seminars and trying to change them. I've asked students to lead various sessions. Casey really did not want to lead the session on listening and reading, and no one seemed inclined to respond. Tim is supposed to lead tomorrow, but he has not yet contacted me about his plans."

I knew that the problem wasn't just the difficulty of the course materials, nor was it the fact that none of the students had ever before been asked to connect theoretical issues raised in the articles to their own practices in the classroom. In retrospect, I realize that their discomfort in the seminar was related to their reluctance to assume teacherly authority, and that this reluctance was not simply a matter of their personal choice but a function of the powerful social and institutional forces that constructed them as "good college students." Although they openly talked about their instructional challenges and about individual students in their groups, they could never define themselves as my composition colleagues nor as writing instructors. In fact, they seemed to think that my desire to extend this authority to them was somehow a trap that would ultimately affect their course grade.

As Rick Evans explains, citing Bruffee, many successful students "typically assume that the only important classroom relationship is that 'one-to-one relationship' between themselves as individual (and isolated) students and their teacher. . . . [T]hese students rarely recognize genuine open-ended interaction or collaboration of any kind among themselves or with their teacher as valid learning experience" (1994, 155–56). Testifying to Evans's observations that high-achieving students often believe that "they learn only when they talk in response to the teacher's questions or when the teacher talks at them" (155), my peer group leaders unself-consciously stated that their own favorite classes were lectures. Anne asserted, "I hate classes where students do all the talking because then you don't know what the teacher wants." Kathy added, "When students sit around and talk, you don't really learn anything. There are so many opinions and you don't know what the right answer is." Tim said, "I like classes where the teacher tells us what he wants us to know and then we can give it back to him."

Evans (1994) notes that education majors in particular expect the instructor to maintain central authority in the classroom and that they anticipate this hierarchical role for themselves when they become teachers. They invest their teachers—and anticipate for themselves—what Mary O'Hair and Joseph Blase categorize as "legitimate power," a view that authority derives uncontested from the teacher's position (1992, 12).[7] Allegiance to this mindset is hegemonic. Successful students learn the roles expected of them, roles that sustain traditional power relations, and they learn to believe that such roles are "good," "right," and wholly "natural" (Grimm 1999, 69; see also Trimbur 1998, 118). From the tutors' comments about learning and teaching, it became clear that although they were themselves working in collaborative frameworks in the basic writing class and in the seminar, they continued to invest in authoritarian, top-down instruction when they characterized their own preferences.

Thus, problems of hierarchy and power cannot be attributed merely to students' predilections or even to their academic insecurity. Power relations are a significant and inevitable feature of every teacher-student engagement, even for those of us who would have it be otherwise. In the first place, as Hubbuch (1989–90) explains, students need an understanding of their teachers' expectations in order to be earn high grades. Asking the instructor "What do you want?" expresses the student's desire to fulfill appropriately a particular social requirement. While Hubbuch recommends class discussions that explain and interrogate alternative classroom arrangements, she stresses the teacher's need to recognize the ways in which apparently egalitarian classrooms mask, but do not eliminate, hierarchical control (37). According to Tobin, teacher authority is especially intrinsic to "democratic" process writing classrooms (1993, 20).

From the perspective of these theorists, I was naive to think that I could surrender my authority in the seminar, even as I attempted to diffuse it. For example, I tried to decenter control by circumventing the issue of seminar grades, but the peer group leaders would not permit me to do this. At the outset, I had indicated that they would each receive an A in the course. I told them that I expected them to do superior work, complete quality assignments, and capably facilitate peer groups, and, in fact, they met my every expectation. However, as Tobin astutely observes, "Stop giving grades and they remain just as significant. In fact, although we like to believe that we can relieve tension by not grading, the opposite is often the case. When we stop giving grades, everyone gets tense" (1993, 70). In my case, tutors' concerns were directly related to my evaluation of the basic writing students' essay grades, which, they believed, reflected their instruction and guidance. If a student's essay was returned with a C or, worse yet, a request for further revision, they worried that this evaluation would affect their grades in the seminar.[8] Although we discussed at length the issue of writers' grades and although they acknowledged that basic writers often need a great deal of practice and feedback to achieve the A's or B's they desire, the peer group leaders continued to feel responsible for their writing group members' final products, and they continued to worry that their students' success was implicated in their grade for the seminar course.[9]

Even more crucial than grades, however, the peer group leaders' apparent reluctance to assume equal power in the seminar was caught up in the conflicting roles that defined them in their various educational communities. In the seminar, I had introduced composition studies research and had hoped that they would develop theoretical insight into the practices they were initiating in their peer groups; I had hoped also that, as future teachers, they would begin to formulate their own set of principles about writing groups and writing instruction. At the same time, I had hoped that their experience with writing groups would help them to appreciate the importance of peer collaboration in their own academic lives. The seminar represented my effort to bridge the tutor-as-teacher versus tutor-as-peer dichotomy by bringing tutors into classroom writing groups equipped with some theory but also with an even stronger inclination to collaborate. I was going for, in Trimbur's words, "just the right amount of expertise and theory mixed with just the right amount of peership and collaboration" (1998, 120).

Ultimately, I failed to see the contradiction inherent in my desire: when peer group leaders affiliated with me, they were participating in the gatekeeping functions of hierarchical academic figuration (Grimm 1999, 34–38); at the same time, when they affiliated with their peers, they were defining the limits of their own authority as students. Furthermore, my hope that the tutors would choose to affiliate with their group members implies that such discursive agency can actually be effected. In the end, the tutors could neither accept my invitation to share authority in the seminar nor could they sustain their roles as peers in the basic writing classroom because the entire structure of institutional power militated against the possibility that such a construct could be sustained.

## THE PARADOX OF AUTHORITY IN DEMOCRATIC CLASSROOMS

This study offers a small window into the relations of power that were constituted, deferred, and reconstituted for particular groups of students in two university classes. But as Alice M. Gillam reminds, "the peer tutorial relationship ought not be considered in terms which ignore the multiple other collaborations which intersect in the peer tutorial encounter" (1994, 50). Thus, I need to acknowledge various other collaborative networks that influenced my basic writing students, including engagements with assigned essays and articles, with me in classroom and conference when the peer group leaders were not present, and with other peers in the writing class. These "sources" likewise influenced how the basic writing students interpreted their writing group activities. Likewise, I need to take into account the operations of power among group members, recognizing, for example, that gender, writing ability, and competition for peer group leader approval may contribute covertly to hierarchies and exclusions. (For a relevant discussion of competition in process classrooms, see Tobin 1993, 89–113). Further, as Lunsford so honestly reveals in her analysis of her graduate seminar, even the most democratic classroom practitioners may fail to recognize or acknowledge the "silent supports" for authority and power historically configured into the instructor's role or unconsciously fueled by his or her own desire (2000, 73).

Thus, I need to reflect on my own behaviors: was I sending mixed signals about my desire to decenter my seminar or basic writing class? Was I inviting the peer group leaders to share authority but all the same revealing doubt about their expertise as tutors or mentors? According to Ellen Cowne and Susan Little (1999), primary and secondary school cooperating teachers often worry that their inexperienced student teachers will not effectively cover the material or will simply teach the material "differently," and as a result, they continue to try to control the instructional environment. College writing teachers too tend to be quite possessive about their classrooms and methods. Certainly, I gave the peer group leaders full responsibility during the group sessions, removing myself from the workshop. Certainly, I encouraged leaders to try out different approaches to writing group facilitation and to peer response, and I praised and rewarded these efforts. Yet it is also true that I felt more separated from my writing students than I am used to feeling and that I worried about whether this group of basic writers had received enough assistance. Thus, while one kind of power struggle involved a desire to "recruit" writing tutors as my colleagues, another may have involved my need to remain in control of the writing instruction, a situation threatened by the presence of tutors in my classroom.

Of course, attributing authoritative conflict to my desires or to the peer group leaders' apparent response suggests that teachers and students can simply take on alternative roles like donning new baseball caps. It does not account for the broader cultural and social implications of role conflict within the peer groups and seminar. Invoking a Newtonian metaphor, we might say that when peership and student collaboration seem to tip the balance in favor of a student collectivity, institutional discourses exert equal and opposite pressure to "center" traditional authority, by "recalling" or clarifying for students their various unequal roles. As Grimm (1999) argues, tutors will strive toward teacher positions because they have internalized a particular culturally based instructional script and thus self-define their teacher-tutor roles. However, competing scripts serve as forceful reminders that tutors are students, not teachers, inscribing self-definitions of powerlessness and limited expertise. Ironically, these latter, persistent self-descriptions engender affiliations that create possibilities for engaged peer group work. But because of competing institutional affiliations, because institutions configure tutors differently than basic writers, their peer relationships are fragile and temporary.

Lunsford (2000) has suggested that our efforts to create newer, more democratic instructional models will be circuitous and complex. Even as we try out these new paths, we observe not only that particular pedagogies promote particular sets of values, but also that these liberating moves are readily co-opted by the discourses they were meant to redress. Yet our publications and practices insist that composition classrooms offer possibilities for interrogating and recasting relations of power. Therefore, if we want our students to experience nonhierarchical forms of learning, we will need to make explicit what is at stake in this effort. When we bring peer group activities to student writers, we must encourage them to reflect on their roles as well: to examine the bases of the choices they believe they are making and to consider the threatening potential of student collaboration. When we introduce students to peer leadership or mentoring roles, those that so readily appear to flatter them as surrogate teachers or construct them as "merely" students, we need to help them to recognize and interrogate the institutional supports that reinforce traditional power arrangements. Finally, our efforts to engage and collectivize our students on issues of authority and institutional power should encourage us as writing instructors and as members of academic communities to face squarely our own complicity with and resistance to these institutional structures.

# 14

# INSTITUTIONAL CHANGE AND THE UNIVERSITY OF WISCONSIN–MADISON WRITING FELLOWS PROGRAM

Jennifer Corroy

Writing fellows are a unique brand of peer tutors who work closely with both university faculty members and other undergraduates. Writing fellows are chosen from a diverse pool of applicants in many majors and serve in many disciplines. They are carefully trained to work across the curriculum helping other students improve their writing skills. In their first semester, fellows enroll in a special training course on the theory and practice of teaching writing. A writing fellow works with twelve to twenty students in a course whose professor has requested fellows' support. Writing fellows comment extensively on student drafts and meet individually with each writer to collaborate on possible revision techniques and strategies. The student is then given time to revise before turning in a final draft to his or her professor. Students remain the authorities of their work, and professors evaluate final drafts without any input from fellows, although professors generally review the first drafts and fellows' comments. The first writing fellows program was started at Brown University in 1982, and in 1997–98 the University of Wisconsin–Madison selected its inaugural class of writing fellows, who began training and work with great success.

The official rhetoric of Madison's writing fellows program does not generally include the notion of institutional change. The program describes itself as beneficial to students, professors, and fellows who gain, respectively, feedback; more polished papers; and community, leadership, and skills. However, some of the program's participants, particularly its founders and fellows, believe that significant institutional change occurs on campus as a result of the work they do. Unfortunately, concepts like "institutional change" lend themselves to abstract generalizations that may inconspicuously fail to materialize. Despite the euphemistic claims and goals of these writing fellows program participants, it remains unclear if and to what extent their visions of institutional change are realized within the university. The following research, interviews, and analysis consider the proposition that Madison's writing fellows are agents of institutional change in the university.

## THE INSTITUTION AND ITS CHALLENGES

Before evaluating whether these alleged changes have been realized, I want to provide a working definition of the term *institutional change* as I use it in this chapter. In the following discussion, *the institution* will most concisely refer to the body (students and faculty) of the University of Wisconsin and the ideas and practices that shape their experiences within the university community daily and over time. To supplement this initial distinction it will be helpful to keep in mind the more extensive definition of *institution* that Kenneth Bruffee develops in *Collaborative Learning: Higher Education, Interdependence, and the Authority of Knowledge*, where the "institution" is "precisely the interests and goals of these people [who, for the time being, walk the quad, teach the curriculum, and enforce the catalogue], what they value, what they know and how they know it, what they learn and how they learn it, what they teach and how they teach it, what they think of one another, and the whole fabric of human relationships that exists invisibly within the walls and bricks and mortar" (1999, 109).

Together these definitions create a picture of the institution as simultaneously comprised of people and practices as well as "interests and goals," and identify these as four potential mediums in which change may occur.

Notably, this definition can be applied both to the university as a whole and to the teaching of writing within it. This study closely examines the institution through the second, more narrow view, but evaluates possible change in the institution at both levels. Specifically, interviews with professors who have worked with writing fellows are the sources of primary research; they address interviewees' experiences teaching writing. Therefore, I assess institutional change most narrowly by examining the long-term impact on the way the professors teach writing as a result of their work with writing fellows and their adoption of the writing fellows program's values and practices. Institutional change more broadly includes potential and realized changes in professors' attitudes about teaching writing and about the typical professor-undergraduate hierarchy that usually subordinates the undergraduate to the professor. Bruffee again provides a helpful definition, this time of the potential changes that peer tutors can help colleges and universities bring about, specifically "changes in human relations—among students, among professors, and between students and professors; changes in classroom practice; changes in curriculum; and even (often the last domino to fall) changes in the prevailing understanding of the nature and authority of knowledge and the authority of teachers" (1999, 110). Challenged hierarchies, redefined social relationships, and other alterations in attitude are among the types of potential change anticipated by definitions such as this one.

Professors are a particularly useful gauge of change because they are a more stable part of the institution than the constantly changing student body. Their individual and collective practices, interests, and goals persist along with their physical presence and remain a critical part of the institution. Their relationships with the writing fellows program are also significant in evaluating the program's impact on the university. Changes in faculty practices, interests, and goals, along with their "human relations" after working with the fellows, can reveal whether Bruffee's potential changes have materialized as a result of the program.

Arguably, the writing fellows program also has the potential for limiting change by reinforcing current practices and hierarchies. Moreover, it may subvert its own institutional change potential while assimilating participants into a kind of static illusion of change that blindly prevents real change from occurring. This may be visible if professors and the writing fellows program, despite the unique relationships they foster, continue to enforce typically rigid hierarchies and attitudes. For example, if fellows fail to assert themselves as partners in teaching with the professors they work with, they may encourage the generally accepted position of undergraduates as totally subordinate to professors. Similarly, if fellows do not approach and respect the students they work with as peers (rather than as authorities), they may jeopardize the delicate and unique collaborative position they represent. Clearly, the examples are endless, involving possible failures by professors, students, and fellows. In any of these cases, Bruffee's "changes in the prevailing understanding of the nature and authority of knowledge and the authority of teachers" (1999, 110) could be threatened.

The structure of the writing fellows program introduces additional challenges in achieving potential changes. Many challenges in detecting, assessing, and perhaps even enacting institutional change through the writing fellows program result from the structure of the program. As mentioned above, the program does not include institutional change among its asserted goals; it defines neither change nor a specific method for achieving it. When fellows are told that they are participating in a program that is capable of effecting institutional change, administrators imply that they are participating in change by simply participating in the program. While this may be true, the context reduces their role in change, rendering it ambiguous, unasserted, and difficult to assess. Similarly, in written descriptions of the program, change is often mentioned in passing or as a final euphemistic statement that ends an article on a high note. This allows claims to evade critical explanations of how the alleged change actually occurs. For example, in his article "The Undergraduate Writing Fellows: Teaching Writing and Much More," which appeared in *Time to Write*, the WAC newsletter in the Letters and Science program at the University of Wisconsin, Bill Cronon, history professor and director of the L&S Pathways to Excellence Project, discusses the usual impacts of the writing fellows program, such as assisting faculty in teaching writing, providing undergraduate writers with useful feedback, and giving fellows a unique opportunity to learn by teaching (1998, 1). After presenting participant quotes expressing satisfaction with the program, the article jumps to a generalization alluding to institutional change. The final sentence of the article states that "the Writing Fellows Program is ultimately about changing the culture of undergraduate education at UW–Madison" (2), although no concrete examples of change are actually presented.

The glossing over of this assertion is likely justified by the intentions of this article (presumably to inform generally and positively about the program). It also illustrates the program's general treatment of its notion of institutional change. Without a clearly defined notion of how the semester-specific, individual impacts of the program lead to a "changing culture" or even how that culture changes, it is hard to determine if Cronon's asserted change is or is not occurring. Unfortunately, the goal or agenda for change remains as ambiguous for the writing fellows program as the alleged achievement of it does for the enthusiasts publicizing it. In "Why Feminists Make Better Tutors: Gender and Disciplinary Expertise in a Curriculum-Based Tutoring Program," Jean Lutes, one of the founders of the UW's program, articulates her own understanding of this fact as a barrier to identifying and realizing goals for change. Lutes states: "In retrospect, I can see that in order to meet my expectation that the Writing Fellows act as agents of change, the program would have to articulate that expectation more explicitly and involve students much more directly in discussion about what kind of change they want to bring about and why" (forthcoming, 29). This also raises the question of whose responsibility it is to define the kind of institutional change desired by the program. An awareness of the kinds of change participants are supporting is necessary to ensure that it is something they even want to or can support.

The writing fellows' role in institutional change must also be considered in light of the participants making up the program. Professors and fellows, two major agents of potential change, are voluntary participants. Therefore, it is reasonable to assume that, specifically in this study, the professors interviewed may have already shared many of the writing fellows program's ideals about teaching writing. This may create a closed system of ideology where participants begin with similar ideas and goals, leaving less obvious room for possible modifications. In that case, it would be expected that minimal or no change would be detected in a professor's approach to teaching writing. At the same time, in these relationships, the writing fellows program may still be a catalyst for change within the greater institution where, although the fellows and professors may remain unchanged, as a catalyst they may simultaneously provide the necessary interaction for a reaction within the institution. For example, a writing fellow may be the agent necessary for bringing a professor's teaching philosophy to light for students, or a writing fellow may help even the most perceptive professor understand more accurately the struggles of his or her students. Thus, in addition to potentially challenging the attitude of any given participant, a writing fellow may help a more receptive individual break less obvious barriers in his or her existing relationships or practices.

With the above considerations in mind the following analyses of interview responses will illustrate two examples of institutional change occurring at the University of Wisconsin–Madison as a result of the undergraduate writing fellows program. In both instances, the changes are specific to the professors involved and intimately related to their preexisting relationships to the institution of the university and to teaching writing. The first interview, with a professor of Scandinavian studies, shows how writing fellows influenced her methods for explaining assignments, commenting on work, and communicating with her students. The second interview, with a professor of English, reveals fewer definitive changes because the professor's teaching philosophies were in agreement with the program even before he worked with writing fellows. The interviews are primarily guided by open-ended questions about the professors' experiences with writing fellows and their personal teaching philosophies before and after working with fellows. Professors' names have been changed.

### INTERVIEW: LESLIE DUAMES, PROFESSOR OF SCANDINAVIAN STUDIES

At the time of the study, Leslie Duames, professor of Scandinavian studies, had worked with the writing fellows program twice, in the same course, and indicated that she would continue to do so in the future. She recently began teaching the course as a Communications-B class, which means writing has become a required focus of the curriculum in order to meet the university requirements for Communications-B credit.

According to Duames, she has always valued writing as an important tool of education, always basing courses on writing rather than examinations. She has a well-developed sense of writing as a tool for life, and believes that teaching students to write well—with strong, well-supported arguments, clarity, and critical thinking—is crucial to her role as an educator. Fitting with writing fellows program pedagogy, she has always commented extensively on student work with a strong focus on high-order concerns such as argument and analysis. Before working with fellows, turning in early drafts for her response was only an occasional option for her students.

Professor Duames considers herself to be approachable to students and views undergraduates as her collaborative partners in learning. When asked how she would describe her writing fellows' position in relation to her students and herself in view of the fact that writing fellows are not teaching assistants who determine grades and that they are undergraduates, she said, "I think this all connects to how I see myself as a teacher. I don't think that I'm a sage on the stage. I work with my students. We work cooperatively and we help each other learn, my students often teach me very, very much. So I would just say that the writing fellows just fit into that pattern of all of us learning together, and that's how I want them to be viewed by the students. . . . Really just part of our group learning project."

This notion of her fellows joining a preexisting collaborative learning structure shows that she values undergraduates in the learning process. It also reveals that she views the typical professor-undergraduate hierarchy more flexibly than some, in her words, "sage on the stage" professors. As a result, the program did not change her perception of undergraduates altogether. It also explains how receptive she has been to the possibility of learning from writing fellows.

With Professor Duames's values and goals, there was not much at stake to change in terms of writing fellows program goals. However, although her values and goals about teaching writing and approaching her relationship to the institution might not serve as significant measures for the type of change writing fellows allegedly foster, specific changes in her writing instruction provide a useful starting point for gauging the impact of the program. When asked if working with writing fellows helped how she teaches her class, she responded:

> It helped me organize the writing assignments better, and realize kind of what was needed for students to be able to understand what I was looking for in a writing assignment. So I think I was much better organized. . . . Possibly, the writing fellows' comments sometimes really made me think to and look at, I think I've become in all of my classes now much more critical of the writing process—I mean, I always look at content, but now I'm very aware, I explain to students I need a thesis statement, need a conclusion. I'm very critical if they don't give me that and I'm looking for topic sentences and all those things. I think it's made me much more aware of that in every class.

Her response reveals that the process of working with writing fellows alerted her to the need to clarify her assignments. Needing to "explain to writing fellows what I wanted from writing assignments" specifically suggested to her the importance of preparation, organization, and clarity. Although the writing fellows program did not set out to change her instructional values, it did provide the catalyst for the change to occur.

Isolated moments of reflection like this depict one type of change occurring through the writing fellows program, specifically, Bruffee's "changes in classroom practice; changes in curriculum" (1999, 110). The program does not conspicuously or even actively set out to alter the way professors write or present writing assignments. It does, however, take credit for a part in the institutional change Professors Duames's new assignments represent. The unidentified missing step here is the change itself: a change in the nature of how one professor thinks about giving assignments and her students' need for clarity. Seeing fellows' comments seems to have helped her grasp where her students were struggling to meet her expectations. Explaining her assignments to undergraduate writing fellows as collaborative teacher figures, rather than as students producing the work, allowed her to see the importance of articulating not only her assignments but also her expectations to her students as a way of helping them produce better work. Through her own reflection on working with fellows, she developed a more useful approach for assigning papers.

This type of change at an individual level is not unique to Professor Duames's experience, nor is the realization of its significance unique as an indicator of institutional change. In *Collaborative Learning*, Bruffee cites similar instances of change occurring through a peer tutoring program as described in a 1988–89 report by Robert L. Hess, then president of Brooklyn College: "Peer tutors have a potential to act as agents of institutional change, as revealed by . . . [the] faculty's acceptance [in one course] of the tutors' request for an all day faculty review of an experiment that proved to be an enormous success and [in another course, the] professor's comment that a presentation to the department by the tutors resulted in changes in the way the course is taught" (qtd. in Bruffee 1999, 81).

Although in Bruffee's examples professors were responding directly to peer tutors' suggestions, they underwent the same types of reflection and instructional revision that Professor Duames illustrates. Bruffee points out that the assertion that "peer tutors can be agents of institutional change . . . is not referring to all kinds of change. It is referring to a particular and crucially important kind: professors changing their course structure and *teaching practices*" (1999, 95; emphasis added). Notably, Professor Duames's revised assignment strategy resulted from standard interaction with writing fellows, rather than a direct "challeng[ing of] traditional prerogatives and assumptions about the authority of teachers and the authority of knowledge" (Bruffee 1999, 95). Without challenging the professor's authority, fellows illustrate in a less aggressive way that through their position alone, "peer tutors can help change the interests, goals, values, assumptions, and practices of teachers and students alike" (95). Thus, it can be argued that Professor Duames changed aspects of how she relates to the "institution" as she thinks about, gives, and evaluates assignments.

In another statement, Professor Duames revealed that her attention to the written work of her fellows influenced her teaching process. She said that she began to "comment more on style" after observing writing fellows at work. Although writing fellows may not describe focus on style as a specific concern of the program, Professor Duames now emphasizes the effects of style on structure and argument presentation, where before she focused solely on content. Thus she indicates increased concern specifically for teaching writing in conjunction with teaching content. While writing was always a tool for teaching content in her classes, she now includes writing itself as a skill that she helps students develop. While many professors use writing to teach in their classes, far fewer actually work to *teach writing* along with their subject matter. The benefit of developing writing and content simultaneously is often overlooked; in this case it seems writing fellows helped Professor Duames see some of those benefits.

In addition, Professor Duames explained that fellows' comments have provided her with new methods for effectively explaining concepts to her students, stating: "[T]heir comments are generally really useful just to look at and sometimes I've used the way that they explain things. . . . sometimes as a professor . . . you're not really communicating with them [the students] very well, so sometimes it helps to look at how a student communicates with another student." This echoes Bruffee's notion of potential change in "the prevailing understanding of the nature and authority of knowledge and the authority of teachers" (1999, 110). While it may be common for a professor to value undergraduates in the classroom, it is another step to learn teaching methods from them. Fortunately, Professor Duames recognized the unique position of the fellow—a student communicating with another student—and learned from her observations of the interaction.

This situation may also involve issues of authority. The nature of peer tutoring removes some of the authority from the "teaching" position a writing fellow assumes. As Professor Duames indicates, there is value in this position, and professors may learn not only from the specific ways fellows communicate, but also from the positions they assume as collaborative learners rather than ultimate authorities.

These examples also represent the potential influence of writing fellows in a variety of situations. While Professor Duames is particularly receptive to learning from writing fellows, other professors encountering similar writing fellow work may be surprised or hesitant, even rejecting the opportunity to learn or change. However, Duames's experiences reveal that although institutional change may not occur across the board, the opportunities for such change do arise. Furthermore, in the instance of professors unlike Duames, the opportunity for change is actually greater because it may instigate reevaluation of not only practice, but also ideology.

## INTERVIEW: SCHNIDER MARQUEE, PROFESSOR OF ENGLISH

At the time of the study, Schnider Marquee, professor of English, had worked with the writing fellows program once and said that he intended to work with the program again in the future. His ideas were always very much aligned with those of the writing fellows program. His practice of teaching writing has always involved many program strategies, such as requiring drafts, commenting extensively, and conferencing with students. This leaves little room for fellows to change his teaching practice but offers fellows a role in the type of change he may already be enacting at the university. From the researcher's perspective, his approach to teaching writing is itself a change from the overwhelming trend of the institution, although statistically supporting this would mandate an evaluation of all writing instruction at the university beyond the scope of this study. However, personal experience with many instructors of writing-intensive courses at the University of Wisconsin gives me confidence in asserting that Professor Marquee's writing pedagogy is not typical practice. Although many professors may agree with his ideas about the value of teaching writing and even of using process (including revision, conferences, etc.), his ambitious and dedicated practice is unique. He, therefore, may represent an individual change within the institution—the addition of a professor intensely involved throughout his students' writing process. As he shared his well-developed philosophies and methods with fellows, Professor Marquee was interacting with students on a different level, and because of fellows' training in current teaching theory they may have challenged him to rethink some of his practices.

Aspects of Professor Marquee's practice in teaching writing and his attitude toward fellows are revealed in his response to questions about why he wanted to work with the writing fellows program:

> I wanted it to save time. . . . One absolute reason was to save time. I was spending an hour per paper, on thirty plus papers, times several drafts of each paper, times several assignments, so I was looking to reduce the time I was spending over drafts of papers. . . . That to my mind was the first way it was going to be useful. . . . [B]efore I started working I could imagine it being useful that students would receive other students' comments, not necessarily better than they would receive my comments but differently in a healthy way.

It may at first appear negative that his initial goal with the program was to save time, as writing fellows are not intended to be a time-saving device for professors. However, Professor Marquee was already doing the tasks writing fellows take on in any class. When he declares that he wants writing fellows to save him time, he refers to time that many professors never bother to take, before or after working with writing fellows. Professor Duames, for example, cited time as a significant factor in her choice not to use mandatory drafts or conferences with her students. In the same way that she has not changed the process she uses to teach writing, neither has Professor Marquee. The difference is that he already used a process consistent with the writing fellows program, a close conjunction with the type of change writing fellows may encourage among other professors. He states, "Writing fellows did not change [the] structure of my assignments. . . . I had drafts, I had conferences, all kinds of things before; that's what was useful and profitable but really burdensome for my time." Thus, at the level of attitude toward and process of teaching writing, no change occurred from working with writing fellows.

Moreover, when asked specifically if working with writing fellows changed anything about the way he commented or taught, Professor Marquee clearly stated: "No. It's not that it didn't; it's that it actually served, rather than my changing, it actually served how I did things quite well." The writing fellows fell in line not only with his specific approach to teaching writing, but also with his rigor and goals. They also did not significantly change his methods; they did not "make me reflect globally on teaching or on writing." He's taught writing for a long time and "published something on writing instruction." He did comment, however, that "[the] writing fellows [program] served me, I don't know that my teaching or notions about writing changed that much. What did change, something did change, I'm quite fond of the program, so what changed is it's something that I'll use and I'm quite happy to have."

While his language throughout the interview represents his declared position of using writing fellows as a tool, he also demonstrated an awareness of how their goals lined up with his own along with his respect for the ambitions of the program. When asked if he had any method that he wanted his fellows to use or if he had discussed ways to help their tutoring fit his style, he responded:

> Yeah . . . it was quite respectful and obedient to the mandate and the mission of the writing fellows, so I don't think my advice to them, or my counsel, or my expectations, or my goals were in any conflict. . . . [I]t wasn't so much having them do certain things that I wanted them to do because I think the writing fellows program trains them to do the sort of things I wanted them to do, but how they went about doing it. I thought I could teach them something and I

think I did; and I gave them ten to twelve pieces of counsel . . . one of them was what it takes to write comments . . . in writing comments you are doing less thinking about students' writing than you are about your own thinking, because it's easy to comment on an A paper, easy to comment on a D paper. What's hard is writing on a B paper and a C paper that's confusing or slightly off . . . because you're not sure . . . you thought it was saying one thing or another . . . your own mind is confused . . . comment involves look[ing] back on your own thinking . . . self-scrutiny.

Thus, he indicates his respect for the goals of the writing fellows program, which he describes as "to help them [fellows] help students develop the strategies to learn how to become successful writers . . . not helping them necessarily become good writers, helping them to *learn* how to become good writers, and not just helping them . . . learn to become good writers but how to develop the skills to become good writers."

His discussion of how to write comments involves a perhaps unrealized awareness of an aspect of writing fellows' training. Writing fellows are exposed to a range of considerations about how to approach commenting and its purpose. Most significantly, during their training they engage a variety of ideas and philosophies about writing, teaching writing, tutoring, commenting, and more. By sharing his ideas with fellows, Professor Marquee not only clarifies his goals, but also provides them with another perspective on the issues they ideally are striving to develop their own sound philosophies about. He is contributing to writing fellow training and providing them with another forum for developing their "interests and goals . . . what they value, what they know and how they know it, what they learn and how they learn it, what they teach and how they teach it" (Bruffee 1999, 109). Professor Marquee stated, "[T]hey were aides to me, they were coteachers in some sense. They were also obedient to me, I clearly had authority with them but they were also doing their job with me and for me; in some way they were peers; in some way they weren't. In some way I took seriously the idea that I was mentoring them so in some way they were students of mine, at least that's how I took it."

Professor Marquee's effect on the fellows' portion of the institution has many possible implications: writing fellows not only gain his insights, but also see professional examples of how some of the teaching theories that they have studied come into practice for him. In this case, change is occurring for fellows because of Professor Marquee's mentoring. Writing fellows who were willing to learn from Professor Marquee's strategies, even by critiquing them, could reap personal benefits from working with him. But this opportunity to learn could not occur without a change in how undergraduates and faculty interact with each other. In peer tutoring programs that remove the professor from the process, opportunities to learn from an instructor are lost to peer tutors. While his mentoring may be useful to any tutor or educator, Professor Marquee's writing fellows are in the unique position of working with the teacher and interacting with the students he teaches. This gives them a view of the writing and thinking his practice produces and an opportunity to work within his well-developed system. As writing fellows continue to bring their knowledge and experience to diverse aspects of the institution over time by working with many students, cofellows, and professors in a range of disciplines, Professor Marquee's philosophies and practices may be shared with a wider range than otherwise possible. Moreover, fellows who reject Professor Marquee's practice will have had a semester to understand why and refine their own philosophies and perhaps encourage Professor Marquee to reconsider aspects of his theory and pedagogy.

Professor Marquee's involvement with the writing fellows program reveals that Professor Duames's experience is by no means isolated or individual. Although Professor Marquee's teaching style, philosophy, and practice remained static over the course of his experience, he demonstrates another avenue for change: his potential impact on fellows and their potential to influence his thinking. He is very conscious of his developed beliefs—where they came from and why they are valuable; it happens that his beliefs are also closely aligned with those of the writing fellows program. Along with his respect for his students and writing fellows, however, Professor Marquee in a way upholds the typical professor-undergraduate university hierarchy, confidently proclaiming that his students "would always prefer if I would look at a first draft." It remains questionable if his opinion about this will ever change, or even if it should. Significantly, he also recognizes that writing fellows' comments may have "profited them [his students] in ways I couldn't have, and then the other way around." This recognition, of the unique value of peer tutoring, may or may not be attributable to writing fellows, but perhaps in time Professor Marquee will understand more specifically the benefits he alludes to and, like Professor Duames, perhaps he too will profit from them.

## ASSESSING INSTITUTIONAL CHANGE

Change comes in at least two forms: realized and potential. Realized changes in practice, such as those directly evidenced by Professor Duames's experience, are happening throughout the writing fellows program. Potential for philosophy refining and sharing is demonstrated by Professor Marquee's involvement with the program. With every relationship forged, a new development occurs. In the hands of anyone attempting to enact change based on these potentially abstract ideals, the evidence presented here may be used as an instrument for measuring change. These examples demonstrate that reflection on the part of participants and case-specific use of such reflections translate into action that may be as mechanical as clarifying assignments or as ideological as sharing philosophies. Both are tangible ways to change the face of the institution at some level; both are occurring through the writing fellows program. Considered in the challenging framework of actual change while maintaining their relationship to the loftier goals of the program and at times failing to align exactly with them, these analyses also provide the complex framework for shaping the way institutional change is discussed while exemplifying how it may be assessed, itself a step toward implementing change.

Change most frequently occurs at the lowest level, that of individual reflections and interactions. If widespread lower-level change happens, the institution will change in an increasingly conspicuous manner. As the writing fellows program grows, many small changes will occur at the levels of practice and potential. Openness to these changes, though individual in many circumstances, will predictably develop patterns: many professors over time may be challenged to clarify how they write assignments; many may share their strong, well-developed philosophies about teaching and writing with fellows and recognize the power they may have. This movement of ideas creates the space for change in many directions. The absence of one given direction for institutional change in the writing fellows program will allow it to progress through the ideas and practices shared by its members. It will encourage personal development that may or may not proceed to impact the greater university. However, identification of these changes and potentials will not eliminate what seems to be one of the most significant difficulties: without a realistic determination of goals, this multidimensional change cannot develop according to the desires of participants. Only by identifying those desires and goals can writing fellows become true agents of, rather than unknowing participants in, institutional change.

## Conclusion

# HYBRID MATTERS
## *The Promise of Tutoring On Location*

Laurie Grobman and Candace Spigelman


We have argued that on-location tutoring should be understood as a hybrid instructional genre that incorporates features, practices, and conceptual frameworks from at least four significant "parent" writing initiatives. We have also emphasized that the products and processes of classroom-based writing tutoring result in a blurred form, exhibiting characteristics of each of its parents but operating in its own distinctive space, neither synthesizing nor rejecting related theories. Indeed, classroom-based writing tutoring "violate[s] decorum and trouble[s] hierarchies," in some of the same ways that Wendy Bishop and Hans Ostrom advocate for contemporary genre theory (1997b, xii): it operates amid contradictions within the productive chaos of writing classrooms; it confuses the nature of classroom authority; it encourages noise and active collaboration at the very scene of writing.

Perhaps we stretch the metaphor too far, but it does seem that Charles Bazerman's notion of genre as *place* powerfully conceptualizes distinctive practices in writing classrooms, writing instruction, and writing support efforts as well as it represents the distinctive discourses invoked within those practices. Thus, we find Bazerman's closing paragraph to "The Life of Genre, the Life in the Classroom" especially relevant to our concerns:

> [H]aving learned to inhabit one place well and live fully with the activities and resources available in that habitation, no one is likely to mistake it for a different place. Nor having moved to a different place do people stint on learning how to make the most of their new home. It is only those who have never participated more than marginally who do not notice where they are, because they do not perceive why all that detailed attention is worth their effort. Once students feel part of the life in a genre, any genre that grabs their attention, the detailed and hard work of writing becomes compellingly real, for the work has a real payoff in engagement within activities the students find important. (1997, 26)

In large part, students come to understand what writing is through their experiences in writing classrooms. Unless their first-year composition classroom is remarkably different from prior sites of writing instruction, they will simply assume that they "know," if not how to write, at least how writing is done. Collaborative writing assignments, writing group activities, support for writing center tutoring—such instructional efforts move students from the margins to frame them as agents, as "real" writers. By combining and extending these initiatives, classroom-based writing tutoring immerses students even more directly in the "compellingly real" and "detailed hard work" of composition.

## PROMOTING SUCCESSFUL CLASSROOM-BASED WRITING TUTORING

At this point, it should be apparent that successful on-location tutoring does not occur by chance. Program coordinators, teachers, and tutors need to prepare well in advance to ensure that programs are adequately funded and carefully orchestrated to serve student writers. Of course, classroom situations will vary depending on discipline, course content, and instructor's needs, so it is difficult to generalize procedures and processes. Furthermore, classroom-based writing tutors will assume various roles and functions to meet the needs of particular tutoring situations and will therefore need to readjust and recalculate their practices on the scene. Recognizing these limitations, we offer the following strategies, which, we hope, will contribute to effective classroom-based writing tutoring experiences for coordinators, teachers, tutors, and student writers involved in these programs.

*Prepare the institutional supports.* Programs gain needed credibility when they receive articulated institutional support. At Penn State Berks–Lehigh Valley College, where we teach, our classroom-based writing tutoring project began with seed grants for tutor training from the university's Schreyer Institute and the Fund for Excellence in Learning and Teaching. We were also fortunate in that our administrators' backgrounds led them to appreciate, and to finance, writing-focused initiatives. At the same time, we want to second Josephine A. Koster's advice to writing center administrators, as it relates to on-location initiatives as well: "[I]t behooves us rhetorically to construct our arguments [for funding and recognition] on grounds that match the concerns and perspectives of our administrative audiences" (2003, 155). This means, for example, knowing the appropriate buzzwords (such as "retention" and "student-centered") for our program proposals and reports.

In addition to generous college funding, our tutors continue to gain status through administrative rhetoric. When our administrators praise the program and describe it as integral to our voluntary communications across the curriculum initiative, instructors begin to perceive writing tutors as a valuable addition to their classes. Moreover, as Marti Singer, Robin Breault, and Jennifer Wing show, material support, such as sufficient supplies of paper, access to copy machines, and dedicated classroom time, contribute to tutors' status and faculty buy-in to the program.

With such support in place, we want to make one caveat: as the research of our contributors confirms, classroom-based writing tutoring should be implemented at the classroom teacher's request, not imposed administratively from above. We note especially, David Martins and Thia Wolf's assessment of a failed writing program, in which instructors were forced to accept classroom tutors, and we emphasize that institutional agendas that do not take into consideration individual faculty needs, interests, and commitments are doomed to failure.

*Train tutors differently.* The work of Teagan Decker, of Melissa Nicolas, and of Singer, Breault, and Wing suggests that on-location tutors should receive initial and ongoing training. Writing center directors will need to anticipate differences between how tutors are customarily understood to provide writing assistance, in relative one-to-one privacy, and how tutors will operate in the relatively public space of classroom life, and they will need to modify their methods to support tutors within this new arena. Experienced and new tutors may need training to facilitate group processes, to lead presentations, or to actively interrupt student writers at work (Grobman; Lui and Mandes; Nicolas). Because they simultaneously bridge the work of tutors and peer class members, they must know how to both "inform" and "model" effective writing processes, academic discourse conventions, and collaborative engagement (Grobman). From another angle, Mary Soliday stresses that, in some cases, tutors will also need to be prepared for writing-intensive classes outside of their own majors; they will need to understand "curricular and institutional aspects of WAC that differ from the traditional writing course," including an apperception of genre conventions for specific disciplines and of expectations within particular classrooms (this volume 42). Tutors also need training to distinguish between high-stakes formal writing assignments and writing to learn activities with relatively low stakes.

Relatedly, tutors must be prepared for the disjunctions that arise from their advanced training in complex literacy instruction and the ways this sophisticated view of literacy positions them as advocates and agents within their tutoring programs in contrast to the more limited view of literacy work held by most content instructors. As Decker astutely observes, classroom-based writing tutoring retains the more "obvious benefits of peer tutoring [found in writing centers] and provides much-needed help to overworked instructors, but leaves the political and social energy of the autonomous writing center behind" (this volume 22) Repeatedly, our contributors stress the importance of clarifying tutors' roles and identities when they are working on location with students and with the classroom teacher. If, as some theorists suggest, tutors are to investigate and challenge institutional codes, they must be given the tools to resist assimilation and be prepared to deal with narrow views of their goals. Specifically, Decker stresses the importance of tutors' gaining a "sense of the complexity of their place in the university when they leave the writing center and visit the classroom" (see also Nicolas in this volume).

Because classrooms configure authority in ways that challenge tutoring models of peership, tutors must have strategies in place so that they can remain facilitators, not "helpers or preteachers," when they enter classrooms, as Decker puts it (this volume 19; see also Corbett; Spigelman). At the same time, they need to have sufficient authority to accomplish their assigned tasks. Thus, Martins and Wolf warn that on-location tutors need help to figure out how they can work together and with their administrators to negotiate these contradictory roles without loss of confidence and agency. They need to learn to adopt a more flexible stance and be willing to modify their usual practices to fit classroom needs. Steven J. Corbett describes how certain classroom situations insist upon directive tutoring practices. Likewise, Barbara Little Liu and Holly Mandes point out that because students don't choose the time and place of their writing assistance, because this assistance occurs while they are in the very act of writing, and because their questions, no matter how superficial (or editorial or lower order) are crucial to their continued writing *at that moment,* writers' needs and concerns must be addressed directly, not deferred or revised in favor of higher-order considerations.

*Prepare the teacher for the program.* Classroom teachers who invite tutors into their classrooms play a central role in the success (or failure) of the initiative. Program coordinators and classroom instructors need to meet well in advance of tutoring days to determine the teacher's needs and to discuss how they envision their tutors' roles. Decisions must be made about the numbers of tutors required at a session, the kinds of work tutors can accomplish, and the limitations (both ethical and practical) on tutors' time and responsibilities. In addition to, or prior to, such discussions, it is useful for faculty to receive printed information, describing various models of classroom-based tutoring support and, especially for noncomposition faculty, highlighting some of the nuts-and-bolts issues writing instructors typically take for granted. In documents we provide for faculty, we suggest, for example, reasonable amounts of time to expect between response drafts and revised copies, depending on the length of the student's paper; we remind teachers to write out their assignments based on their specific instructional goals; and we invite faculty to consider their students' writing in relation to particular, listed genre conventions.

It often happens that teachers need additional background relating to such theories as collaborative learning, the social construction of knowledge, and models of composing. They may need training to work with their classroom-based tutors, to learn how to share instructional information and course expectations as well as how to share their authority with tutors and to empower tutors to share their knowledge with students, as Singer, Breault, and Wing and Martins and Wolf suggest. Hopefully, faculty members who use tutors will value writing in their classrooms, emphasizing to their students the tutor's knowledge and the importance of writing instruction and support.

*Prepare the class by explaining the classroom tutor's anticipated roles and activities.* Students in classrooms must be kept in the loop: they should be told why the tutors have been invited in and what their instructor understands their role to be. Such conversations should emphasize the peer relationship between students and tutors, so that the tutors are not perceived as still another level in the institutional hierarchy. Likewise, such conversations should convey the instructor's expectation that the tutor will not "fix" essays or evaluate class members' essays or report on students' behaviors. According to Susan Georgecink, teachers contribute to the success of classroom-based tutoring by preparing their students to welcome and use tutors, perhaps engaging some positive writing activities and collaborative methods in advance of the tutors' initial visit. Teachers' support for and enthusiasm about on-location tutoring is usually contagious. Students respond positively and work more productively when their instructor actively invests in the tutoring project.

We have also found that if the classroom instructor retains highest authority, introducing the tutor and the concept, establishing the tutor's knowledge, defining the tutor's zone of activity, and valuing the tutor's practices, everyone is more comfortable. Tutors should not be in collusion with teachers and usually don't want to be. Keeping the instructor in charge limits potential conflict about staking authority, while it gives students permission to reject or collaboratively negotiate the tutor's advice.

At the same time, tutors must have some authority and autonomy. Our contributors have shown repeatedly that on-location tutoring is most effective when the tutors are acknowledged and empowered as legitimate sources of knowledge. Ideally, the classroom teacher will provide tutors with an articulated job description, clear expectations for the course, and his or her supporting materials and handouts. Likewise, tutors will be encouraged to create additional materials and experiment with various instructional strategies to meet the needs of their writing peers.

*Maintain the appropriate number of tutors for the tasks required.* From peer response group facilitation to writing workshop troubleshooting to one-to-one class time tutorials to brief small- or large-group presentations, each mode of writing support poses specific staffing requirements. In a class of eighteen basic writers, for example, five to six tutors will be needed for weekly fifty-minute writing group meetings, while two to three tutors could deftly manage a writing workshop. Increasing that ratio can create competing demands for tutors' attention, resulting in writers' drifting off task or addressing only lower-order concerns. Our classroom-based writing tutors recommend that when too few tutors are in attendance the instructor allow some students or groups to work independently or that, in these situations, students be asked to address a finite number of specific concerns in order to ensure that all writers receive feedback. However, anticipating the appropriate distribution of tutors to students will go a long way toward ensuring the productive chaos of collaborative inventing, composing, and revising activities.

*Encourage start-of-the-course warm-up activities.* If the classroom teacher is willing, prior to the start of actual tutoring work, one full class period should be devoted to conversation and tasks geared toward integrating the tutor into the classroom community. While our newer tutors often worry that icebreakers seem artificial or silly, our more experienced tutors remain convinced that such activities help to build trusting relationships among tutors and students. They suggest simple get-acquainted games, like offering a roll of toilet tissue and directing each student to reveal a number of facts about himself or herself corresponding to the number of sheets torn from the roll, or distributing color-coded cards or Skittles candies, with each color representing a category of information (for example, green can represent "random personal information" like siblings, hometown, or pets, while orange may call for "wacky facts" like an embarrassing attribute, school awards received, or even the number of students in the residence hall, and so on). In these introductory meetings, it is also effective to have students and tutors working together to answer an assigned question or to resolve a curricular or campus "problem." For first-year students, for example, the instructor might divide the class into tutor-led groups and challenge them to develop the longest list of strategies for being an effective student. Alternatively, tutors may assist students in answering "quiz" questions on assigned readings, or in staging mock peer reviews or workshop sessions using sample essays supplied by the instructor or program coordinator. At this early stage, both teacher and tutors should privilege the cultivation of peership and process over any products that might be produced during these meetings and conversations.

*Wherever possible, keep the same students and tutors together throughout the course.* Time and again, we have debated the advantages and disadvantages of consistent working relationships and, although we have no empirical data relating to our own programs, our experience suggests that, most often, students develop more confidence and exhibit more willingness to confer with the tutor and with each other when relationships remain consistent over time. We also draw from writing group research, which advises keeping group formations constant, owing to, as Karen Spear explains, the "fragility" of group life and the "complexities of group process" (1988, 7). Advising writing teachers to "make group membership permanent," Hephzibah Roskelly explains that writers and readers are more likely to share opinions and ideas if they "feel that others are listening and *believing* in them" and that such "trust takes time to nurture" (2003, 138). Like Casey You, who writes about the impact of trust on group processes, Roskelly emphasizes that trust "can flourish when groups know they will stay together for the term." In her "second-chance" tutor-led peer response groups in her current school, Melissa Nicolas's students remain together throughout the semester, engaging together in many activities in addition to peer response, and seem to feel more "invested" in one another and their work. We believe a parallel case can be made for consistency among students and classroom-based tutors. Just as writing center tutees often become "regulars" because they've established a relationship with a particular tutor, whom they will seek out in subsequent visits, our classroom-based tutors report their students' eagerness to meet repeatedly with the same tutor. In our own classes, we have also noted our students' discomfort, reticence, and higher levels of absenteeism when established tutor-tutee partnerships are altered in the course of the semester. As one tutor commented, when he resumed work with his established tutees, they seemed so relieved to be back together that their level of productivity actually increased.

*Ask for feedback.* It is likely that the tutoring program coordinator will receive feedback from his or her tutors about how the class is going. Typically, tutors in training will record their tutoring work and reflections in journals. More advanced tutors may log their hours and activities as part of the program's record keeping or meet periodically with their coordinator to discuss progress and problems. Martins and Wolf emphasize that administrators need to take into account tutors' expressions of concerns and evaluations of a program's effectiveness. In Georgecink's view, tutors should be allowed to try their wings, unencumbered by overly controlling program directors. Although we agree, we believe that supervisory personnel must be involved in day-to-day classroom tutoring operations, through regular conversations with the classroom instructor, classroom visitations, or brief meetings with the instructor, the students, and the tutors. We stress that the classroom teacher should expect and insist upon a high level of coordination and consultation.

Therefore, the classroom teacher and students should also be part of the conversation. Ideally, classroom tutors should work directly with the instructor to discuss program goals or to plan sessions, but some of those meetings should also highlight the successes and discuss the concerns of all parties. By speaking openly with the instructor of a basic writing class, my tutors discovered how much he valued their practice of insisting students read their drafts aloud, and he learned that his literary criticism assignment was too difficult for his developing writers. In that class, we also polled the writing students, using check sheets and short fill-in questionnaires, which we shared with all participants, to gauge students' perceptions and their level of satisfaction with the program.

Classroom-based writing tutoring, Muriel Harris wrote in a 1990 essay, "may be a particularly encouraging trend" for integrating tutoring, collaborative writing activities, and composition instruction. "In addition," Harris pointed out, "it offers us some interesting new ways to expand the role of the tutor" (24). We believe that with careful planning, external and internal support, and open dialogue among all participants, on-location tutoring can be more than an "interesting" intervention: it can be a significant practice for teaching students, tutors, teachers, and coordinators about the social construction of knowledge and the collaborative realities of writing.

## FUTURE SITES OF INQUIRY

As a relatively new practice, tutoring on location requires continued investigation. Stephen North's suggestion that "[w]riting centers, like any other portion of a college writing curriculum, need time and space for appropriate research and reflection if they are to more clearly understand what they do, and figure out how to do it better" (1984, 445) applies twenty years later to classroom-based writing tutoring. The chapters in *On Location* have begun the crucial work of theorizing and assessing the many incarnations of classroom-based writing tutoring, and we look forward to future published accounts advancing the work initiated here. As we bring this chapter to a close, we want to suggest future sites for practicing, evaluating, and theorizing this fruitful, albeit complicated, pedagogy. Specifically, we turn our attention to two of composition's central concerns: difference and technology.

### Locating Difference When Tutoring On Location

Research on exclusions based on gender, race, ethnicity, and other categories of difference during the processes of collaboration can usefully inform future directions for classroom-based writing tutoring. Taken together, these studies suggest that marginalized voices and perspectives have less access to the knowledge-making activities of collaborative writing groups and, thus, less opportunity to influence change. Moreover, research indicates that even if minority voices are present, they may not be heard (Myers 1986). Citing Nancy Grimm's call for writing center scholars to consider categories of difference, Melissa Nicolas asserts that "literature on race, class, culture, and educational differences in writing centers is embarrassingly scant" (2002, 10). As practitioners and researchers continue to work with classroom-based writing tutoring, it behooves all of us to think carefully about how gender, ethnic, racial, class, and other differences potentially affect this practice.

Evelyn Ashton-Jones's (1995) work points to the impact of gender on peer collaboration, noting that collaboration and feminism have long been viewed as partners. Collaborative methodologies work in sync with feminist pedagogies to disrupt traditional male forms of knowledge and teaching and to open up new spaces for women in the classroom and the academy. In addition, many feminist scholars view collaborative learning as a more authentic form for female writers, enabling them to construct ideas unmediated by hegemonic, patriarchal culture (Ashton-Jones, 1995, 9, citing Carol Stanger). However, Ashton-Jones observes that feminist theorists have also critiqued collaborative learning as a reaffirmation of patriarchal teaching and as useful only for all-women groups (citing Howe 1971; Friedman 1985; Cooper 1989). She points out that the presence of males in collaborative work may sustain unequal power relations, as writing group participants take on socially constructed gender roles. For example, males tend to control knowledge building (17–19) and females tend to bear most of the interactional work (11–16).[1]

Classroom-based writing tutoring research might fruitfully address the relationship between gender and collaboration or peer tutoring. With membership, however tentative, in both peer and instructor discourse communities, might properly trained classroom-based tutors help students shed socially constructed gender patterns in male-female conversations and thus assist students to become more egalitarian in their collaborative work? Do tutor-led mixed-gender response groups work more effectively based on the tutor's gender? Do male and female tutors help students to work more productively in groups, in workshops, and in other classroom configurations? And what do the results suggest for training tutors or facilitating classroom activities?

From a somewhat different perspective, future work in classroom-based writing tutoring might consider Melissa Nicolas's critiques of the "feminization" of writing centers (2002, 12), a perspective that primarily assumes that most of the tutors, administrators, and tutees of writing centers are women; that writing centers are on the margins of composition studies; and that writing center theory and pedagogy should be based on a "feminine ethic of care." Following Nicolas, scholar-teachers implementing on-location tutoring can employ the critical reflection necessary to examine reified assumptions and thus to avoid gendering and marginalizing classroom-based writing tutoring programs.

Studies of peer collaboration and ESL students likewise have much to teach us about classroom-based writing tutoring. Dave Healy and Susan Bosher's (1992) work with curriculum-based tutoring for ESL learners provides a model of the kinds of work researchers might conduct. Healy and Bosher examined the effects of linking curriculum-based tutors with ESL students in peer response groups and in one-to-one follow-up grammar sessions with promoting more egalitarian tutoring arrangements.

Moreover, Sara Kurtz Allaei and Ulla Maija Connor have studied writing groups with mixed language abilities to determine conflicts that arise due to students' varying communication styles and perspectives of "good" writing (1990, 20). Their study, which provides specific strategies for peer response with multicultural groups, can inform future work in classroom-based writing tutoring. This might include explorations of informal introductory meetings, in which class members can discover their cultural communication differences, or studies of semester-long group arrangements in which participants must directly address their diverse communication styles. Continued research is needed to reach more definitive conclusions about the nature of classroom-based writing tutoring and cross-cultural communication.

Research considering the impact of racial and ethnic difference on peer collaboration can also guide on-location investigations. One important discussion is Gail Okawa's study of the EOP Writing Center at the University of Washington. At UW, the EOP Writing Center acts as a "bridge" between student and teacher and student and institution (1993, 169), assuming multiple and complex roles. According to Okawa, in a writing center devoted to students of color and nontraditional students, tutees feel encouraged to talk about their writing, their experiences with language, and their experiences within a largely monocultural institution; as a result, they are more likely to find their voices and to challenge authority structures (170). We believe that classroom-based tutoring is likewise situated to explore the needs of minorities and other historically marginalized students. Since tutors on location already cross and recross institutional, structural, and pedagogical borders, they may help to encourage more enlightened views of literacy practices. In this volume, Martins and Wolf and Jennifer Corroy describe ways in which classroom writing tutors can alter teachers' traditional notions of literacy when program coordinators, faculty, and tutors work collaboratively, and many of our contributors have emphasized the need for such open, collaborative conversations. In the future, we would especially encourage research focused on such negotiations in multicultural classrooms, where the dynamics tend to be even more complicated.

Moreover, Okawa suggests that tutors in the EOP Writing Center should acquire a critical understanding of personal, cultural, political, and educational issues related to literacy and that they need to be trained dialogically and collaboratively in order to work effectively with minority students (1993, 171). It seems reasonable to apply these same expectations and supports to classroom-based tutors as well. In addition, studies of racial and ethnic difference as it affects classroom-based writing tutoring can identify specific strategies for helping tutors acquire critical multicultural understandings. Of central concern to classroom-based writing tutoring is Okawa's assertion that tutors in writing centers serving multicultural populations need to "mirror the students' diversity" to become role models and effective writing tutors. Okawa believes that for minority and nontraditional students, issues of authority and voice take on great urgency, raising the critical issue of "who has the *right* to control ownership of a text? Who has the *right* to write in the academy?" (171; emphasis in original). Research in classroom-based writing tutoring could address these concerns by asking questions like the following: To what extent does race or ethnicity matter in the tutor-tutee relationship? Can white tutors working with minority students assist them in the acquisition of academic authority while maintaining their home languages? Must classroom-based tutors mirror students' diversity to be effective? [2]

## Technologies and Classroom-Based Writing Tutoring

Technologies have altered the traditional notion of writing center work and space, as peer tutoring has moved outside the walls of the writing centers to online environments. Online tutoring is proliferating, whether by way of e-mail tutoring, synchronous chat systems, automated file retrievals, or newsgroups (see, for example, Harris and Pemberton 1995). Indeed, online writing labs (OWLS) experiment with emerging technologies as they become available. More than ten years ago, Dawn Rodrigues and Kathleen Kiefer described their plans for a cross-curricular electronic writing center, where students across the university would have access to tutors as well as bulletin boards for electronic peer response groups. Students seeking tutoring help would no longer go to the writing center; indeed, they claimed that students "need not ever meet with their tutors face-to-face" (1993, 223). As composition continues to merge online technologies with writing pedagogies, research must ask whether classroom-based writing tutoring, which stresses face-to-face, "on-the-scene" collaborative practice, can find an ally in technology.

Advocates of online tutoring believe it offers numerous advantages, including reduced stereotyping in the tutoring relationship (Harris and Pemberton 1995, 156), fewer vocal and social inhibitions (Harris and Pemberton 1995, 156; Coogan 1995), written records that describe previous sessions and reduce duplication of effort (Healy 1995), and extended tutoring sessions (Coogan 1995). Many note its disadvantages, including the lack of *immediate* back-and-forth dialogue, the elimination of voice and body cues, fewer clues to learning disabilities, a tendency to move away from genuine peer collaboration to more authoritative response and/or editing, and, most important, the lack of "personal contact" and the nurturing of caring relationships (Harris and Pemberton 1995, 156–58).

It is our sense that e-mail or other kinds of online tutoring could productively be used to augment on-location tutoring work: to extend the tutoring time over several days and to provide another means for students to interact with the tutors they have worked with in class. But we believe the tutor's presence *in the classroom*, with its attendant elements of collegiality, mentoring, and nurturing, is classroom-based writing tutoring's central feature. We are wary that the disadvantages identified with online tutoring might be even more pronounced with on-location tutoring. Given some classroom teachers' traditional notions of literacy, for example, extension of classroom-based tutoring online may readily revert to editing sessions. Furthermore, although much of the initial impetus for online writing tutoring was to reach new populations of students (Healy 1995; Harris and Pemberton 1995), this situation is obviated by classroom-based writing tutoring, which brings tutoring to students in a wide variety of classes, and, as Decker points out, significantly expands the center's reach.

As technologies continue to alter the way we teach writing, however, there may be additional ways to combine classroom-based writing tutoring with technology. We might explore research on the relationship between revision, writing efficiency, and community, an early interest of computer and composition specialists, who focused on word processing and its relationship to students' composing processes. Lui and Mandes in this volume have argued that students benefit from instant tutor feedback as they compose through on-location tutoring. Studies of classroom-based writing tutoring might examine the impact of computer classrooms on students' revision strategies, where revision is facilitated immediately after or even during tutoring sessions of various kinds, and on community building.

Computer-mediated composition (CMC) on local area networks and the Internet may also have a fruitful role to play in classroom-based writing tutoring.[3] Generally, CMC is thought to democratize the classroom, for it enables students to create their own diverse community, participate in written dialogue in the classroom, and engage in a process that mirrors their own initiation into academic discourse (Cooper and Selfe 1990). Absent academic authorial presence, online forums more readily enable students to participate in cultural critique, challenging social and political definitions of good writing and acceptable knowledge, and empowering their own voices in an atmosphere of egalitarianism.[4] Thus classroom-based writing tutoring, which also resists classroom hierarchical structures and recenters authority with tutors and students, may be a likely fit with CMC.

Laurie Grobman's study of tutor-led peer response groups using MOO conferencing in the classroom is one model for allying CMC with on-location peer tutoring, although the CMC dimension of the project was not the focus of her study. In designing the project, Grobman had hoped that the democratizing potential typically associated with CMC would foster more honest and authoritative responses, since basic writers, for many reasons, often hold back in response sessions. Certainly, further research can assess this potential in CMC tutor-led response sessions. Moreover, by conducting sessions online, students, tutors, and instructors can "reexperience" and thus assess the peer group process through logged transcripts, potentially benefiting student response and revision as well as tutor training.

Finally, as the notion of the classroom itself extends into virtual spaces through the proliferation of online and distance courses, tutoring on location may expand along with it. We can envision specific tutors attached to particular students in online classes, where the tutors are involved in curricular matters and work collaboratively with teachers as virtual classroom-based tutors. Of course, in such situations, issues of authority, collaboration, negotiation, and tutor training become even more complicated, demanding further inquiry and analysis.

In this volume, we have tried to expose teacher-scholars to current models of on-location tutoring, to identify its advantages and disadvantages, and to suggest possibilities for further exploration and practice. Most important, we hope to have initiated dialogue so that other models can be designed, implemented, and shared.

The myriad configurations of classroom-based tutoring highlight composition's concern and respect for students as meaning makers. Placing students and tutors at the center of classroom practice, on-location tutoring reforms classroom hierarchical relations and institutional structures; it shows students (tutors and the students with whom they work) that their work as knowledge makers matters and that they have much to contribute to one another, to faculty, and to the institution as a whole.

# NOTES

### INTRODUCTION

1.   Our understanding of genre is closely related to Kenneth Burke's sense: each genre produces its own *orientation*, a "sense of relationships" (1984, 18) or "view of reality" (3). From Hans George Gadamer, we have borrowed the parallel notion of conceptual "horizon" (Weinsheimer 1985, 157).

2.   As Brian Stross observes, the "cultural hybrid is a metaphorical broadening" of the biological hybrid, which is the "offspring of a mating by any two unlike animals or plants" (1999, 254). The cultural hybrid is "heterogeneous in origin or composition."

3.   While such work for multiculturalists is steeped in contentious and perhaps irreconcilable debates about power, culture, and social otherness (see Grimm 1999 for an examination of cultural issues regarding tutoring work), the notion of generic hybridism helps us to emphasize the "play" among the various theoretical and methodological influences that have helped us to theorize classroom-based writing tutoring.

4.   According to Brian Stross, cultural hybridity is marked by the "heterogeneity of relevant elemental factors contributed by the 'parents'" (1999, 256).

5.   Since at least the early 1970s, writing centers have served as models for tapping the power of peer influence. Writing centers are marked by collaboration that is student-centered, nonhierarchical, and equally respectful of "the voice of everyone involved" (M. Harris 2001, 436). Moreover, writing center theory and practice stress liberation from institutional structures and constraints (436). The best writing centers are abuzz with informal, energized peer interaction and learning (437). In general, tutors do not hold the same kinds of evaluative authority that teachers do and, as a result, student writers are more likely to regard tutors as allies who will help them to overcome institutional obstacles (M. Harris 1995a, 27–28). At tutoring sessions, tutors and writers exchange information and build on each other's ideas in informal and, at times, circuitous, freewheeling conversations; peer tutors also offer encouragement, support, and "insider" knowledge about being

a student as well as about being a writer. Because writing centers have traditionally asserted that their central role is "to produce better writers, not better writing" (North 1984, 438; see also M. Harris 1992a), they emphasize instruction rather than correction and the attendant processes of inventing, reseeing, composing, and revising through readers' and writers' conversations.

6.    Muriel Harris implores her colleagues in composition and English studies to "step in [to writing centers] and look around" in order to "envision alternative forms of writing instruction" (2001, 439). Pragmatically, too, offering expanded services, including training, resources, and theoretical perspectives for tutors working in classroom settings, helps to secure for writing centers an integral role within their institutions.

7.    It was their observing the benefits of students' working one-to-one with tutors in writing centers that prompted some writing teachers to seek similar applications in their own classrooms, initially adding a required lab component to first-year or basic writing classes and later "expand[ing] the scope of [lab] activities in new and much more sophisticated directions" (Kail and Trimbur 1987, 6). One of the earliest published reports of such a project is Mary Soliday's program at CCNY, in which writing center tutors were appointed to several sections of a two-semester experimental course, College Writing I and II (Soliday 1995, 59).

8.    Writing across the curriculum initiatives emphasize writing in (what are commonly called) "content" courses. Even more than writing centers, WAC programs focus on writing to learn, although they have a complementary goal of teaching students to write in their specific disciplines (McLeod and Maimon 2000, 577). Writing is thus considered "an essential component of critical thinking and problem solving . . . a way of constructing knowledge" (McLeod et al. 2001, 3; see also McLeod and Maimon 2000). WAC approaches encourage ungraded exercises, in which students write for themselves in order to figure out what they mean and what they don't understand. WAC goals may also include fostering disciplinary knowledge about writing through programs that help teachers to construct effective writing assignments or guide students in particular genre conventions. Both writing to learn and learning to write activities encourage instructors to reflect on course objectives and methods (McLeod and Maimon 2000, 580). Like writing centers, WAC programs encourage "profound change[s] in pedagogy and curriculum" based on an active, engaged learning paradigm (578).

According to WAC historians, WAC programs trace a course parallel to writing center expansion, intersecting with tutoring assistance in the disciplines (McLeod et al. 2001, 13). In terms of genealogy, it is difficult to assign primary parenthood because "two basic models drive WAC-writing center connections: writing centers beget WAC programs or WAC programs beget writing centers" (Mullin 2001, 183). Often the WAC–writing center association occurs when faculty in the disciplines request peer tutors to augment discipline-specific writing instruction or to provide feedback to students' papers. Because they do not view themselves as writing teachers, "content" faculty often deem themselves ill equipped to describe methods or explain ways of thinking about how to write. Therefore, they may seek support from tutors who can address students' assignments in disciplines besides English. At some schools, WAC initiatives remain apart from writing centers, separately training and linking tutors with faculty who teach courses outside of English studies.

9.     In 1992, Tori Haring-Smith reported over one hundred writing fellows programs (in various incarnations) at numerous schools (182). Margot Soven's 1993 survey of ninety-five institutions that had requested information from Brown University or had attended workshops on curriculum-based tutoring at the 1988 or 1990 CCCC convention yielded twenty-six returned surveys (59). Of the twenty-six, eighteen reported some kind of curriculum-based tutoring program (59–60), and anecdotal information suggests to us that interest is growing.

WAC tutoring programs have these common features: tutors are integral to the course, coming to class to introduce themselves, collect papers, and set up conference times with students; tutors work with all students in a particular course, not just those identified as "needy" by self or teacher; tutors assist faculty members with assignment design; and they present the classroom instructor with strategies for responding to student papers (Haring-Smith 1992, 178; Soven 2001, 203–4).

The writing fellows program at Brown University has become the model for many curriculum-based peer tutoring initiatives. Initiated by Harriet Sheridan and developed by Tori Haring-Smith in the early 1980s, the Brown University Writing Fellows Program involves undergraduate peer tutors who serve as first readers for papers written for particular courses in the university. In the Brown model, tutors come from a variety of majors and fields and act as "educated lay readers" without particular discipline-specific knowledge (Haring-Smith 1992, 179); however, other programs find it advantageous to match writing fellows with courses in their majors (Soven 2001, 211–15).

10. Developing in tandem with writing centers and WAC initiatives but focused on content acquisition rather than on writing to learn or learning to write, SI was initially designed as academic support for students in courses designated "high risk," or extremely difficult. SI aims at assisting students in a wide range of courses and of wide-ranging academic abilities, serving an estimated quarter million students each academic term (Arendale 2002, 19–21). Numerous studies reveal that SI programs contribute to student participants' increased self-esteem, lower attrition rates, and higher grades (see, for example, Blanc, DeBuhr, and Martin 1983; Commander et al. 1996; Arendale 2002).

11. Although SI is curriculum-based and similar to some writing fellows initiatives, typically such programs emphasize course-content acquisition and course-related learning strategies, not writing as a skill or as a strategy for learning. However, some SI practitioners have used SI in writing classes. Gary Hafer argues that it is a common misperception that tutoring works better than SI in composition courses, which are not identified as "high-risk" courses and which are thought by those outside the discipline to be void of "content" (2001, 31). Hafer asserts that SI and composition pedagogy share many similarities, including their focus on learning strategies; on problem solving; on process, not content; and on collaborative group work with student interaction and peer support (32,34). In Hafer's view, the goals of SI have more in common with collaborative composition pedagogy than do the one-to-one tutorials of writing centers.

12. More than two decades ago, collaborative learning and collaborative writing theories reinvigorated composition studies' appreciation of both peer tutoring and writing classroom peership activities. Kenneth Bruffee's early articles called for educators to tap the "powerful educative force of peer influence" (1984, 638; 1998, 127) and to dismantle traditional, authoritarian instructional practices (1972, 1973). In "Collaborative Learning and the 'Conversation of Mankind'" (1984), which argues for the importance of peer response in writing instruction, and "Peer Tutoring and the 'Conversation of Mankind'" (1998), which extols writing center tutoring, Bruffee stresses "conversations to promote intellectual growth." In Bruffee's view, students develop knowledge by reflecting on their products and processes, while reflection is "learned" socially by talking with others (1998, 129). Therefore, Bruffee argues, students must engage in conversation at various points in their writing process (131) in order to externalize and reflect on their composing activities as well as on their written texts.

Despite the many valid critiques of consensus and community that define Bruffee's work, composition scholarship confirms that peer writing groups benefit student writers. Whether they are imagined as cities in which conflict and dissensus thrive (J. Harris 1989) or as "social networks" that support learning and student needs (Wiley 2001) or as something in between, peer writing groups create practicable settings for stimulating peer conversation. In his most recent effort to rethink the notion of community in favor of "more open, contested, and heteroglot spheres of discourse," Joseph Harris proposes three alternative terms: public, material, and circulation (2001, 4). In the most effective writing groups, members share drafts, offer response, and collaboratively construct knowledge.

13.    Peer group communities are configured as sites of autonomy; fostered by writing teachers, their independence from teachers often marks their success. According to Karen Spear, in effective writing groups, "students explore and resolve ideas together. Writers share with readers the responsibility for generating and testing ideas, while readers . . . pool opinions and reactions, explore differences, and come to conclusions" (1988, 57). In peer groups, Spear stresses, the reader "shares responsibility for the content of the revised piece" and is not only involved in "asking questions and making suggestions, but also in thinking through new possibilities *with* the writer" (59; see Bishop 1988, 121).

Today, writing groups are so intrinsic to composition classrooms that they may seem unremarkable. Yet, instructors continue to seek better ways to orchestrate writing groups where trusting and meaningful talk leads to active draft revision and a more comprehensive understanding of what it means to be a writer (see, for example, Brooke, Mirtz, and Evans 1994a; Roskelly 1999; Moss, Highberg, and Nicolas 2003). As a result, some teachers invite more experienced peer writers to serve as writing group facilitators or "leaders," thus combining peer writing group theory with writing tutoring to implement a classroom-based tutoring model.

14.    Carino explains that for many early theorists, "center" represented a first "move toward empowerment," from the marginalized idea of "clinic" and the more negative connotations of "lab," to a conception of collaboration that "claim[s] to be central to all writers" (1995, 43; see also Addison and Wilson, 1991).]

15.    Although the writing fellows program at the University of Wisconsin–Madison is *curriculum-based* rather than *classroom-based* as we use the

terms in this book, we chose to include Jennifer Corroy's chapter because the salient issues she addresses are pertinent to classroom-based writing tutoring.

## CHAPTER THREE

1.    My study does not account for the particular characteristics of online tutoring. However, as Candace Spigelman and I suggest in our concluding chapter in this volume, electronic forms of classroom-based writing tutoring beg further exploration.

2.    Margaret Weaver (1995) rightfully acknowledges the debate over authority and peer response groups in basic writing research. That is, some theorists advocate consensus, that peer response enables students to join our conversations, while others advocate dissent, that peer response groups enable basic writers to resist academic discourse, though she perhaps creates a false dichotomy. Nevertheless, because I believe the use of peer group leaders can facilitate both dissensus and consensus, debating the issue itself is beyond the scope of this essay.

3.    I received this grant in conjunction with a former colleague, Claudine Keenan. Claudine used a peer group leader in her basic writing class at the Lehigh Valley campus of Penn State University, Berks–Lehigh Valley College; my study involves my class at the Berks campus.

4.    Throughout this article, I use pseudonyms for both the peer group leader and the students in my basic writing class.

5.    Melissa Nicolas's chapter in this collection also addresses Harris's discussion of peer collaboration.

6.    I am not encouraging teachers to disappear completely, however. Indeed, I introduced a writing rubric to my students, one that closely resembled my own set of writing assessment criteria, with greater emphasis on content and meaning than mechanics, and throughout the semester, we circled back to these issues in numerous ways. However, my attention to rhetorical issues had more to do with my general approach to teaching academic discourse, rather than specifically focused on modeling for peer response groups.

7.    I have edited the transcripts to make them intelligible (students writing online tend to rush and transcripts can be difficult to read), but I have been very careful not to appropriate their words or language.

## CHAPTER FOUR

Our thanks to the following writing center consultants for their contributions to the pilot Bridge Program in 2000 and to this article: Nick

Aguina, Sharon Gissy, Dana Lord, Benjamin Miller, Joseph Ruzich, and Julie Shannon.

1. Jim Ottery is former coordinator of the basic writing program and Bridge Program writing instructor; Jean Petrolle is director of composition and Bridge Program writing instructor; Derek Boczkowski is assistant director of the writing center; and Steve Mogge is former coordinator of college reading and Bridge Program reading.

2. Elizabeth Silk, Columbia College's director of institutional research, was hesitant to provide statistics regarding students in the pilot Bridge Program because "the size of the cohort was really not large enough from which to draw any conclusions" (e-mail, 23 April 2002).

3. Since this chapter was drafted, the economic downturn that has affected colleges, universities, and their programs across the country has taken its toll on Columbia College's Bridge Program. During the summer of 2002, while class size remained small, the roles of teachers and writing center consultants changed. Two consultants were still assigned to work with two teachers, but they split their three hours of class time between the teachers' separate classes. Two consultants were thus responsible for working with up to thirty students and for only half the time as in 2000 and 2001. As one professor of reading who taught in the summer of 2002 told me, this watering down of the consultants' role made it impossible for them to establish close relationships with students, faculty members, and course subject matter as they had in the past.

## CHAPTER FIVE

I would like to thank Professor Candace Spigelman for her guidance on this project.

1. The students' names are pseudonyms, and they have given written permission expressing their willingness to participate in the study. The project received approval to conduct research on human subjects from the Penn State University Compliance Office.

## CHAPTER SIX

1. While North was not the first or only author to advocate a nonintrusive, noneditorial model for writing center tutorials, his essay stands as one of the most-cited statements of writing center philosophy. It is referenced in numerous writing center mission statements, as well as the predominance of subsequent writing center scholarship. At Eastern, when our president expressed interest in establishing a writing center, our writing program director immediately sent him a copy of North's

essay in order to provide him with an enlightened understanding of what such a center would be about.

2.    That handbook, entitled *It's a Whole New Ballgame*, contained classroom-based tutoring strategies that Holly had discovered in her work as a tutor and that Barbara suggested from her perspective as instructor. It comprised the first incarnation of what has become this article.

## CHAPTER SEVEN

1.    With George Dillon, I focus on issues of power and authority in another decentralizing-writing-centers essay, "The Rhetoric of Online Conferencing" (forthcoming).

2.    The issue of plagiarism is given considerable treatment, most notably for our purposes here, by Clark; Haviland and Mullin; Shamoon and Burns; and Spigelman in the 1999 *Perspectives on Plagiarism and Intellectual Property in a Postmodern World*.

3.    Beginning in the mid-1980s, immediately following North's (1984) impassioned argument for writing center autonomy (see Decker, chapter 1), writing center theorists/practitioners began to (counter)argue the need for writing centers to decentralize by sending tutors into classrooms. In a *WCJ* 2003 special reprint of "Independence and Collaboration: Why We Should Decentralize Writing Centers," first published in 1986, Louise Z. Smith critiques North's "Idea of a Writing Center" (1984) by drawing upon the Queens College model and, especially, the UMass–Boston's tutoring program to illustrate how "the idea of the 'center' has gotten in the way" of productive writing center/classroom collaborations (22). Smith urges writing center directors and faculty across the curriculum to look at the "choreography" between UMass–Boston's English department and writing center. This dance pairs one tutor to each section of first-year English. Tutors and professors negotiate the role of the tutor according to the teachers' pedagogical preferences. Tutors, in turn, help teach in the class with the professor with the goal of trying to present to students an approachable, knowledgeable person who functions more as a concerned peer (listener) than a judger or grader (Smith 2003, 20). And over fifteen years later she still believes in the relevancy of this original message. In a brief introduction to the 2003 reprint, Smith jokes, "As pink-bewigged Mrs. Slocombe on the British sitcom 'Are You Being Served?' proclaims, 'I am unanimous!' In fact, today I am even more unanimous than when *WCJ* published this article in 1986" (15). In 1990, Muriel Harris recognized that this trend "is the melding of our pedagogy with classroom instruction in interesting new ways. . . .

As a way to help our colleagues learn about what we do, this may be a particularly encouraging trend. In addition, it offers us some interesting new ways to expand the role of the tutor" (24). In that same edition of the *WCJ*, Thomas Hemmeter argues that "we can recognize in classroom practices traces of writing center instruction. . . . Similarly, the group instruction assumed to belong to the classroom belongs as much to the writing center, suggesting that the writing center always contains within itself this trace of the classroom" (1990, 43). And in her essay "Shifting Roles in Classroom Tutoring: Cultivating the Art of Boundary Crossing" (1995), Mary Soliday talks of the potential for richer collaborations between classrooms and centers where the lines between teachers and students are blurred, where the roles of tutors can be more teacherly or studently, where tutors can use their outsiderness or insiderness to advantage. But this hybridized role, Soliday admits, turning to the work of Kail and Trimbur (1987), is politically charged and the potential for conflict exists with each expedition.

4.  Other IWCA/ NCPTW 2003 Joint Conference sessions that emphasized classroom negotiations among students, tutors, and instructors further contributed to my thinking about directive versus nondirective tutoring efforts. Ackerman's session discussed the importance of tutors' establishing trust and helping students in classrooms feel comfortable. Interestingly, the presenters emphasized how to negotiate some of the logistical and collaborative issues among classroom teacher, tutors, and writing fellow director. Ryan, Zimmerelli, and Wright's session offered rationales for tutors' leading peer response groups, including: being able to see and react to the instructor's concerns about writing on their turf and noting how much students appreciate tutors visiting them versus the typical writing center visit.

## CHAPTER EIGHT

1.  Occasionally, we had PWCs and 110W students who were nontraditional students, returning to college after an extended absence. The interpersonal dynamics in groups in which there are significant age differences are often very different from same-age groups. Many of the differences are related to issues of life experience. Unfortunately, exploring these dynamics is beyond the scope of this essay.

## CHAPTER NINE

1.  The students participating in the study have been given pseudonyms and have given approval to be part of this study through written consent.

**CHAPTER ELEVEN**

1.    Our strongly felt alliance with faculty arose not only because of our relationships with them, but also because we faced direct institutional pressure for our funded program to show results. Biweekly meetings between the WAC administrators and a representative of the Provost's Office were requested by administration for updates on efforts and results. In addition to the biweekly meetings, written reports were required weekly. And by Fall 2001, the state's growing budget crisis left us with a sense of emergency: if we could not prove the program's merits, we feared it would be cut. (Indeed, our worst fears were realized during the fall term when we received word that the program could not be funded for the spring.)

2.    For an excellent discussion of ways that tutors are viewed as authorities, see Gillam 1994.

**CHAPTER TWELVE**

I would like to thank Noreen Groover Lape for her insightful reading of an earlier draft of this essay.

**CHAPTER THIRTEEN**

1.    As part of my grant, peer group leaders received free textbooks for the seminar and also texts for my developmental writing course, so that they could stay abreast of the readings and assignments that their writing group members were doing. In the seminar, we discussed articles relating to response group processes, writing processes, revising, basic writing, and so on. The peer group leaders also kept journals, recording the problems, breakthroughs, and activities of their weekly group meetings. As the culminating activity for the seminar, each tutor conducted qualitative research, in which, with their permission, writing group members became research subjects. In this way, the students at both levels found they were integral to each other's academic progress. In succeeding years, our classroom-based writing tutoring program grew and evolved. Today, sophomore-, junior-, and senior-level students in a dozen different majors enroll in the seminar each fall semester, train in classes taught by instructors other than me, and become writing fellows in classrooms across the college.

2.    The students remained within their assigned writing groups throughout the semester. Using an opening-day writing sample, I organized the groups according to their apparent writing ability. In each group, I tried to balance strong writers with those who appeared to have moderate

or limited writing experience or skill. However, early in the semester, some of the peer group leaders observed expressions of inadequacy from weaker group members, which suggests that this was not the best arrangement (see Gonzalez in this volume). In later semesters, I tried to group students of similar ability together, and I have encouraged this model when instructors request group leaders for their writing classes.

3. With the exception of Casey You, the names of all peer group leaders are pseudonyms. You's article (pulished as Gonzalez), "Building Trust While Building Skills," appeared in *Journal of Teaching Writing* (Spring 2002), and is reprinted with modifications in this volume.

4. While I agree that tutors do face various crises of authority arising out of their conflicted status as peers and instructional assistants, I question the absolute distinction between writing center–based and classroom-based arrangements. In "'Peer Tutoring:' A Contradiction in Terms?" (1998), Trimbur shows that role conflict occurs in writing center tutoring too. When good students begin tutoring in the writing center, they too struggle with their desire to identify with teachers or to seek teacher approval marked by grades. Furthermore, Kail and Trimbur (1987) and Healy (1993) assume that peer tutors and tutees will naturally build knowledge together. Quite often, however, the writing center tutor in the role of "expert" will guide, suggest, and edit, deriving authority from his or her tutor status and from the tutees' expectations of learning center instruction (see, especially, Grimm 1999).

5. Basing her arguments on the distinctions drawn by Muriel Harris, Nicolas asserts that training for tutoring and peer group work must remain separate and distinct "because, as the separate models imply, there are different skill sets required to have effective tutorials and productive peer response groups" (1999, 6). Interestingly, Soliday (1995) calls for greater integration of consultants into classroom life while Nicolas's critique of her initial Ohio State tutoring project suggests off-site tutoring, more like the present CUNY model (1999).

6. For student writing, the spelling has been standardized.

7. Contrasting this perspective with other forms of "teacher power" in K–12 classrooms, O'Hair and Blase confirm that egalitarian, student-centered approaches seem to increase student learning, while "coercive power" and "legitimate power" both decrease student learning (1992, 15). They advocate small doses of "expert power," in which the teacher derives authority from his or her subject-area knowledge, but emphasize an approach that uses "referent power," in which teachers use a form of communication that responds directly to the personal and academic needs of their students (13).

8. According to John Trimbur (1998), such concerns are typical of new writing center tutors as well. Because higher education makes grading the absolute measure of success, tutors gauge their instructional effectiveness by their tutees' grades (117).

9. Over the years, I have found that portfolios help to diminish grade anxiety in classes where this kind of classroom-based writing tutoring occurs. In portfolio classes, peer group leaders can engage with the instructor in ongoing formative response while summative evaluation concerns only teacher and student writer at the end of the semester.

## CONCLUSION

Special thanks to the following Penn State Berks writing fellows for their assistance with the section of this essay entitled "Promoting Successful Classroom-Based Writing Tutoring": SaraLouise Howells, Natalie Kakareka, Nicolas Moyer, and Ray Rishty.

1. Ashton-Jones (1995) cites numerous studies about male-female group and one-to-one conversations that she applies to collaborative learning in writing classes. For example, she refers to Pamela Fishman's studies of conversational dynamics, pointing to the finding that men's attempts to get topics to become conversations succeeded 97 percent of the time, while for women it was 38 percent (Fishman 1983, 97; cited in Ashton-Jones 1995, 12). "Thus," Fishman asserts, "the definition of what is appropriate or inappropriate conversation becomes the man's choice" (98; qtd. in Ashton-Jones 1995, 13). Furthermore, Helena M. Leet-Pellegrini's study indicates that even when women have expertise and power, men's "conversational advantage" remains (cited in Ashton-Jones 1995, 15).

2. Grobman's chapter in *On Location* did not specifically address issues of race or other forms of difference, but her article points to the need for study in this arena. The peer group leader, Tyisha, is a female African American sophomore who worked with white students in a basic writing class.

3. From another vantage point, James A. Inman and Donna N. Sewell observe the myriad ways electronic media have "enable[d] writing center professionals to stay connected to each other" (2003, 177); we envision electronic media to function similarly for faculty, administrators, and tutors involved in classroom-based writing tutoring.

4. Stan and Collins note, however, that some studies suggest that CMC silences some students while providing safe venues for others (1988, 27).

# REFERENCES

Ackerman, David, Candace Spigelman, Laura Gamble, Sara Louise Howells, Natalie Kakareka, Nicholas Moyer, and Ray Rishty. 2003. Navigating New Waters: Writing (Back) on the Rocky Seas of Classroom-Based Writing Tutoring. Paper presented at the IWCA/NCPTW Joint Conference, October, Hershey, PA.

Addison, Jim, and Henry Wilson. 1991. From Writing Lab to Writing Center: Reinventing, Expanding, and Advancing. In *The Writing Center: New Directions*, edited by Ray Wallace and Jeanne Simpson, 56–72. New York: Garland.

Allaei, Sara Kurtz, and Ulla Maija Connor. 1990. Exploring the Dynamics of Cross-Cultural Collaboration in Writing Classrooms. *Writing Instructor* 10:19–28.

Arendale, David R. 2002. History of Supplemental Instruction (SI): Mainstreaming of Developmental Education. In *Histories of Developmental Education*, edited by Dana Britt Lundell and Jeanne L. Higbee, 15–27. Minneapolis: Center for Research on Developmental Education and Urban Literacy, General College, University of Minnesota.

Ashton-Jones, Evelyn. 1995. Collaboration, Conversation, and the Politics of Gender. In *Feminine Principles and Women's Experience in American Composition and Rhetoric*, edited by Louise Wetherbee Phelps and Janet Emig, 5–26. Pittsburgh: University of Pittsburgh Press.

Bakhtin, M. M. 1986. *Speech Genres and Other Late Essays.* Translated by Vern W. McGee and edited by Caryl Emerson and Michael Holquist. Austin: University of Texas Press.

Bardine, Bryan A., Molly Schmitz Bardine, and Elizabeth F. Deegan. 2000. Beyond the Red Pen: Clarifying Our Role in the Response Process. *English Journal* 90:94–101.

Barnett, Robert W., and Jacob S. Blumner, eds. 2001. *The Allyn and Bacon Guide to Writing Center Theory and Practice.* Boston: Allyn and Bacon.

Bartholomae, David. 1986. Inventing the University. *Journal of Basic Writing* 3:4–23.

———. 1987. Writing on the Margins: The Concept of Literacy in Higher Education. In *A Sourcebook for Basic Writing Teachers*, edited by Theresa Enos, 66–83. New York: Random House.

Bartholomae, David, and Anthony R. Petrosky. 1986. *Facts, Artifacts, and Counterfacts: Theory and Method for a Reading and Writing Course.* Upper Montclair, NJ: Boynton/Cook.

Baumlin, James S., and Margaret E. Weaver. 2000. Teaching, Classroom Authority, and the Psychology of Transference. *Journal of General Education* 49.2:75–87.

Bawarshi, Anis. 2003. *Genre and the Invention of the Writer: Reconsidering the Place of Invention in Composition*. Logan: Utah State University Press.

Bazerman, Charles. 1997. The Life of Genre, the Life in the Classroom. In Bishop and Ostrom, 1997, 19–26.

Beason, Larry, and Laurel Darrow. 1997. Listening as Assessment: How Students and Teachers Evaluate WAC. In Yancey and Huot, 1997, 97–121.

Behling, Laura L. 2003. "Generic" Multiculturalism: Hybrid Texts, Cultural Contexts. *College English* 65:411–26.

Benesch, Sarah. 1985. Improving Peer Response: Collaboration between Teachers and Students. *Journal of Teaching Writing* 4:87–94.

Berkenkotter, Carol. 1984. Student Writers and Their Sense of Authority over Texts. *College Composition and Communication* 3:312–19.

Berthoff, Ann E. 1984. Is Teaching Still Possible? *College English* 46:743–55.

Bishop, Wendy. 1988. Helping Peer Writing Groups Succeed. *Teaching English in the Two-Year College* 15:120–25.

Bishop, Wendy, and Hans Ostrom, eds. 1997a. *Genre and Writing: Issues, Arguments, Alternatives*. Portsmouth, NH: Boynton/Cook.

———. 1997b. Introduction. In Bishop and Ostrom 1997a, ix–xv.

Bizzell, Patricia. 1999. Hybrid Academic Discourses: What, Why, How. *Composition Studies* 27:7–21.

Black, Laurel. 1998. *Between Talk and Teaching: Reconsidering the Writing Conference*. Logan: Utah State University Press.

Blanc, Robert A., Larry E. DeBuhr, and Deanna C. Martin. 1983. Breaking the Attrition Cycle: The Effects of Supplemental Instruction on Undergraduate Performance and Attrition. *Journal of Higher Education* 54:80–90.

Boquet, Elizabeth H. 2000. Intellectual Tug-of-War: Snapshots of Life in the Center. In Briggs and Woolbright 2000, 17–30.

———. 2002. *Noise from the Writing Center*. Logan: Utah State University Press.

Bosker, Julie. 2000. Dilemmas of Collaboration for the Tutor with Work Experience. *Writing Lab Newsletter* 25.9:5–9

Brannon, Lil, and Stephen North. 2000. The Uses of the Margins. *Writing Center Journal* 20.2:7–12.

Briggs, Lynn Craigue, and Meg Woolbright, eds. 2000. *Stories from the Center: Connecting Narrative and Theory in the Writing Center*. Urbana, IL: NCTE.

Brodkey, Linda. 1987. Modernism and the Scene(s) of Writing. *College English* 49:396–418.

Brooke, Robert. 1994. Invitations to a Writer's Life: Guidelines for Designing Small-Group Writing Classes. In Brooke, Mirtz, and Evans 1994b, 7–30.

Brooke, Robert, Ruth Mirtz, and Rick Evans. 1994a. Our Students' Experiences with Groups. In Brooke, Mirtz, and Evans 1994b, 31–51.

———, eds. 1994b. *Small Groups in Writing Workshops: Invitations to a Writer's Life*. Urbana, IL: NCTE.

Brooks, Jeff. 1991. Minimalist Tutoring: Making the Students Do All the Work. *Writing Lab Newsletter* 19.2:1–4.

Bruffee, Kenneth. 1972. The Way Out. *College English* 33:457–70.

———. 1973. Collaborative Learning: Some Practical Models. *College English* 34:634–43.

———. 1978. The Brooklyn Plan: Attaining Intellectual Growth through Peer-Group Tutoring. *Liberal Education* 64:447–68.

———. 1984. Collaborative Learning and the "Conversation of Mankind." *College English* 46:635–52.

———. *Collaborative Learning.* 1993. Baltimore: Johns Hopkins University Press.

———. 1998. Peer Tutoring and the "Conversation of Mankind." In Capossela 1998, 127–38. First published in *Writing Centers: Theory and Administration,* edited by Gary A. Olson 1984, 3–15. Evanston, IL: NCTE.

———. 1999. *Collaborative Learning: Higher Education, Interdependence, and the Authority of Knowledge.* 2nd ed. Baltimore: Johns Hopkins University Press.

Buranen, Lise, and Alice M. Roy, eds. 1999. *Perspectives on Plagiarism and Intellectual Property in a Postmodern World.* Albany. State University of New York Press.

Burke, Kenneth. 1984. *Permanence and Change: An Anatomy of Purposes.* 3rd ed. Berkeley: University of California Press.

Capossela, Toni-Lee. 1998. *The Harcourt Brace Guide to Peer Tutoring.* Fort Worth: Harcourt Brace.

Carino, Peter. 1995. What Do We Talk about When We Talk about Our Metaphors: A Cultural Critique of Clinic, Lab, and Center. In Murphy and Law 1995, 37–46. First published in *Writing Center Journal* 13.1 (1992): 31–42.

———. 2003. Power and Authority in Peer Tutoring. In Pemberton and Kinkead 2003, 96–113. Logan: Utah State University Press.

Clark, Irene L. 1988. Collaboration and Ethics in Writing Center Pedagogy. *Writing Center Journal* 9.1:3–12.

———. 1999. Writing Centers and Plagiarism. In Buranen and Roy 1999, 155–67.

———. 2001. Perspectives on the Directive/Non-Directive Continuum in the Writing Center. *Writing Center Journal* 22.1:33–58.

Clark, Irene L., and Dave Healy. 1996. Are Writing Centers Ethical? *WPA: Writing Program Administration* 20.1–2:32–48.

Commander, Nannette Evans, et al. 1996. A Learning Assistance Model for Academic Support. *Journal of Developmental Education* 20:8–12, 14, 16.

Coogan, David. 1995. E-Mail Tutoring, A New Way to Do New Work. *Computers and Composition* 12:171–81.

Cooper, Marilyn M. 1989. Women's Ways of Writing. In *Writing as Social Action,* edited by Marilyn M. Cooper and Michael Holzman, 141–59. Portsmouth, NH: Heinemann–Boynton/Cook.

Cooper, Marilyn M., and Cynthia L. Selfe. 1990. Computer Conferences and Learning: Authority, Resistance, and Internally Persuasive Discourse. *College English* 52:847–69.

Corbett, Edward P. J. 1990. *Classical Rhetoric for the Modern Student.* 3rd ed. New York. Oxford University Press.

Corbett, Steven J. 2002. The Role of the Emissary: Helping to Bridge the Communication Canyon between Instructors and Students. *Writing Lab Newsletter* 27.2:10–11.

Corbett, Steven J., and George L. Dillon. 2003, The Rhetoric of Online Conferencing. *Academic Exchange Quarterly* 7.4:273–77.

Cowne, Ellen, and Susan Little. 1999. Giving Up My Kids: Two Mentor Teachers' Stories. In *Teacher/Mentor: A Dialogue for Collaborative Learning*, edited by Peg Graham, Sally Hudson-Ross, Chandra Adkins, Patti McWhorter, and Jennifer McDuffie Stewart, 46–52. New York: Teachers College Press.

Cronon, Bill. 1998. The Undergraduate Writing Fellows: Teaching Writing and Much More. *Time to Write* (September): 1–2. University of Wisconsin–Madison.

Driver, Felix. 1994. Bodies in Space: Foucault's Account of Disciplinary Power. In *Reassessing Foucault: Power, Medicine, and the Body*, edited by Colin Jones and Roy Porter, 113–31. London: Routledge.

Duffey, Suellyn, and Donna LeCourt. 1991. English 693 Syllabus. Ohio State University, Columbus.

Dunbar, Melissa. 1999. A Hybrid of a Hybrid: Tutoring Peer-Response Groups. Paper presented at the National Conference on Peer Tutoring in Writing, 29 October, University Park, PA.

Durst, Russel K. 1999. *Collision Course: Conflict, Negotiation, and Learning in College Composition*. Urbana, IL: NCTE.

Dylan, Bob. 1969. Lay Lady Lay. In *Nashville Skyline*. Columbia.

Elbow, Peter. 1973. *Writing without Teachers*. New York: Oxford University Press.

———. 1990. *What Is English?* New York: MLA.

Evans, Rick. 1994. Changing the Frame: Writing, Reading, and Learning about Writing in Small Groups. In Brooke, Mirtz, and Evans 1994b, 154–71.

Fisher, Roger, and William Ury. 1981. *Getting to Yes: Negotiating Agreement without Giving In*. Boston: Houghton Mifflin.

Fishman, Pamela. 1983. Interaction: The Work Women Do. In *Language, Gender, and Society*, edited by Barrie Thorne, Cheris Kramarae, and Nancy Henley, 89–101. Rowley, MA: Newbury.

Fishman, Stephen M., and Lucille Parkinson McCarthy. 1992. Is Expressivism Dead? Reconsidering Its Romantic Roots and Its Relation to Social Constructionism. *College English* 54:647–61.

Foucault, Michel. 1988. *Politics, Philosophy, and Culture: Interviews and Other Writings, 1977–1984*. Edited by Lawrence D. Kritzman. New York: Routledge.

Freedman, Aviva. 1995. The What, Where, When, Why, and How of Classroom Genres. In Petraglia 1995, 121–44.

Freire, Paulo. 1970. *Pedagogy of the Oppressed*. Translated by Myra Bergman Ramos. New York: Continuum.

Friedman, Susan Stanford. 1985. Authority in the Feminist Classroom: A Contradiction in Terms? In *Gendered Subjects: The Dynamics of Feminist Teaching,* edited by Margo Culley and Catherine Portuges. Boston: Routledge and Kegan Paul.

Gay, Pamela. 1991. Questions and Issues in Basic Writing and Computing. *Computers and Composition* 8:63–81.

Gere, Anne Ruggles. 1987. *Writing Groups: History, Theory, and Implications.* Carbondale, Southern Illinois University Press.

Gillam, Alice M. 1994. Collaborative Learning Theory and Peer Tutoring Practice. In *Intersections: Theory-Practice in the Writing Center,* edited by Joan A. Mullin and Ray Wallace, 39–53. Urbana, IL: NCTE.

Gillespie, Paula, and Neal Lerner. 2000. *The Allyn and Bacon Guide to Peer Tutoring.* Boston: Allyn and Bacon.

Goffman, Erving. 1959. *The Presentation of Self in Everyday Life.* New York: Anchor Books-Doubleday.

Goodburn, Amy, and Beth Ina. 1994. Collaboration, Critical Pedagogy, and Struggles over Difference. *JAC: A Journal of Composition Theory* 14:131–47.

Graham, Joan. 1992. Writing Components, Writing Adjuncts, Writing Links. In McCleod and Soven 1992, 110–33.

Grimm, Nancy Maloney. 1999. *Good Intentions: Writing Center Work for Postmodern Times.* Portsmouth, NH: Boynton Cook.

Grumet, Madeleine R. 1988. *Bitter Milk: Women and Teaching.* Amherst: University of Massachusetts Press.

Hacker, Tim. 1996. The Effect of Teacher Conferences on Peer Response Discourse. *Teaching English in the Two-Year College* 23:112–26.

Hafer, Gary R. 2001. Ideas in Practice: Supplemental Instruction in Freshman Composition. *Journal of Developmental Education* 24:30–37.

Haring-Smith, Tori. 1992. Changing Students' Attitudes: Writing Fellows Programs. In McLeod and Soven 1992, 175–88.

Harris, Joseph. 1989. The Idea of Community in the Study of Writing. *College Composition and Communication* 40:11–22.

———. 2001. Beyond Community: From the Social to the Material. *Journal of Basic Writing* 20.2:3–15.

Harris, Muriel. 1983. Modeling: A Process Method of Teaching. *College English* 45:74–84.

———. 1988. Peer Tutoring: How Tutors Learn. *TETYC* 15:28–33.

———. 1986. *Teaching One-to-One: The Writing Conference.* Urbana, IL: NCTE.

———. 1990. What's Up and What's In: Trends and Traditions in Writing Centers. *The Writing Center Journal* 11.1:15–25.

———. 1992a. Collaboration Is Not Collaboration Is Not Collaboration: Writing Center Tutorials vs. Peer-Response Groups. *CCC* 43:369–83.

———. 1992b. The Writing Center and Tutoring in WAC Programs. In McLeod and Soven 1992, 154–74.

———. 1995a. Talking in the Middle: Why Writers Need Writing Tutors. *College English* 57:27–42.

————. 1995b. What's Up and What's In: Trends and Traditions in Writing Centers. In Murphy and Law 1995, 27–36. First published in *Writing Center Journal* 11.1 (1990): 15–25.

————. 2001. Centering in on Professional Choices. *CCC* 52:429–40.

Harris, Muriel, and Michael Pemberton. 1995. Online Writing Labs (OWLS): A Taxonomy of Options and Issues. *Computers and Composition* 12:145–59.

Haviland, Carol Peterson, Sherry Green, Barbara Kime Shields, and M. Todd Harper. 1999. Neither Missionaries nor Colonists nor Handmaidens: What Writing Tutors Can Teach WAC Faculty about Inquiry. In *Writing Centers and Writing across the Curriculum Programs: Building Interdisciplinary Partnerships*, edited by Robert W. Barnett and Jacob S. Blumner, 45–57. Westport, CT: Greenwood Press.

Haviland, Carol Peterson, and Joan Mullin. 1999. Writing Centers and Intellectual Property: Are Faculty Members and Students Differently Entitled? In Buranen and Roy 1999, 169–81.

Hawkins, Thom. 1980. Intimacy and Audience: The Relationship between Revision and the Social Dimension of Peer Tutoring. *College English* 42:64–68.

Healy, Dave. 1993. A Defense of Dualism: The Writing Center and the Classroom. *Writing Center Journal* 14.1:16–29.

————. 1995. From Place to Space: Perceptual and Administrative Issues in the Online Writing Center. *Computers and Composition* 12:183–93.

Healy, Dave, and Susan Bosher. 1992. ESL Tutoring: Bridging the Gap between Curriculum-Based and Writing Center Models of Peer Tutoring. *College ESL* 2.2:25–32.

Hemmeter, Thomas. 1990. The "Smack of Difference": The Language of Writing Center Discourse. *Writing Center Journal* 11.1:35–48.

Hilgers, Thomas, Ann S. Bayer, Monica Stitt-Bergh, and Megumi Taniguchi. 1995. Doing More Than "Thinning Out the Herd": How Eighty-Two College Seniors Perceived Writing-Intensive Classes. *Research in the Teaching of English* 29:59–87.

hooks, bell. 1994. *Teaching to Transgress: Education as the Practice of Freedom.* New York: Routledge.

Howe, Florence. 1971. Identity and Expression: A Writing Course for Women. *College English* 32:863–71.

Hubbuch, Susan M. 1988. A Tutor Needs to Know the Subject Matter to Help a Student with a Paper: ___Agree___Disagree___Not Sure. *Writing Center Journal* 8.2:23–30.

————. 1989–90. Confronting the Power in Empowering Students. *Writing Instructor* 9:35–44.

Inman, James A., and Donna N. Sewell. 2003. Mentoring in Electronic Spaces: Using Resources to Sustain Relationships. In Pemberton and Kinkead 2003, 177–89.

*Innovative Teaching at City College: A Handbook for Faculty across the Disciplines.* Prepared by the CCNY Writing Fellows and Mary Soliday.

Johns, Ann M. 1995. Teaching Classroom and Authentic Genres: Initiating Students into Academic Cultures and Discourses. In *Academic Writing in a Second Language*, edited by Diane Belcher and George Braine, 277–91. Norwood, NJ: Ablex.

Jones, Rachel L. 1992. What's Wrong with Black English? In *Encountering Cultures: Reading and Writing in a Changing World*, edited by Richard Holeton, 17–19. Englewood Cliffs, NJ: Blair.

Kail, Harvey, and John Trimbur. 1987. The Politics of Peer Tutoring. *Writing Center Journal* 11.1–2:5–12.

Kiedaisch, Jean, and Sue Dinitz. 1993. Look Back and Say "So What": The Limitations of the Generalist Tutor. *Writing Center Journal* 14.1:63–74.

Kinkead, Joyce A., and Jeanette G. Harris, eds. 1993. *Writing Centers in Context: Twelve Case Studies*. Urbana, IL: NCTE

Kleine, Michael. 1985. What Freshmen Say—and Might Say—to Each Other about Their Own Writing. *Journal of Teaching Writing* 4:215–33.

Koster, Josephine A. 2003. Administration across the Curriculum: Or Practicing What We Preach. In Pemberton and Kinkead 2003, 151–65.

Latterell, Catherine G. 2000. Decentering Student-Centeredness: Rethinking Tutor Authority in Writing Centers. In Briggs and Woolbright 2000, 104–20.

Lawrence, Sandra M., and Elizabeth Sommers. 1996. From the Park Bench to the (Writing) Workshop Table: Encouraging Collaboration among Inexperienced Writers. *TETYC* 23:101–11.

Leet-Pelligrini, Helena M. 1980. Conversational Dominance as a Function of Gender and Expertise. In *Language: Social Psychological Perspectives*, ed. Howard Giles et al. 1980. Oxford: Pergamon. 97–104.

Leverenz, Carrie Shively. 1994. Peer Response in a Multicultural Composition Classroom: Dissensus—A Dream (Deferred). *JAC* 14:167–86.

Levine, Judith. 1990. Using a Peer Tutor to Improve Writing in a Psychology Class: One Instructor's Experience. *Teaching of Psychology* 17:57–58.

Lunsford, Andrea. 1992. Intellectual Property, Concepts of Selfhood, and the Teaching of Writing. *Journal of Basic Writing* 11:61–73.

———. 1995. Collaboration, Control, and the Idea of a Writing Center. In Murphy and Sherwood 1995, 36–42.

———. 2000. Refiguring Classroom Authority. In *The Ethics of Writing Instruction: Issues in Theory and Practice*, edited by Michael A. Pemberton, 65–78. Stamford, CT: Ablex.

Lunsford, Andrea, and Lisa Ede. 1990. *Singular Texts/Plural Authors: Perspectives on Collaborative Writing*. Carbondale: Southern Illinois University Press.

Lutes, Jean Marie. Forthcoming. Why Feminists Make Better Tutors: Gender and Disciplinary Expertise in a Curriculum-Based Tutoring Program. In *Centered Research: New Perspectives on Writing Center Research*, edited by A. Gillam and P. Gillespie. Mahwah, NJ: Erlbaum.

Marx, Karl. 2000. Economic and Philosophical Manuscripts. In *Karl Marx: Selected Writings,* 2nd ed., edited by David McLellan, 75–112. Oxford: Oxford University Press.

Marx, Karl, and Friedrich Engels. 2001. The Fetishism of Commodities and the Secret Thereof. In *The Norton Anthology of Theory and Criticism,* edited by Vincent B. Leitch, 759–88. New York: W.W. Norton.

McAndrew, Donald, and Thomas Reigstad. 2001. *Tutoring Writing: A Practical Guide for Conferences.* Portsmouth, NH: Boynton/Cook.

McLeod, Susan H., and Elaine Maimon. 2000. Clearing the Air: WAC Myths and Realities. *College English* 62:573–83.

McLeod, Susan H., Eric Miraglia, Margot Soven, and Christopher Thaiss, eds. 2001. *WAC for the New Millennium: Strategies for Continuing Writing-across-the-Curriculum Programs.* Urbana, IL: NCTE.

McLeod, Susan H., and Margot Soven, eds. 1992. *Writing across the Curriculum: A Guide to Developing Programs.* Newbury Park, CA: SAGE.

Meyer, Emily, and Louise Z. Smith. 1987. *The Practical Tutor.* New York: Oxford University Press.

Moss, Beverly, Nels Highberg, and Melissa Nicolas, eds. 2004. *By Any Other Name: Writing Groups Inside and Outside the Classroom.* Mahwah, NJ: Lawrence Erlbaum.

Mullin, Joan A. 2001. Writing Centers and WAC. In McLeod et al. 2001, 179–99.

Murphy, Christina. 2001. Freud in the Writing Center: The Psychoanalytics of Tutoring Well. In Barnett and Blumner 2001, 296-301. First published in *Writing Center Journal* 10.1 (1989): 13–18.

Murphy, Christina, and Joe Law, eds. 1995. *Landmark Essays on Writing Centers.* Davis, CA: Hermagoras.

Murphy, Christina, and Steve Sherwood. 1995. *The St. Martin's Sourcebook for Writing Tutors.* New York: St. Martin's Press.

Murray, Donald M. 1978. Teach the Motivating Force of Revision. *English Journal* 67:56–60.

Myers, Greg. 1986. Reality, Consensus, and Reform in the Rhetoric of Composition Teaching. *College English* 48:154–73.

Newkirk, Thomas. 1984. Direction and Misdirection in Peer Response. *CCC* 35:300–11.

Nicolas, Melissa. 2002. Re-Telling the Story: An Exploration of the Feminization of the Writing Center Narrative. Ph.D diss., Ohio State University.

Nicolas, Melissa, Taia Altiero, Kathryn Brauchle, Mary Domsicz, Bryan J. Drunin, Dolores Hooper, Andrew Kleiner, Joseph Makari, Jamie Razar, and Brad Wlazelek. 2003. Writing Fellows, Peer Group Members, and Teachers: Many Voices, One Program. Paper presented at the IWCA/NCPTW Joint Conference, October, Hershey, PA.

North, Stephen M. 1984. The Idea of a Writing Center. *College English* 46:433–46.

———. 1994. Revisiting "The Idea of a Writing Center." *Writing Center Journal* 15.1:7–19.

O'Hair, Mary, and Joseph Blase. 1992. Power and Politics in the Classroom: Implications for Teacher Education. *Action in Teacher Education* 14:10–17.

Okawa, Gail Y. 1993. Redefining Authority: Multicultural Students and Tutors at the Educational Opportunity Program Writing Center at the University of Washington. In Kinkead and Harris 1993, 166–91. Urbana, IL: NCTE.

O'Reilley, Mary Rose. 1998. *Radical Presence: Teaching as Contemplative Practice.* Portsmouth, NH: Heinemann.

Palmeri, Jason. 2000. Transgressive Hybridity: Reflections on the Authority of the Peer Writing Tutor. *Writing Lab Newsletter* 25.1:9–11.

Pemberton, Michael A., and Joyce Kinkead, eds. 2003. *The Center Will Hold: Critical Perspectives on Writing Center Scholarship.* Logan: Utah State University Press.

Pepper, Karen. Reading to Revise. 2001. Paper presented at the National Conference on Peer Tutoring in Writing. 3 November. Allentown, PA.

Petraglia, Joseph, ed. 1995. *Reconceiving Writing, Rethinking Writing Instruction.* Mahwah, NJ: Lawrence Erlbaum.

Prior, Paul. 1998. *Writing/Disciplinarity: A Sociohistoric Account of Literate Activity in the Academy.* Mahwah, NJ: Lawrence Erlbaum.

Raines, Helon Howell. 1994. Tutoring and Teaching: Continuum, Dichotomy, or Dialectic? *Writing Center Journal* 14.2:150–62.

Rodrigues, Dawn, and Kathleen Kiefer. 1993. Moving toward an Electronic Writing Center at Colorado State University. In Kinkead and Harris 1993, 216–26.

Roskelly, Hephzibah. 1999. The Cupped Hand and the Open Palm. In *The Subject is Writing*, 2nd ed., edited by Wendy Bishop, 125–35. Portsmouth, NH: Boynton/Cook.

———. 2003. *Breaking (into) the Circle: Group Work for Change in the English Classroom.* Portsmouth, NH: Boynton/Cook Heinemann.

Russell, David. 1991. *Writing in the Academic Disciplines, 1870–1990.* Carbondale: Southern Illinois University Press.

———. 1995. Activity Theory and Its Implications for Writing Instruction. In Petraglia 1995, 1–77.

Ryan, Leigh, Lisa Zimmerelli, and Elliot Wright. 2003. Conducting Small Group Tutoring Sessions. Paper presented at the IWCA/NCPTW Joint Conference, October, Hershey, PA.

Sarup, Madan. 1978. *Marxism and Education.* London: Routledge and Kegan Paul.

Shamoon, Linda K., and Deborah H. Burns. 1999. Plagiarism, Rhetorical Theory, and the Writing Center: New Approaches, New Locations. In Buranen and Roy 1999, 183–92.

———. 2001. A Critique of Pure Tutoring. In Barnett and Blumner 2001. 225–41, First published in *Writing Center Journal* 15.2 (1995): 134–51.

Shaughnessy, Mina P. 1977. *Errors and Expectations.* New York: Oxford University Press.

Singh-Gupta, Vidya, and Eileen Troutt-Ervin. 1996. Preparing Students for Teamwork through Collaborative Writing and Peer Review Techniques. *TETYC* 23:127–35.

Smith, Louise Z. 2003. Independence and Collaboration: Why We Should Decentralize Writing Centers. *Writing Center Journal* 23.2:15–23. First published in *Writing Center Journal* 7.1 (1986): 3–10.

Smulyan, Lisa, and Kristin Bolton. 1989. Classroom and Writing Center Collaborations: Peers as Authorities. *Writing Center Journal* 9.2:43–49.

Soliday, Mary. 1995. Shifting Roles in Classroom Tutoring: Cultivating the Art of Boundary Crossing. *Writing Center Journal* 16.1:59–73.

Sommers, Nancy. 1980. Revision Strategies of Student Writers and Experienced Adult Writers. *CCC* 31:177–86.

Soven, Margot. 1993. Curriculum-Based Peer Tutoring Programs: A Survey. *WPA: Writing Program Administrator* 17.1–2:58–74.

———. 2001. Curriculum-Based Peer Tutors and WAC. In McLeod et al. 2001, 200–32.

Spear, Karen. 1988. *Sharing Writing: Peer Response Groups in English Class.* Portsmouth, NH: Boynton/Cook.

Spigelman, Candace. 1999. The Ethics of Appropriation in Peer Writing Groups. In Buranen and Roy 1999, 231–40.

———. 2000. *Across Property Lines: Textual Ownership in Writing Groups.* Carbondale: Southern Illinois University Press.

Spigelman, Candace, Nancy Ditunnareillo, Josalyn Gebhardt, Charles Howells, Laura Lawfer, June Brown, and Bithyah Shaparenko. 2003. Where the Action Is: Peer Tutors as Writing Group Members. Paper presented at the IWCA/NCPTW Joint Conference, October, Hershey, PA.

Stan, Susan, and Terence G. Collins. 1988. Basic Writing: Curricular Interactions with New Technology. *Journal of Basic Writing* 17.1:18–41.

Stay, Byron L. 1985. Talking about Writing: An Approach to Teaching Unskilled Writers. *Journal of Teaching Writing* 4:248–52.

Stross, Brian. 1999. The Hybrid Metaphor: From Biology to Culture. *Journal of American Folklore* 112:254–67.

Sultan, Gerry. 1998. No More Sixes, Nines, and Red Lines: Peer Groups and Revision. *English Journal* 77:65–68.

Suskind, Ron. 1998. *A Hope in the Unseen: An American Odyssey from the Inner City to the Ivy League.* New York: Broadway Books.

Thaiss, Christopher. 2001. Theory in WAC: Where Have We Been, Where Are We Going? In McLeod et al. 2001, 299–325.

Thaiss, Christopher, and Terry Zawacki. 1997. How Portfolios for Proficiency Help Shape a WAC Program. In Yancey and Huot 1997, 79–96. Greenwich, CT: Ablex.

Thompson, George J. 1978. Revision: Nine Ways to Achieve a Disinterested Perspective. *CCC* 29:200–2.

Tobin, Lad. 1993. *Writing Relationships: What Really Happens in the Composition Class.* Portsmouth, NH: Boynton/ Cook.

Tong, Rosemarie. 1989. *Feminist Thought: A Comprehensive Introduction.* Boulder: Westview Press.

Trimbur, John. 1989. Consensus and Difference in Collaborative Learning. *College English* 51:602–16.

———. 1998. "Peer Tutoring": A Contradiction in Terms? In Capossela 1998, 117–23. First published in *Writing Center Journal* 7.2 (1987): 21–28.

Varone, Sandy. 1996. Voices from the Computer Classroom: Novice Writers and Peer Response to Writing. *Teaching English in the Two-Year College* 23:213–18.

Vygotsky, L. S. 1978. *Mind in Society: The Development of Higher Psychological Processes.* Cambridge: Harvard University Press.

Walvoord, Barbara, and Lucille P. McCarthy. 1990. *Thinking and Writing in College: A Naturalistic Study of Students in Four Disciplines.* Urbana, IL: NCTE.

Wauters, Joan K. 1988. Non-Confrontational Critiquing Pairs: An Alternative to Verbal Peer Response Groups. *Writing Instructor* 7:156–66.

Weaver, Margaret E. 1995. Using Peer Response in the Classroom: Students' Perspectives. *Research and Teaching in Developmental Education* 12:31–37.

Weinsheimer, Joel C. 1985. *Gadamer's Hermeneutics: A Reading of Truth and Method.* New Haven: Yale University Press.

Willis, Meredith. 1993. *Deep Revision.* New York: Teachers and Writers Collaborative.

Wiley, Mark. 2001. Rehabilitating the "Idea of Community." *Journal of Basic Writing.* 2.2:16–33.

Wingate, Molly Sue. 2000. What Line? I Didn't See Any Line. In *A Tutor's Guide: Helping Writers One to One,* edited by Ben Raffoth, 9–16. Portsmouth, NH: Boynton/Cook.

Wolch, Jennifer, and Michael Dear. 1989. Introduction to *The Power of Geography: How Territory Shapes Social Life,* edited by Jennifer Wolch and Michael Dear. Boston: Unwin Hyman.

Yancey, Kathleen Blake, and Brian Huot, eds. 1997. *Assessing Writing across the Curriculum: Diverse Approaches and Practices.* Greenwich, CT: Ablex.

Zhu, Wei. 1995. Effects of Training for Peer Response on Students' Comments and Interaction. *Written Communication* 12:492–528.

# CONTRIBUTORS

CANDACE SPIGELMAN is an associate professor at Penn State Berks–Lehigh Valley College, where she serves as co-coordinator of professional writing and teaches composition, rhetorical theory, English language analysis, and peer tutoring in writing. Her publications include *Across Property Lines: Textual Ownership in Writing Groups, Personally Speaking: Experience as Evidence in Academic Discourse,* and articles in *College English, CCC, JAC,* and *Composition Studies.* She received the 2002 Richard Ohmann Award for her article "Argument and Evidence in the Case of the Personal."

LAURIE GROBMAN is an associate professor of English at Penn State University, Berks–Lehigh Valley, where she is co-coordinator of the degree in professional writing. Her work as a teacher-scholar focuses on how written language, as it is produced and consumed, can play a substantial role in making connections across cultural differences. She has published a book, *Teaching at the Crossroads: Cultures and Critical Perspectives in Literature by Women of Color* (2001), and several articles in *MELUS, JAC, Pedagogy, College Literature,* and *Journal of Basic Writing.* Grobman also coedits *Young Scholars in Writing: Undergraduate Research in Writing and Rhetoric.*

DEREK JOHN BOCZKOWSKI is the assistant director of the writing center at Columbia College, Chicago, and an adjunct faculty member of the Columbia English department. His teaching and research focus on peer tutor training and development, cultural and textual analysis, and writing across the curriculum.

ROBIN BREAULT completed her doctoral work at Georgia State University and graduated in August 2004. There she worked as a research and teaching assistant for the WAC program and taught business writing courses in the English department. Currently Robin is an instructor at the University of Arizona, Business Communications Program, in Tucson, where she teaches business writing and technical communication courses. Her dissertation, "Building Doors: A Narrative of Literacy and Possibility", is a work of ethnographic creative nonfiction that describes and analyzes the community literacy efforts of a private day treatment program in an urban environment.

STEVEN J. CORBETT is a Ph.D. student in English language and rhetoric at the University of Washington, where he teaches first-year composition and founded the Dance Program Writing Center, which he directs. His teaching and research interests include peer teaching and tutoring, critical pedagogy, and creative nonfiction. His essays have appeared in the *Writing Lab Newsletter, Academic Exchange Quarterly,* and *University Week,* and he is currently conducting an ongoing research project involving tutor training.

JENNIFER CORROY teaches middle school language arts in Roma, Texas. She graduated from the University of Wisconsin–Madison with degrees in English and history. While in Madison, she spent three years as an undergraduate writing fellow and served for one year as the program's undergraduate assistant director.

TEAGAN DECKER is a Ph.D. student at the University of Washington–Seattle, where she formerly directed the English department's writing center. She is currently a teaching assistant in the expository writing program. Her research interests include basic writing, interdisciplinary writing, affirmative action in higher education, and discourse analysis.

SUSAN HRACH GEORGECINK is an assistant professor of English at Columbus State University, where she serves as writing center director and teaches expository writing as well as early British and world literature. Her research interests include historical and contemporary literacy practices and English cultural history. She is at work on a study of seventeenth-century advice books for mothers.

KELLY GIGER will graduate from Penn State University in fall 2004 with a degree in elementary education. She is a member of the Pi Lambda Theta National Honor Society in Education. She presented research at the 2001 National Conference on Peer Tutoring in Writing. She has worked for the Penn State Education Partnership Program and the America Reads Program while attending Penn State.

BARBARA LITTLE LIU is an assistant professor of English at Eastern Connecticut State University, where she also coordinates the first-year writing program. Her teaching and research focus on composition theory and pedagogy and rhetorical theory and criticism, especially political and religious rhetorics.

HOLLY MANDES is a doctoral candidate in the rhetoric, composition, and teaching of English program at the University of Arizona. Her current interests include rhetorics of the body—specifically disability rhetoric—writing program administration, and peer tutoring in online spaces. She coauthored this chapter while she was an undergraduate at Eastern Connecticut State University, where she worked as a senior tutor in the writing associates program.

DAVID MARTINS is an assistant professor at California State University–Chico, where he formerly coordinated the writing across the curriculum program and now teaches full-time in the Department of English. His teaching and research focus on theories of literacy, disability, and rhetoric.

STEVE MOGGE is an assistant professor of education at Towson University, where he teaches graduate courses in literacy and research. He has written and presented on adolescent and adult literacy, second-language immigrant literacy and reader response, and elementary reading matters. He was formerly a professor at Columbia College, Chicago, where he created a developmental reading program for the open-admissions arts and media institution.

MELISSA NICOLAS is an assistant professor of English at the University of Louisiana–Lafayette. In her previous post at Penn State–Lehigh Valley, she held the positions of composition program co-coordinator, writing center director, and writing fellows coordinator. Nicolas has presented her research on writing centers and peer groups at CCCCs, IWCA, and NCTE. Most recently, she coedited *By Any Other Name: Writing Groups Inside and Outside the Classroom.*

JIM OTTERY is an assistant professor of English at the University of Illinois–Springfield, where he teaches first-year composition, modern and multicultural literature, and upper-level classes and graduate seminars in the history of rhetoric and teaching composition. His teaching and research focus on composition pedagogy and rhetoric and epistemology.

JEAN PETROLLE is a professor at Columbia College, Chicago, where she has served as coordinator of basic writing, Bridge coordinator, and director of composition. She coedited the anthology *Women and Experimental Filmmaking* (forthcoming) and has published in a variety of journals and anthologies about twentieth-century film, literature, and painting. Her teaching and research focus on personal narrative and the spiritual dimensions of public rhetoric.

MARTI SINGER is an associate professor of English at Georgia State University. She was formerly the director for training writing consultants for the WAC program and is currently the director for lower-division studies in English. She develops programs and resources for instructor training for nearly one hundred graduate students and visiting instructors who teach first-year composition and literature survey courses at Georgia State. In addition, she teaches advanced composition and rhetorical theory courses for both undergraduates and graduate students. Her research focuses on composition history and pedagogy, program development, and teacher beliefs.

MARY SOLIDAY is an associate professor of English at the City College of New York, where she is currently a campus coordinator of the City University of New York Writing Fellows Program. She has published articles in many composition journals and book chapters and is the author of *The Politics of Remediation: Institutional and Student Needs in Higher Education,* winner of the 2004 4Cs Outstanding Book Award.

JENNIFER WING, is a graduate student at Georgia State University, where she is a research and teaching assistant. While working as a research assistant for the WAC program, she helped to compose a handbook for WAC tutors. Currently, she is completing her Ph.D. program in nineteenth-century American literature and literary theory. Jennifer teachers composition and American literature at Georgia State and has published in American literature journals and encyclopedias.

THIA WOLF is a professor of composition studies at California State University, Chico. She has twice been a co-coordinator of the WAC program and is mst recent past coordinator of the university writing center. Currently, she serves as the administrator for English composition. Her publications explore successful and unsuccessful collaborative learning strategies in classrooms across the disciplines.

CASEY YOU is a substitute teacher and a graduate of Penn State University in elementary education. She began her research for this chapter as a writing fellow at Penn State Berks and completed the project during her junior year at the University Park campus.

# INDEX